SCARFACE NATION

Also by Ken Tucker

Kissing Bill O'Reilly, Roasting Miss Piggy:
100 Things to Love and Hate About Television

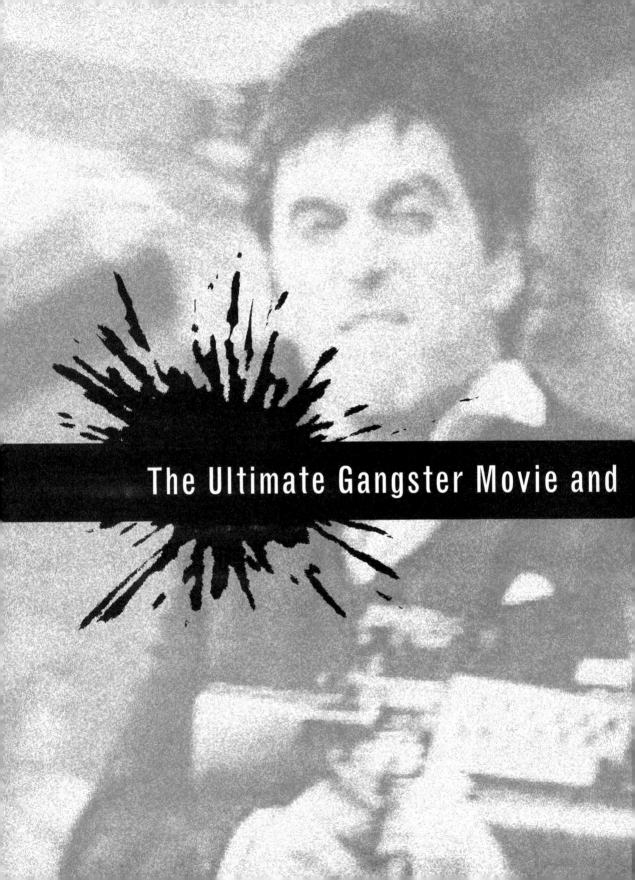

The Ultimate Gangster Movie and

Ken Tucker

SCARFACE

How It Changed America

NATION

St. Martin's Griffin ❦ New York

www.stmartins.com

Book design by Kathryn Parise

Library of Congress Cataloging-in-Publication Data
Tucker, Ken, 1953–
   Scarface nation : the ultimate gangster movie and how it changed America / Ken Tucker.
   —1st ed.
     p. cm.
   ISBN-13: 978-0-312-33059-0
   ISBN-10: 0-312-33059-6
1. Scarface (Motion picture : 1983) I. Title.
   PN1997.S195T83   2008
   791.43'72—dc22   2008021152

First Edition: November 2008

10 9 8 7 6 5 4 3 2 1

To Anne, of course

Contents

Introduction   1

PART I

1.   Scarface Lives Among Us   13
2.   The Movie   33
3.   Making a *Scarface*   41
4.   Four Creators   75
5.   *Scarface* Music   99

Contents

PART II

6.	The Origins: Howard Hawks's *Scarface*	125
7.	The Origins: Armitage Trail's *Scarface*	149
8.	Alterna-*Scarface*s: Movies, TV Shows, Novels, and Comic Books	159
9.	President Scarface	193
10.	*Scarface*: Its Money, Its Women, Its Power	203
11.	A Meaning of *Scarface*	253

Appendix: *Scarface* as a Business Plan   259
Notes   267
Acknowledgments   271
Index   273

Introduction

Pauline Kael once noted that it's difficult to explain what makes a piece of popular art "great," and that this is "particularly difficult with movies." She was writing about *Citizen Kane,* which she described as "a shallow work, a shallow masterpiece." I don't think even *Scarface*'s most ardent admirers would compare it to *Citizen Kane*—although Charles Foster Kane/William Randolph Hearst *was* his own sort of autodidact-gangster in the manner of Tony Montana/Al Capone.

No, what *Scarface* is, in a sense, is something bigger, more outsized than that. It is a great and shallow masterpiece of pop, a work of diverse, mongrel artistry. It's *all* surface, but, boy, what Brian De Palma, Oliver Stone, and Al Pacino applied to that surface. It glows, it glistens, it retains its sheen of power, glory, and shimmeringly decadent rot a quarter-century after its release. It remains a tremendously exciting and dismaying piece of moviemaking, unique in the careers of every one of its various creators.

Scarface keeps on inspiring more versions of itself. *New York Times* television critic Virginia Heffernan noted in May 2007, regarding the announcement of a new CBS series *Cane,* a kind of Miami-Cuban *Dynasty,* that it resembled a "prime-time version of *Scarface,* [which] has lodged itself in the lizard brain of the popular imagination." Unlike most Hollywood movies, *Scarface* doesn't merely exist as a period film—year after year, it inspires other people to make *Scarface* gestures, whether those gestures are to quote its dialogue in movies and TV shows; to use it as an inspiration for music, TV shows, and books; to brand Al Pacino's scarred face as an image to sell everything from T-shirts to shower curtains. *Scarface* is the only movie that is *its own franchise*: It didn't require sequels—as *Star Wars* or *Spider-Man* or even *The Godfather* needed sequels—to cement the status of an ongoing cultural and commercial enterprise in which art, popularity, and merchandising have now long met, melded, and flourished.

"Say hello to my l'l fren!" "All I have in this world is my balls and my word, an' I don' break them for anyone." "Don't get high on your own supply."

When a movie becomes best known for its catchphrases, it can come to seem like a lesser creation—a novelty, a fad, eventually tiresome, even disposable. This is not what happened with *Scarface*.

When a movie enters the culture so thoroughly that even people who never saw it think they know what it's all about, can refer to it with a knowingness that has nothing to do with really comprehending it, or have formed an original opinion of it—that movie can seem like a dead letter sent from America's collective memory. This is not what happened with *Scarface*.

But here are three of the many things that *did* happen with *Scarface*. It was not a huge hit upon its initial release. It became an item of massive cult veneration. It remains an ever-changing thing, inspiring—by various turns—wit, invention, and sometimes reprehensible responses from every corner of pop culture.

Scarface—released in 1983 as a blood- and obscenity-fueled remake of a 1932 movie, which few of its eventual rabid fans were even aware existed—stands as a singular phenomenon in American moviemaking. Created by a group of middle-aged white men (director De Palma, screenwriter Oliver Stone, producer Martin Bregman), the audience it would eventually attract has been largely young, black, and Hispanic; women as well as men. The areas of pop culture it has most omnivorously influenced—hip-hop music, videos, and fashion— were quite beyond its original creators' understanding. In all the interviews I conducted and read for this book, none of them suggests that De Palma and company to this day has a clue as to who, say, the rapper Scarface is, or why—to take just one of many examples of *Scarface*-provoked cultural artifacts—the movie inspired, in a roundabout way, the rapper Paris's 1992 song "Bush Killa."

Scarface is, in a sense, a movie that got away from its creators.

From the start, it took on an unruly life of its own. Conceived as a project meant to be Hollywood-controversial—that is, in show-biz parlance, "tackling" a few "issues," such as drug use and the glamorization of the gangster—it proved troublesome (it was a tough shoot, requiring the entire production to pick up and leave Miami for Los Angeles two months into location-shooting), difficult (behind-the-scenes squabbles between the director and the writer; many scenes elaborately tricky and expensive to film), and widely, sometimes willfully, misinterpreted (one man's harsh-critique-of-crime is five others' *wow-look-at-those-guns-I-can-do-that-too!*).

I'm not talking here of geek culture, such as accrues around the *Star Wars, Star Trek,* or *Lord of the Rings* movies. I'm talking about *deep* culture. And not deep in the sense of profound (*Scarface* is, above all, about surface, about the obviousness of man's corruptibility, and about how superficial pleasures are at once the most immediately gratifying and the most enduringly corrosive), but "deep" in the sense of burrowing-in, of digging down to expose the source of so many varied pleasure centers.

Few pieces of pop culture can withstand the ferocious celebration, examination, and marrow-gnawing dissection that we—as audience; as fans; as self-made media experts—now routinely subject all of the bright and showy pieces of entertainment that aspire to being phenomena, if not art. From *The Matrix* to *Lost*; from *American Idol* to *Heroes*; from the movie spectacle *300* to the TV serial *24,* we like to chew over the knottier meanings of our movies, TV shows, and music in ever-more-thorough ways—on the Internet or via sequels; as video games and on blogs. And like most pop culture, once a hit or a cult phenomenon has been thoroughly consumed, it goes the way of Davy Crockett's Disney-fied coonskin cap in the 1950s, or of *The Brady*

Bunch in the 1970s—it becomes mere nostalgia; a relic; an item of camp devotion or derision.

Not so with *Scarface*. A quarter-century after its release, it remains elusive yet pervasive, the movie that will not go away, but which pops up where you least expect it. What began life as a remake that was it-self an adaptation of a 1925 novel has not followed the usual trajec-tory of an American pop icon. The 1983 movie was a nonoriginal idea whose creators had less to do with its sustained life than the audi-ence that has sought to salute it, emulate it, and rip it off. Certainly, Brian De Palma, like a father whose child grows up to be someone he barely recognizes; who wonders from whose genes his progeny really sprang, never expected the movie to take on the life it did. A child of the counterculture, De Palma has always been a bit baffled about the movie's ongoing, ever-morphing, and sprouting subcultural life.

It is the story of the rise and fall of Tony Montana, a Cuban refugee—portrayed by an Italian-American actor and brought to life by a screenwriter who was shaking an addiction to the drug the movie glorified. It was overseen by a producer who eventually gave up trying to explain its power by saying, "It's not just the hip-hop community—white college students have *Scarface* parties. The film just keeps going. It's bizarre and amazing."

Scarface—which traces its origin to the real-life gangster "Scarface Al" Capone—has long since severed ties to even the most cursory sort of historical/biographical work. Transplanted to Miami, set to the rhythms of disco and, later, hip-hop, featuring a performance some consider one of the finest the profession has yielded and others con-sider a joke, in a role that smacked of commercial sellout and artistic self-parody, *Scarface* is by now its own myth, its own mythmaker.

Tony Montana arrives in America a few thousand miles south of the Statue of Liberty but every bit the core constituency of the lady-with-the-torch: tired, hungry, and poor. Yet he hits our shores as part of the Fidel Castro/Jimmy Carter Mariel Boatlift (see p. 52), and is thus immediately deemed not merely an illegal but a criminal. Proclaiming himself—as so many minority radicals had in the 1960s—a "political prisoner," he's got nowhere to go but up.

This was not the stuff of your average gangster picture—or even a transcendently nonaverage one like Francis Ford Coppola's *The Godfather,* released eleven years earlier. Looking to update director Howard Hawks's Prohibition-era *Scarface* as a cocaine-era *Scarface,* screenwriter Stone and director De Palma were both political-minded yet doggedly commercial filmmakers. The Ivy League–bred, Vietnam-veteran Stone had already proven himself capable of diving lustily into severed-limb exploitation fare with his first auteurist phantasmagoria, the bomb *The Hand* (1981), while De Palma, who'd both satirized and saluted radical politics in his first, independent films, was looking for the big studio hit he hadn't had since he'd poured blood on a telekinetic teenager in *Carrie* (1976).

As this book will demonstrate, they succeeded beyond their most extravagant imaginings by, initially, failing: The De Palma/Stone *Scarface,* produced by a veteran Hollywood player, Bregman (*Dog Day Afternoon, Serpico*), was Universal Studios' big 1983 Christmas release. What a holiday surprise for America: a bullet- and profanity-riddled action flick with lugubrious crane shots and a chain-saw scene that rivaled anything in movies this side of a Texas massacre. Greeted with not a few jeers from the always dependably middle-brow/prude wing of the film-critic establishment, *Scarface* was the little killer that could. Opening nationwide to mixed-to-negative reviews, it was in urban theaters that the movie found its first great appreciators: non-middle-class youths who got off not merely on the violence but on its *message*, its *themes,* its *philosophy,* all of whose details this particular audience-demographic filled in and expanded upon well beyond the confines of what was up on the screen or in the screenplay.

Soon enough, lines like "Never underestimate the greed of the *other* guy" and others I mentioned earlier began to cohere as a code of honor, as business ethics, as a declaration of loyalty, and of capitalism trickling down inexorably to Reaganomics. What trickled *up* was a cult hit whose base grew broader with the increase in home-entertainment technology—the release of the film after its initial the-atrical run on, first, VHS tape and subsequently DVD. Then there was the Internet, which leant itself to millions of words spent sussing out the *Scarface* devotion that resided in so many hearts, as well as prov-ing a site for its own creativity: the posting not just of clips from the movie but conceptually daring creative acts themselves. This included many amateur recuttings of the nearly three-hour *Scarface* down to a three-*minute* montage whose scenes were only the ones containing the word "fuck"—yet which, when strung together in sequence, told the entire tale of the movie with complete coherence. These and other Web videos, such as Dick Cheney bringing Scarface to the 2004 Re-publican National Convention, were acts of pop democracy-in-action, guerilla warfare every bit as ruthless as the hero being extolled.

Scarface was birthed at the same time that hip-hop had turned hard. As mainstream movie-culture settled into a period of glossy es-capism with hits like *Flashdance, Risky Business, Trading Places,* and *Octopussy* (to name just four of the highest-grossing crowd-pleasers released the same year), *Scarface* began its second life as a new musical paradigm. Its "The World Is Yours" message informs hip-hop business dealings and countless lyrics of the then-nascent gangsta rap genre, even as the film's grandly languid displays of ostentatious wealth became the backdrop to many hip-hop videos, with their men and women sipping champagne, flashing their jewelry, and striking poses in big cars and bigger swimming pools.

But these are merely the most obvious products of *Scarface*'s infiltration of America. There are so many other ways in which the movie made connections—sparked inspirations—that render its afterlife at least as exciting and provocative as the movie itself. For its creators, *Scarface* became something of a trap. De Palma and Pacino have both said it is the movie they're asked most about, yet *Scarface* stands as an anomaly, even an aberration, in their resumes. But for its audience, including other artists, hucksters, and ordinary citizens inspired by some scene, some phrase, some bit of *Scarface* attitude, it became gloriously inspirational.

All this, for a character whose triumph and happiness are short-lived, whose existence is presented to us book-ended by desperate ambition and depressed, despairing decadence. Among its numerous paradoxes, *Scarface* became an inescapable American touchstone during the rise of the "feel-good movie," the "high-concept" film, and the kind of ironic humor popularized in such places as *Spy* Magazine. *Scarface* is a feel-bad, complex, utterly unironic saga. Like everything dead-serious in our society, it became the object of parody—Tony's machine-gun envoi, "Say hello to my l'l fren!" becomes a T-shirt slogan and a cell-phone ringtone; everyone from *The Simpsons* to HBO's *Curb Your Enthusiasm* takes their licks at ridiculing *Scarface*.

But unlike the way a comparable phenomenon—*The Godfather* or *The Sopranos*, say—ultimately withstands pop parody because of those projects' bottom-line seriousness, *Scarface* absorbs ridicule and overexposure and just keeps on going, making something new out of its ever-shifting meaning in the culture and the marketplace. This book will explore all of this, and more.

The story of *Scarface America* as I have assembled it is structured as a series of loops and twists; this film, a disruptive saga itself, seemed to demand its own form. And so it does not follow a strict chronological order; in fact, I've reversed it. I decided to begin with the Al Pacino/Brian De Palma *Scarface,* retelling its story for readers both familiar and new to it, with frequent interruptions, interpretations, opinions, and, where appropriate, production details. Then I take one step back, to Howard Hawks's *Scarface,* which has its own tale, its own myth, to tell, and then a step back farther still, to Armitage Trail/Maurice Coons's source-novel.

After these chapters, the Scarface tale takes off in a number of directions, making its mark in other media (video games, novelizations, TV shows, comic books), in politics, and most pervasively, in music. You can read this book straight through, for the good ride I hope I have constructed. You can also jump around and read parts of it out of order, as suits your fancy. At this point I'd write, "Say hello to my l'l fren," but I suspect you know him a bit already. I just want you to get to know *Scarface* better.

PART I

Scarface Lives Among Us

MAJOR IMMIGRANT SMUGGLING RING IS BROKEN IN PHOENIX, POLICE SAY

The New York Times
February 15, 2008
By Randal C. Archibold

PHOENIX—In a case highlighting this city's prominent role in the smuggling of illegal immigrants across the border, the authorities conducted a series of raids on Thursday, arresting what they said were the leaders of a ring that helped transport hundreds of people to way stations in Phoenix. . . .

The authorities made 20 arrests, including those of two Cubans accused of directing the operation. . . . Oddities abounded along the way. . . .

"We often see 'Scarface' or 'Godfather' posters," said Lt. Vince Piano of the Phoenix Police Department, a lead investigator. "That's the mentality."

MAN SHOWS "SCARFACE" T-SHIRT AND DEMANDS CHECK AT BANK
By The Associated Press
March 28, 2007

MICHIGAN CITY, Ind.—A 24-year-old Michigan City man entered the City Savings Bank just before noon Tuesday and asked to see the manager, the police report said. Brian Nelson, vice president of consumer lending at the northwestern Indiana bank, brought him into his office and the man demanded a check for $10,000, Nelson told Michigan City police. The man . . . lifted up his T-shirt, which was inside out, to display an image from *Scarface*. It showed Pacino's character, Tony Montana, brandishing a gun and the words "Straight to Hell," the report said. The man at the bank told Nelson "You see what I mean."

OUT WITH OLD, IN WITH THE TEEN TOUCH
Simple tips to turn kids' rooms into dream spots
By Casey Capachi
Contra Costa Times **Teen Correspondent**
Article Launched: 06/15/2007

"Every self-respecting guy needs a *Scarface* poster in his room," says senior Robert Carrington from Acalanes High School. "If you put up that giant black-and-white *Scarface* poster, some of the manliness is sure to rub off."

"SCARFACE" POSTER NEAR 37 POUNDS OF COKE, DETECTIVE SAYS

Posted by *Birmingham News* **staff, Birmingham, Alabama, July 26, 2007 3:08 PM**

A poster from the movie *Scarface* adorned a hallway wall near a closet where Birmingham police found more than 37 pounds of cocaine inside a tote bag, testimony in a Jefferson County drug trial

showed today. The poster depicts Al Pacino, who starred in the 1983 movie, in front of a large amount of cocaine. In addition to the 17 kilograms of cocaine in the hall closet, police also found nearly a half-kilogram more of cocaine and pills of the illegal drug Ecstasy, according to testimony today in the trial of Derrick Phillip Ervin.

Suburban and Wayne Times, **March 3, 2006**

"Radnor, PA: A man was robbed while walking on Conestoga Road near County Line Avenue on Jan. 27 around midnight. Four black men . . . accosted the victim, punching him in the head several times and taking a white leather coat with 'Scarface' written on it valued at $1,500 and a cell phone valued at $200."

"SCARFACE MANSION" TO BECOME CLINIC
Tom Kington in Rome
Monday, July 9, 2007
The Guardian

Gangsters the world over have long looked up to Tony Montana, the fictional Cuban drug dealer in the 1983 film *Scarface*, who dies in a hail of bullets in his kitsch, neo-classical Miami villa.

One Naples mobster, Walter Schiavone, was so enamoured of the character played by Al Pacino he built a [$3 million] replica of the villa.

But instead of meeting the glorious fate of his hero, Schiavone was arrested on murder charges in 1999 while trying to escape over his garden wall.

The brother of the boss of the feared Casalesi clan, Schiavone commissioned his villa by handing a video of *Scarface* to a local architect and telling him to build what he saw.

Hollywood Reporter, July 2006

"NBA star Shaquille O'Neill celebrated his 34th birthday with a *Scarface*-themed party in Miami. The venue was decked out like a 1980s *Scarface* set, complete with Elvira Hancock look-alikes, a "The World Is Yours" statue, and a tiger. Shaq wore Scarface's signature white suit and black shirt, and Steven Bauer, who plays Manny Ribera in the movie, even put in an appearance."

As soon as I started work on this book, I was immediately inundated, impressed with, and sometimes overwhelmed by the way *Scarface* has continued its ceaseless commercial intrusions into the marketplace, its non-stop permeation into all media, the way it continues to influence a new generation of pop-culture creators.

Consider the following current phenomena:

Scarface as Video Game

Scarface: The World Is Yours (Vivendi/Sierra) was first released for the Xbox in late 2006, and even more sucessfully in the Wii format in 2007, featuring a what-if-Tony-didn't-die scenario conceived by screenwriter Dave McKenna, who wrote the Edward Norton feature film *American History* X. "I wrote forty hours' worth of dialogue [for the video game]," McKenna told me. "Because you have to write for every possible situation that the gamer moves Tony into: If he walks

Scarface by the Numbers

In 2006–2007, *Scarface: The World Is Yours* was the number-one-selling game in the Wii, PlayStation2, and X-Box formats, selling over two millions copies combined, according to numerous video-game estimates.

Scarface's 2003 two-disc DVD release sold over five million units in '03 alone; its 2006 "Platinum" edition has sold over four million copies.

into this room, he talks to his lawyer; if he walks outside, he talks to a babe at the pool. It's basically how many different ways can I invent to have him tell people to fuck off." Although Al Pacino declined to record new dialogue, a surreally diverse voice cast includes Bauer and a posse that didn't appear in the movie: James Woods, Wilmer Valderrama, Bai Ling, Tommy Lee, *Desperate Housewives* ghost-voice Brenda Strong, and the semi-reunion of the head-trip comedy duo Cheech (Marin) and (Tommy) Chong (they recorded their parts separately). The video game—which has sold more than two million copies— takes place in a post-*Scarface* landscape where Tony has survived his movie-finale shoot-out and must rebuild his empire, attacking Sosa and other villains and obstacles which even include the tigers Tony stocked his estate with. Manny and Gina are dead, their ashes kept in urns that the game-player can find in a remote room and buy for safe-keeping. *Scarface: The World Is Yours* features a "Blind-Rage Mode," which when set compels Tony Montana to spray machine-gun bullets indiscriminately, at anyone or anything he encounters, and has a "Fuck You button" that when pressed causes Tony to utter obscenities. (*Scarface* in the gaming world is nothing new; one of the genre's most popular games, 2002's *Grand Theft Auto: Vice City,* was heavily based on *Scarface* plotlines. The game's protagonist, Richard Diaz, has an opulent mansion, and the climactic battle that takes place in it at the game's end, is very similar to those in *Scarface.* (There is a hidden apartment room with blood on the bathroom walls and a chain saw.)

Scarface Telephone

Scarface wouldn't be vibrant without a ringtone: From scarfacemobile .com, you can download wallpaper images and ringtones with *Scarface* theme music or cleaned-up versions of the most famous lines from the film. The *Scarface* franchise is licensed from Universal via Starwave Mobile, owned by the Walt Disney Company, which results in the nice irony that "Say hello to my little friend" could possibly refer to Mickey Mouse or Donald Duck. By mid-2007, more than two million downloads had been reported—more than 1 percent of all mobile consumption revenue—with more lines and scenes from the movie planned for release. These include "Scarface Casino," which is described by the company as "a casual game" inspired by poker and card games where players strategize against one another, and "Scarface: MPR (Money. Power. Respect.)," a "more immersive game that's task-driven." (I think that's tidy corporate-speak for: "Kill the cocaine-cartel guards, seize the product.")

A Starwave Mobile executive was quoted in the *Hollywood Reporter* in May 2007 as saying that *Scarface* is "such an iconic brand that it can reach pretty broadly and continues to inspire us. Thinking broadly about how to drive that story line to new story lines, and thinking about the content as part of a new entertainment platform, has made it successful."

It's Not TV, It's HBO-*Scarface*

It makes sense that a TV show such as *The Sopranos* would have its *Scarface* moment . . . and it did, in fact, in its very first, pilot episode: Christopher, always the fledgling screenwriter, bleats to Tony, passionately urging a bloody showdown with a rival mobster: "This is *Scarface*, final scene, fuckin' bazookas under each arm, say-hello-to-my-little-friend time!"

✳ Indeed, anything-goes pay-cable HBO is a logical locus for *Scarface* humor: On Larry David's *Curb Your Enthusiasm*, a rapper calling himself Krazee-Eyez Killa (played by Chris Williams) gives David a tour of his mansion, saying he fantasizes about having a big-screen plasma TV on his bedroom ceiling in order to "play *Scarface* 24/7."

✳ On the same cable network's *Entourage*, an ongoing subplot introduced during the series' second season involved pretty-boy movie-star Vince Chase hoping to do a little indie film called *Medellin* in which the young actor would portray drug lord Pablo Escobar: "This movie is gonna be, like, the new *Scarface,*" says Vince Chase; he then does an imitation of Pacino snorting coke off a desk. A few episodes later, Vince's agent Ari Gold crows of *Medellin,* "This could be your *Scarface!*" By the third season, *Entourage* was working old *Scarface* cast members themselves into the show: a May 2007 episode featured Harris Yulin (the film's corrupt cop Mel Bernstein) as the aging producer of *Medellin* who decides Jeremy Piven's Ari is too much of a pain to deal with, and shuts the project down. (Yet, neither this producer nor Ari takes a bullet to the gut as Mel did from Tony.)

❋ Finally, *Scarface* looms unexpectedly in HBO's *The Wire*, the great urban drama of the new century, a pitiless, wrenching, often stingingly funny look at the effects of the drug trade on poor black

HBO's *Entourage:* Adrian Grenier as Vincent Chase playing Pablo Escobar

neighborhoods in Baltimore. There, in the show's fifth and greatest year, which launched in 2006, the terrifyingly cold-blooded young drug dealer Snoop (the awe-inspiring Felicia Pearson, in her first professional acting role), wears a *Scarface* jacket in one episode. One can't help but view it as emblematic of her ruthless determination to nullify her opponents and competition in the drug trade. Al Pacino's face on Snoop's clothing is a debonair, nonchalant act of homage by this young woman: not by Simon and his fellow scenarists, who have no use for *Scarface*'s baroque excess—who, in fact, by their muted style of storytelling and the sophistication of their moral layering, probably view De Palma's work as melodramatic, if not crude—but who nonetheless on some level have been forced by *Scarface*'s cultural pervasiveness to recognize that even some of the young fictional characters they have created would inevitably find the movie's street code embedded in *Scarface* DNA.

Cartoon *Scarface*

The Simpsons, South Park, and *The Family Guy* have all Scarfaced:

* In the sixth-season episode of *The Simpsons* called "Lisa's Rival," Homer assumes a Cuban accent to speak of one of his favorite topics—donuts and their allure: "First you get the sugar, then you get the powder, then you get the women."
* In the ninth season of *South Park,* the squat bully Cartman addresses a school assembly dressed in a white Scarface disco suit and addresses the students as "cock-a-roaches." "You need people like me,"

says the 'toon series' prime "bad guy," "so you can point your fingers . . . Well, say good-night to the bad guy!" Cartman concludes; the auditorium curtain is hastily closed.

✳   On YouTube.com, you can see a section of *The Family Guy* re-cut so that its precocious baby, Stewie, becomes Scarface: http://youtube.com/watch?v=BPH9BIGbyLM.

Harry Potter as Scarface

On numerous Internet sites, you'll find *Harry Potter* fan-fiction that makes a connection between gangster and fantasy hero: The lightning bolt that creases young Harry's face earns him a fan's fond nickname: Scarface. Of course, Harry Potter is the mannerly Tony Montana, not so much rebellious underdog as magical scamp, yet he is still a perse-cuted youth who slowly, steadily, discovers his enormous power.

Scarface Country

Most people know at least something about *Scarface*'s hip-hop influ-ence. But there's a different-genre music-video that's striking: Johnny Cash's recording of Nine Inch Nails's "Hurt," set to a well-edited, slowly paced sequence of wordless scenes from *Scarface*, in black-and-white, drained of color: http://www.youtube.com/watch?v=WasMSZZCt-w.

Tagged on YouTube as "Johnny Cash Meets Scarface," it shows

Montana in his final stages of cocaine stupor, as Cash sings in the solemn croak of his own final years, "I focus on the pain/The only thing that's real." While scenes of Montana shooting Manny and Gina play as if they're memories Tony is having shortly before picking up his machine gun one final time, Cash sings, "What have I become . . . Everyone I know goes away in the end . . ." and during the last blazing shoot-out, Cash's voice rings like a death knell as Tony is torn by bullets: "My empire of dirt/I will let you down/I will make you hurt." It's spookily effective.

Scarface the Merchandiser

The Internet offers a cornucopia of *Scarface* merchandise. Aside from the obvious—posters, T-shirts, coffee mugs, key chains that when pressed say, "Say hello to my little friend!"—there are items such as *Scarface* dartboards, poker chips, flip-flop sandals, and a set of shower curtains that sold for over $300 on eBay. Among the more pricey items of clothing are short-sleeved, Hawaiian-style shirts into which the word "Scarface" is woven into the shirttail, and the character's initials, T.M., are discreetly embroidered on the sleeves. As *The New York Times* reported in a 2005 trend piece, "[Tony Montana's] initials grace

the buttons, too: no detail spared. The orange buttons glow in the dark like sinister fireflies, real attention-getters at nightclubs."

I visited a Greenwich Village store selling these shirts—"one hundred percent polyester!" crowed the owner. These fancy, loose-hanging, Hawaiian-style shirts sell for between $60 to $80, and include versions with Scarface reclining in the tub with a cigar, or brandishing an Uzi. I admit it: I passed. Now, an Izod shirt with a little Tony-head instead of an alligator—*that's* something I might invest in.

✳ Want to be Scarface in October? There's a $49.95-retailing Halloween costume consisting of a white disco-era suit, a red wide-collar shirt, and a machine gun. (The package notes that the gat is "not available in some states": One supposes you then trick-or-treat saying, "Say hello to my leettle thumb-and-forefinger pointing!")

✳   There are, of course, posters galore, but the most unusual one is a hand-drawn, pointillist portrait of Pacino/Scarface shooting a big automatic rifle in full going-to-glory grimace: When you move in closely, you see that the picture was formed by writing out *the entire script of the movie*—every word of it—in a tiny hand, in black and red ink. Los Angeles Pop Art, the company that manufactures the poster, refers to this method as "micrography"—"tiny writing to render the illusion of an image," says the company Web site. Well, there's nothing illusory about it: you can read *Scarface* with one's face pressed to the poster, or stand back to look at the Pacino *in extremis* photo-image.

Scarface in Prime Time

On TV, *Scarface* references range from the most generic to the most specific, assuming a knowledge of the movie's details. The NBC sitcom *My Name Is Earl,* whose premise is built around a list of sins for which Earl must atone, found a way to imply a Scarface-favorite four-letter word without uttering it. One of Earl's sons tells the show's hero that his ex-wife, Joy, calls his piece of paper "the 'idiot list.'" "But," says the little boy, "she puts another word in front of it. But I don't know what it means—the guy in *Scarface* says it a lot . . ."

On a September 2006 episode of *Law & Order: Criminal Intent,* Chris Noth's Det. Mike Logan explains to a colleague the definition of a "police surgeon" as they examine a doctor's murdered body: "He stitches up cops when they don't want to look like Scarface."

During a September 2006 *Saturday Night Live* "Weekend Update," coanchor Seth Meyers told the following joke: "A South Florida teenager used his father's credit card to run away from home and back to Cuba. For more on this story, see *Scarface: In Reverse*."

The teen drama *The O.C.* likes the movie: In the second-season finale, after a drug deal turns into a shoot-out at the kids' hangout the Bait Shop, Rachel Bilson's Summer is hungry for some pancakes: "After that scene from *Scarface* we just lived through, I could use a short stack, stat." And in the show's final, 2006–07 season, Adam Brody's Seth is seen playing the *Scarface* video game.

Scarface as Pop-Culture Influence

Does all of this have any collective meaning? Certainly. In the firestorm debate that flared in 2007 over radio and TV personality Don Imus's racist jokes and subsequent firing, the media turned its gaze once more to the gangster culture that *Scarface* helped to implant in our collective mind. Once again, the argument about how much violence and misogyny in pop culture seeps into real life was brought to the fore. And here again, De Palma was prescient. In a 1984 interview-essay about De Palma, the novelist Martin Amis wrote, "Brian De Palma once described, with typical recklessness, his notion of an ideal viewership. 'I like a real street audience—people who talk during and *at* a movie, a very unsophisticated, 42nd Street crowd.' He is right to think that he has an affinity for these cineastes," Amis continued, going in for the kill, spilling his contempt on both the director *and* his audience as "[people] who have trouble distinguishing filmic life from the real thing. De Palma movies depend not on a suspension of disbelief, but on a suspension of intelligence such as the 42nd Street crowd have already made before they come jabbering into the stalls."

Amis, go home: The sneery novelist's cheap condescension entirely bypasses the independence and originality of moviegoers' response to *Scarface*—their refusal to do what so many haughty culture observers like Amis usually accuse the masses of doing: of falling for the hype—or in the case of *Scarface*, the initial film-critic hype-dismissal that this was not a movie worth attending to.

A November [6] 2006 *New Yorker* piece by Nick Paumgarten proposed that a new primary text for the gangsta code of honor is Robert Greene's 1998 book, *The 48 Laws of Power*, with its Scarfacian dictates such as "Crush your enemy totally," and "Play a sucker to catch a sucker." Quincy Jones III, son of the music producer, goes so far as to say that hip-hop has evolved beyond its gangsta period, which was, Paumgarten writes, "exemplified by its fixation with the movie *Scarface*, [but is now] into a more mature phase, for which the cold-eyed but buttoned-up ethos of *The 48 Laws* is better suited." For music's sake, one can hope Jones and Paumgarten are right: the gangsta tropes snatched from *Scarface*—the ostentatious jewelry, the glorification of drug-taking as well as drug-selling, and the images of women as near-naked arm-candy—are largely played out, exhausted via endless repetition, leaving behind a few but significant albums or songs that retain, and sometimes exceed brilliantly, the brute power and angry despair of the film.

Paumgarten's promotion of *The 48 Laws* does not mean, however, that *Scarface* itself will dissipate as a pop-cultural influence. By now, its effect is deeply ingrained in the realism of the hard stare, in the romanticism of loyalty and respect, and in the efficiency of the big gun—all of that permeates action movies from directors such as Quentin Tarantino, John Woo, and an upcoming generation of young directors.

These directors include Geo Santini, twenty-eight years old, a pro-lific director of music videos and director of the 2008 urban thriller *Hotel California,* starring Yancey Arias (the title star of a prime-time *Scarface*-influenced TV series, *Kingpin*) as a drug dealer trying to go straight. Santini says he has "a *Scarface* tattoo on my arm—my right arm, with Al Pacino's face as Scarface. Underneath that, is written, 'El niño sin amor,' which means 'A child without love' in Spanish. I've had it since I was seventeen.

"I did a video for [the rapper] Cuban Linx, who also has a *Scarface* tattoo, also on his right arm: he has the actual poster [for *Scarface*]. We were talking about the movie and we agree: We all want the cars, we all want, like Tony wanted, to prove to his mom, 'Hey, I'm better, I made it, I'm a good son, I can provide.'

"He's using a negative avenue [drug-dealing, to achieve his goals], but that's the only avenue he can follow . . . [But] he crossed the line, and that's when everything went wrong: When he killed Manny, he killed a guy who had his back, the guy that helped him get to where he was. And that's also what drowns a lotta people: their egos; getting too infatuated with who they are. That was his downfall. That hap-pens a lot with any person in business, in the music or movie game—whatever. It affects their work and they start to decline."

Santini has a theory about why *Scarface* has such lasting power. "I call it 'The Guy Romance.' It's a movie about the young man who comes from the gutter, and doesn't let nobody stand in his way. He just used whatever way he could to get to the top, to get the things he wanted. And he earned the respect of the people around him. So I think it's the guy romance–movie: he got the woman he wanted; he saw something, he took it. It's what a lotta guys fantasize about, just like a lotta of girls fantasize about, 'Oh, that guy's so sweet, he comes back to the girl at the end.' In our case, he goes after and gets what he wants and takes it to the top."

Yancey Arias, Santini's star in *Hotel California,* says he was "only eight years old the first time I saw it. One of my aunts brought me. I think over the years what the movie has glamorized was that kind of rags to riches thing, but even more exotic is that this guy did something that, in order to make that kind of money, you had to take the riskiest job around which was, you know, selling drugs.

"People come to this country looking for that American dream and several options are closed off to them and they find themselves saying, 'Well, to hell with it—I'm gonna be Scarface,' you know? Which is unfortunate, but it does happen, and Brian De Palma did an excellent job of evoking not just that world, but that *attitude.* Because if you take the drugs out of the equation, the little man with the big heart who just wants to make himself into somebody—you know, the guy says 'the world is yours'?—for guys like myself, who make an honest living, you can still apply a lot of the metaphors or a lot of those phrases in your own life. There was definitely a code of honor in that film. It becomes a profound experience to a lot of people who say, 'You know, I'm not going to be a timid person; I'm not going to let people exploit or manipulate me.' "

Arias calls *Scarface* "the godfather of all the drug movies, and no one else has ever gotten it as right again. They can't touch it. Even [De Palma's] *Carlito's Way* didn't come close. I remember sitting in the audience the night *Carlito's Way* came out. Everyone around me was a big *Scarface* fan, and they couldn't wait to see Al Pacino. He had just won an Oscar for *Scent of a Woman,* he was a huge mainstream star, but this was in a big movie theater in Times Square, and you have all these urban kids, not just black and Hispanics, white people as well, and they wanted not *Scent of a Woman*–Al, they wanted *Scarface*-Al. So they went nuts when [in *Carlito's Way*] he finally opened fire in Grand Central Station, because that to them is what the grandeur of *Scarface* was about, the final scene when he's fighting the Colombians.

"It's like these people weren't even watching a movie called *Carlito's Way*. They were literally trying to revisit *Scarface*."

Another Hispanic actor who feels an intense, ongoing connection to *Scarface* is Vincent Laresca, best known as the terrorist Hector Salazar in the 2003–04 season of TV's *24*. He saw *Scarface* at the tender age of ten, and as he grew up, he says, "as a Latino man in New York it was like, 'I wanna be Tony Montana; I have a shot at *being* Tony.' It really hit my generation of Latinos as, 'Man, that guy looks like *me*. That could *be* me.' He was the first character that, it wasn't about the mob position you held, or about the mob tradition and all this 'made-man' stuff—he was a Marieleto; he came here on a boat and he was gonna live the American dream, at any cost, by any means necessary."

Notes Laresca, "All these rappers that are out there rapping about how much money they got, and all the drugs they sell—that's who they're emulating: They're living their little Tony Montana dream.

"It's hard to say: Had that movie not come out, would pop culture be the way it is? I honestly don't know. When you listen to a song by Jay-Z or a young rap star like a Young Jeezy, what are they talking about? 'Yeah, man, I sold drugs and I got away with it.' That was the whole story of Tony Montana, he sold drugs and got away with it.

"He's a real contradiction—a real hero, and a real tragedy."

Scarface is in many ways a simple-minded movie—a big-budget exploitation film—that has taken on a moral complexity only because of what its viewers have brought to it, read into it, and made of it. It's not what's onscreen so much as how what is onscreen altered the lives of its viewers. Sometimes these alterations are merely crass and knee-jerk (getting off on the carnage and the obscenities), and sometimes these alterations verge on the profound. It's not within this book's scope to speculate on this with any thoroughness, but I do ask this: How many young lives—urban *and* suburban—might be less caught up in criminal behavior had *Scarface* not codified a certain set of rules to live (and die) by?

What follows is what is known about *Scarface*'s impact on entertainment and the world—and that world, to quote the words that appear in the film's bitter, mock-triumphant final image, is ours.

The Movie

Looking for a big commercial hit that had eluded him since *Carrie,* Brian De Palma signed on to *Scarface,* working from a script by Oliver Stone, who in turn was looking for the big commercial hit he hadn't had since writing his Oscar-winning *Midnight Express.* Like tinder and flint, the two sparked a fire that grew into a conflagration that could not be contained.

Scarface tells the story of Tony Montana (Pacino), a young Cuban, a petty criminal, who comes to this country during the 1980 Mariel Boatlift. Along with his friend Manny (Steven Bauer), this indigent illegal proves crafty and ambitious beyond anyone's reckoning. Enlisted by

Frank Lopez, a Miami drug kingpin (Robert Loggia), to make a simple drug score in a seedy motel, the result is a chain-saw massacre from which Tony emerges not just alive but with cash in hand, baptized in the blood of his enemies—and a close friend's. He's christened into gangsterdom by his boss, and lusts after the boss's wife, Elvira (Michelle Pfeiffer).

Tony's employer recognizes the younger man's amoral calculation too late: Tony and Manny murder him, and Tony takes Elvira as his wife and most prized possession. Tony rises to prominence by being more ruthless and wily than any hood around him. The only elements in his life he cannot intimidate into being controlled are his family— his mother, who despises what he has become, and his sister, who eagerly succumbs to the trappings of quick wealth and to her attraction to Manny.

As Tony acquires more—more responsibility, more money, more drugs, more enemies—his marriage turns into a sad, cocaine-addled,

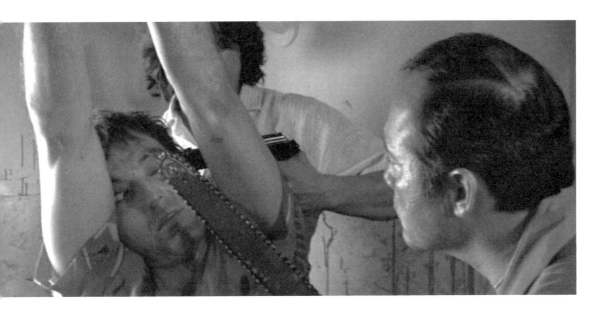

rage-infused joke. He becomes paranoid, haunted: by his crimes; his sins; his failures as a son, brother, husband, and friend. He recognizes the realities of the true danger to his empire too late—only when his worst enemy mounts an all-out assault can Tony rouse himself for one final confrontation with the evil he has brought upon himself, and goes out with a blasting gun and a tragic refusal of repentance.

What I have written above is *Scarface* in a nutshell. I'm assuming you are not a *Scarface* virgin. I'm assuming you've seen the movie at least once, or you wouldn't be here. You probably remember the rhythm of the movie, and key moments such as these:

 ✳ Rounded up by U.S. immigration authorities, Tony proclaims himself a "po-*lit*-i-cal prisoner," but is dismissively thrown into an inhumane, open-air detention center, from which he is sprung by committing a murder. He kills a Castro loyalist among the prison population, and for his work gets another assignment: the drug score for his new boss, Frank Lopez (Loggia).

 ✳ The score turns very bad when Tony and three friends arrive at the Sun Ray Motel to trade money for drugs, and encounter Hector the Pig and his yellow chain saw. Tony's friend Angel is hacked to death before his eyes—eyes that go dead: Tony has entered the realm of soulless criminality and revenge, gaining new impetus to acquire enough control over his life so that such a thing never happens again.

 ✳ For surviving this ordeal—and for meting out his own lethal punishment upon his attackers—Tony arrives, with the drugs in hand, to Lopez's fancy Miami digs and is taken as Frank's guest to the posh-garish Babylon Club. Two crucial things occur in these scenes. Tony

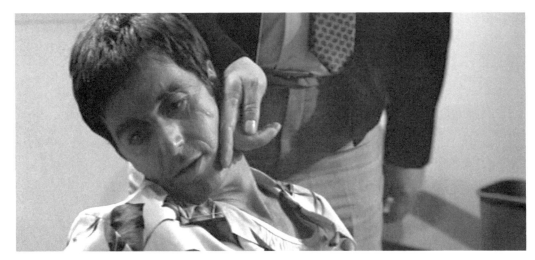

first sees Elvira (Pfeiffer) as she descends in a glass elevator in a way that makes her seem, to Tony, a heaven-sent princess (albeit one with a foul mouth and a nose for toot). And Frank and Elvira give him a couple of rules to live by: "Don't get high on your own supply" and "Never underestimate the greed of the *other* guy."

✳ Soon, Tony and his best pal Manny (Bauer) are moving up in the world, dressing better, driving better cars. But when Tony visits his poor mother (Miriam Colon) and his sister Gina (Mary Elizabeth Mastrantonio) in their shabby little house, his mother rejects the ill-gotten wad of cash he proffers, and his sister, who adores her brother, is intrigued by his new lifestyle . . . and her innocent beauty attracts the attention of Manny.

✳ Tony discerns that Frank Lopez is getting "soft," complacent—he's ripe to become a victim of a Tony Montana power grab. As Tony's ambition becomes known to Frank, he survives a gun-down in the Babylon Club. Tony takes it all: Lopez's life, and Elvira as his wife.

✳ Big business keeps getting bigger: Hooking up with Lopez's foreign supplier, the Bolivian drug lord Sosa (Paul Shenar), Scarface takes over Lopez's operation, cutting new and bigger deals. Tony's

pledge to Sosa: "All I have in this life is my balls and my word, and I don't break 'em for nobody." With Sosa's South American drugs in his Miami pipeline, Tony makes massive amounts of money—money that must be laundered and which attracts the attention of the government.

✳   Unfazed, for the moment, Tony gets caught up in his lifestyle—grandly opulent, crassly decadent. (Key Tony proclamation here: "You know what capitalism is? 'Get fucked.'") Elvira, always melancholy in a way that expresses itself in hostility and solitary drug-taking, withdraws further from him. They have a drunken, drug-addled fight in a restaurant, which culminates in Tony's ejection, as he shouts to the wealthy diners, "You don't have the guts to be what you want to be. You need people like me so you can point your fingers and say, '*That's* the fucking bad guy' . . . Me, I always tell the truth, even when I lie. So say good-bye to the bad guy. It's the last time you're gonna see a bad guy like this again!"

✳   Inevitably, Tony finds himself made a target for a banal but relentlessly pursued crime: tax evasion. A Bolivian politician comes to America to give testimony for the crimes the Sosa-Montana cartel have committed. It's decided to blow up the car the man is traveling in. But when Tony, in another car, behind the wheel with a thug who's rigged a bomb under the Bolivian's car, sees that the man's wife and children are with him, his moral border has been found. Instead of killing the intended target, Tony shoots the bomber.

✳   As if things weren't bad enough for the bad guy, Tony hasn't noticed that Manny and Gina had fallen in love, something that Tony, with protectiveness that inevitably tips over into the irrational, has forbidden. He kills Manny, and in doing so, begins his final descent into guilt, rage, paranoia, and paranoia-justified.

✳   His dealings with Sosa ruined, addicted to cocaine to such an extent that he keeps a small volcano of the stuff on his desk to dip his head into with alarming regularity, Tony prepares for a final face-off when South American gunmen invade his Miami compound. Tony pulls out the big gun—"Say hello to my little friend!"—and tries to blam-blam-blam his way out of his jam, but it's too little, too late. Tony is riddled with enemy fire, and falls from his balcony into his indoor fountain, the one topped with a shiny ball that proclaims, "The World Is Yours."

It never really was, but Tony's extravagant overreaching is its own reward: money, power, sex, and ultimately, the death he now truly desires most of all.

Making a *Scarface*

For a movie of such comparatively recent vintage, there are many aspects of the 1983 production whose details differ depending on who you talk to or read about. Even the origin of the project is a matter of mild dispute.

Producer Martin Bregman, once Pacino's manager and at the time a close friend and advisor, told me that the notion of remaking Hawks's original "was mine. The concept was to do a film about the rise and fall of an American gangster, or the rise and fall of an American businessman. Or somebody with power. And that's what [excited] the audience for this. If you go into the hip-hop world, they consider

it a story about coming up—do you know what 'coming up' means? Coming from nothing. Which, let's face it, most of the people in this country—in this world—come from nothing. We weren't all blessed with rich fathers."

Bregman does acknowledge another figure's crucial contribution in the notion of moving the tale from gangland Chicago to then-contemporary Miami. "It was [director] Sidney Lumet's idea. When I first went to Sidney, with whom I disagreed later on a political issue"—more about that in a bit—"in the initial discussion, he had a great idea. Sidney said, 'Well, liquor is no longer outlawed, there's no such thing as Prohibition, and why don't you look into the cocaine world,' which at the time was reaching epidemic proportions as an illegal import into the country, and largely through ports in southern Florida. And that was it. That was a brilliant idea of his."

But wait, back up a minute. Pacino has said that *he* had the idea for *Scarface*. Talking to host James Lipton in a 2006 *Inside the Actors Studio* interview, with Bregman sitting and smiling in the audience, the actor said, "I had always wanted to see the Paul Muni *Scarface*, because he was an actor I admired tremendously. And one night in Hollywood, on Sunset Boulevard, I passed by a theater, a revival house that was showing the [old] *Scarface*. Well, I was just floored by it. I came out of that theater and I called Marty Bregman and I said, 'I really think there's a movie here—we can contemporize this and really make something special.'

In a 2006 *E! True Hollywood Story* documentary on *Scarface*, the actor retold the same story, adding, "I'd never built up a character in quite that way, from the outside"—as opposed to the inner, clockwork-mechanics of characterization that this most brooding, "interior" of major film actors usually deployed.

While completing the editing of *Blow Out*, De Palma was approached by producer Martin Bregman about remaking Hawks's *Scarface* with Pacino as its star. De Palma was intrigued by Bregman's idea—which at that point was *Scarface* as a period piece, set during the early 1930s—and began working on a script with the playwright David Rabe. (De Palma had collaborated with Rabe off-Broadway, in a revival of the 1971 play *The Basic Training of Pavlo Hummel,* and on an early version of *Prince of the City,* which, with a different script, would eventually be directed by Sidney Lumet.)

But De Palma and Rabe never found a way to do the story that pleased them, and so they bowed out of Bregman's project, which the producer then took to—in a tidy coincidence—Sidney Lumet. Bregman paired Lumet with Oliver Stone. "I brought Stone in," Bregman told me. "I'd known him for years. I'd once optioned a script he'd written that I couldn't get anyone to make and that film was *Platoon.*" (Ah, the ones that get away, eh?)

"Oliver was a wonderful writer and had experienced the ups and downs of cocaine. I'm not telling you anything out of school, because he'd tell you the same thing." And indeed Stone has, to me and in numerous interviews. (For my own interview with Stone on the genesis of *Scarface,* see Chapter 4, "Four Creators.")

Stone's druggy days are, even in his own mind, legion. "I'll admit that cocaine kicked my ass. It's one of the things that beat me in life," he's said. "Cocaine took me to the edge."[1]

Stone ticks off this era of his filmography as something of a pharmaceutical event: "*Conan* was written on cocaine and downers. The drug period was from *Conan* through *The Hand,* and into my research for *Scarface*."[2]

Stone seized on Lumet's idea to transform *Scarface* from a '30s Chicago gangster to an '80s Cuban immigrant-turned-gangster. "*Scarface* grew out of this Lumet idea of the Marielitos coming to America, the brazenness, the drug trade, making it big, taking over from the old Cuban mob." Stone has said, "The Marielitos at the time had gained a lot of publicity for their open brazenness. The Marielitos were the 'crazies.' They were deported by Castro in 1981 to America . . . it was perceived he was dumping all the criminals into the American system. According to the police enforcement in Miami Beach, they were the poorest people, the roughest people in the prisons, who would kill for a dollar. How could you get this outlandish, operatic character inside an American, contemporary framework? . . . That was the artistic challenge."

Stone did a lot of first-person research "in Florida and the Caribbean. I had been in South America [and] I saw quite a bit of the drug trade from the legal point of view as well as the gangster point of view . . . There's no law down there; they'll just shoot you in your hotel room. It got hairy; it gave me all this color. I wanted to do a sun-drenched, tropical, Third-World gangster, sexy Miami movie."

Bregman told me that he, too, went with Stone on some of these expeditions: "We spent a good deal of time in Florida. Pretty much everything I saw was in the film. The way the big drug lords were depicted were [as] very successful businessmen, and their business was cocaine."

Stone lit out for Paris to complete the script. "I moved to Paris and got out of the cocaine world," he told *Creative Screenwriting.* "I was an addictive personality. I did it . . . to where I was stale mentally . . . I moved to Paris to try and get into another world . . . and I wrote the script totally fucking cold sober."

But when Stone turned in his script, Lumet balked, considering Stone's work florid, melodramatic, and simplistic—more the blueprint for an exploitation film than the movie of ideas that Lumet had envisioned. He wanted to explore the politics and human plight of an immigrant who is forced by circumstance into crime. Stone says, "Sidney did not understand my script, whereas Bregman wanted to continue in that direction with Al."

Bregman put it to me more bluntly: "When I had completed the script"—these producers, they take credit for *everything,* don't they?— "Pacino wanted Sidney, okay? I had made two successful films with Lumet and Al, *Dog Day Afternoon* and *Serpico,* so I wasn't opposed to that. Sidney's a good director, and in my discussions with him, that's how the whole liquor [theme] changed to cocaine. But then Sidney said, 'I have a problem with this script. The problem is it's not political enough. I see the Reagan administration being heavily involved in the cocaine world.' Which was a crock of shit. There was nothing political about [the cocaine trade]—it was a business."

For his part, Lumet says that he objected to "the corny elements" in the script, specifically the sentimental portrayal of Tony's mother and sister. "I also wanted to introduce political ramifications, exploring the CIA's involvement of drugs as part of their anti-Communist drive. I didn't want to do it on just a gangster or cop level. As it stood, it was a comic strip."[3]

"And I wasn't about to do anything that would indict [then-President] Reagan, over something he had nothing to do with," retorts Bregman. "He wasn't involved in the cocaine world. At that point I said to Sidney, 'We're talking about a different film. Go make it. It's not this film.' So we separated."

As far as Lumet's dismissal of the script as cartoonish is concerned, Bregman has been quoted by writer Andrew Yule as saying, "De Palma and I had no intention of making a comic strip. We wanted to give the whole thing a larger-than-life, *operatic* quality." The italics are Yule's; the "operatic" is, as I've said, the adjective that will be used by all principals in this production to give a high-culture gloss to its grand-grunge melodrama.

Pacino said of Stone's script, "The text was magnificent. Oliver Stone, he's going to speak about things that are going on in society. He can't help himself, God bless him."[4]

With this new-angle script, Bregman reapproached De Palma with the project, describing De Palma as strictly "a director for hire. He did not design the film, he did not have anything to do with the creation of the film."

De Palma Commits

De Palma was in the mood to do a remake: He'd been thinking of shooting a modernization of John Huston's *The Treasure of the Sierra Madre*, so the *Scarface* theme of greed destroying loyalty appealed to him. In an early *Scarface* scene that was cut, Tony and Manny watch *Sierra Madre* in the Mariel camp, the movie projected against a sheet in a kind of double-reference to a similar scene in Preston Sturges's *Sullivan's Travels*. The script cited a specific *Madre* scene—the one in which Humphrey Bogart laments, "Conscience, conscience: what a thing." Conscience: the thing Tony lacks near the end; what brings about his downfall.

"Did they leave in the *Sierra Madre* stuff?" Stone asked me when I interviewed him in 2006 for this book. "I forget. I was pretty pleased with myself for layering that in there; I think it's a nice touch."

What remains of *Madre* in *Scarface* is a few seconds of Tony and Manny leaving the movie. After watching *Madre,* Tony praises Humphrey Bogart's performance by saying, "He's always looking over his shoulder, like me." All of which is to say: De Palma was game. "*Scarface* is a new way of working for me," he said at the time. "Here I've got a very strong script, an actor who knows what he wants, and a producer who is in on every detail. This is more like a collaboration."

This is putting the best face on Bregman's he-was-a-gun-for-hire interpretation. It also served as a commercial bridge between two of De Palma's most personal films, 1981's *Blow Out* and 1984's *Body Double*. Certainly, at its best *Scarface* achieves some of the sense of tragic inevitability that makes *Blow Out* more moving every time you see it. While there is nothing in *Scarface* that matches John Travolta's anguish when he realizes he has unwittingly led Nancy Allen's character into mortal danger, De Palma lifted what could indeed have been creepy comic-strip incest symbolism in the relationship between Tony and his sister by tapping into the roiling emotions that Paul Muni exhibited for his Scarface's sister a half-century before.

John Travolta in *Blow Out* (Everett Collection)

The Casting

After Pacino was locked in, a young actor, Steven Bauer, a twenty-five-year-old Miami-born Cuban, was chosen over De Palma's first choice, Travolta. Bauer was a perfectly good choice for Manny—he had the right dashing looks, he spoke Spanish, and he could help Pacino work on his own accent (and he was then married to Melanie Griffith, who'd later star in *Body Double*). Pacino told James Lipton on *Actors Studio*, "Bauer and I spent months preparing for this. He's Cuban, so I spent a lot of time with him . . . building the character. I'd never quite thought of a character that way, from the outside, too [i.e., in addition to the "inside," Method-style]. Starting with the scar and the accent and the body language."

Other parts were cast in New York, where Pacino was then based. Auditions were set up at the Puerto Rican Traveling Theater on West 47th Street in Manhattan, a company cofounded by Miriam Colon, who was cast as Pacino's mother (this, despite the fact that Colon

Steven Bauer and then-wife, Melanie Griffith, at the *Scarface* premiere in New York City
(Walter McBride/ Retna)

was only four years older than Pacino). It was here that *Scarface* costars such as Michelle Pfeiffer and Robert Loggia were cast.

Bregman says the casting of Pfeiffer was a cinch—sort of. "Her agent called, because we were auditioning girls in a theater on the west side of New York, he [was an] agent I knew who worked for the William Morris agency, and said, 'Marty, I *have* Elvira!' I said that's terrific, let me get a look at her, because we only had two days left to complete the casting. He said, 'Let me convince you to bring her [from Los Angeles] to New York.' I said, 'I can't do that because first of all, this is a girl I've never heard of before, a big unknown.'" (Bregman had apparently not been aware of the tremendous hype Pfeiffer had been given leading up to her starring-ingenue role in the bomb *Grease 2*.) But, he told the agent, "'If she wants to come, she can come.' Now, in anything I've done, when somebody wants to pay their way and pick up their own tab [to audition], I'll reimburse them for it. But I didn't feel it was up to me to reimburse someone who I'd never heard of. I would be auditioning ten thousand women from all over the country if I did that."

Pfeiffer arrived on her own dime, therefore, and, she told James Lipton in a separate interview, that the audition "was a rough one . . . intense." Pfeiffer says she was called back more than once, and at one point was asked to do a squabbling marriage-feud scene with Pacino that required her to break dishes and throw them around, one shard of which "cut Al's hand—I saw the blood on the floor, I thought it was *my* blood, but no, I'd cut this big movie star!"[5]

Says Bregman, "She came in and she went up onstage and read with Al and she was sensational. Brian and I looked at each other and I said, 'That's Elvira.' We shook hands, and that was it."

But Pacino had qualms. "Al didn't feel that way until some time later," says Bregman. "We continued auditions, but I knew it was going to be Michelle [in the role]. And so did Brian. But it took a little time to convince Al. He was concerned that she was not experienced enough and that she didn't look right. She didn't fit the image of Elvira he had in his mind. But he was dead wrong. To put a long-standing rumor to rest: It wasn't Brian, it was Al who had the resistance to Michelle."

When I asked Bregman whether there was someone else Pacino had in mind, someone with more experience, Bregman hesitated, then said, "I won't mention her name. She was so wrong for this."

Aw, come on.

"Okay, it was, oh, what the hell's her name—it was Glenn Close."

Really? Boy, would *that* have been a mistake, I said.

"*Oh* boy would that have been wrong!" Bregman agreed. "I had a long, old relationship with Al, and I told him he didn't know what the hell he was thinking. I told him he didn't know his ass from his elbow. I said this character is partly a courtesan, and she has to be half a hooker. Glenn Close is many things, but she is *not* half a hooker."

Robert Loggia's casting as Tony's first boss, Frank Lopez, also occurred at the New York sessions. Loggia, by that time a well-established character actor, chafes a bit at the memory: "They flew me to New York; it was Miriam Colon's theater company, [housed] in a church. It was like open season for actors, the producers were sitting in the pews watching people audition for different scenes. Which is unusual—usually an audition is a very private matter. But this one was like a public offering. My audition was delayed, it was taking so long that I was ready to say, 'Fuck you,' and leg it out of there home [to Los Angeles]. I studied Spanish in high school and college and I was stationed in Panama for a couple of years, 1951 to '53 during the Korean War, and Frank Lopez was a Sephardic Jew brought up in Cuba. So I was able to draw on real life; I was able to nail Frank Lopez with great authority.

"Pacino had a lot of power right from the get-go, as to who would play the roles, et cetera," says Loggia. "He liked me; I liked him. Marty Bregman was just interested to the extent that he had Pacino [signed as the star], and as far as everyone else was concerned, he was just doing us a favor. He'd say things like, 'Don't take it personally, but it's a privilege you're in the movie'—it was that kind of [attitude]."

Still, Loggia appreciated that Pacino's power also extended to an insistence with Universal, the studio bankrolling the film, that a few weeks of rehearsal be built into the $20 million budget. ("Pacino was in his heyday, when he loved to rehearse," Stone has said.[6]) Pacino was concerned about getting his accent down, and De Palma wanted the actors to know their lines and the emotional arc of the movie so that he could execute more efficiently some of the elaborate establishing crane shots and intricate action scenes he envisioned. "We had a lot of rehearsal time," Loggia says—at least two weeks, according to Bauer[7]—and the future Frank Lopez says that "We were in such a zone when we were doing the picture; we spoke the Cuban accent on the set and off the set and during dinner, all the time."

Shooting *Scarface* in Miami

Principal photography on *Scarface* began in November 1982. Two years earlier, over a period of six months in 1980, Fidel Castro had, as Stone noted earlier, released over 125,000 Cubans in what became known as the Mariel Boatlift. As Joan Didion wrote in her 1987 book *Miami*, Mariel "meant not just the place [a Cuban port] and not just the boatlift and not just what many see as the 'trick,' the way in which Fidel Castro managed to take his own problem and make it Miami's." Most of these refugees landed in Miami: 26,000 of them had criminal records; many had histories of mental illness. Fifty-seven-thousand Mariels camped out under the bleachers of the Orange Bowl, which was used as an emergency shelter, or lived in makeshift tent cities in the stadium's parking lot and under the ramps of I-95. A Drug Enforcement Agent (DEA) for the FBI, Mark Trouvile, has said that one result, in Miami, was "a Wild West situation" where crime almost immediately became rampant, and that "*Scarface* caught that mood."[8]

Caught it a bit too well, for some Miamians. In 1981, *Time* magazine did a cover story on the city entitled "Paradise Lost," which explored Miami's rising crime rate, and how the stereotype of the town as a haven for doddering senior citizens looking for a place to warm their brittle bones had been replaced as a haven for muscular drug merchants who'd found a handy port of entry for cocaine shipments from South America.

This *Time* magazine piece did not sit well with the town's civic leaders. So, when they got wind of a Universal Pictures production company invading their town to make a bloody movie about a Miami drug lord—and a Cuban-refugee one at that—squawking commenced immediately. Miami Commissioner Demetrio Perez introduced a resolution to the city council that would have prohibited the production from getting a permit to shoot on any piece of city property—that is, almost everywhere (even if Universal rented out private houses and restaurants, they still needed to put their equipment on city streets).

Freely admitting he hadn't read the *Scarface* script, Perez waged a pretty successful one-man war against the production, countering the usual movie-company claim—that making a movie in a town brings it millions of dollars in publicity and tourism—by saying *Scarface* would actually drive people away from Miami, that more people would see this film than had read the *Time* article, and look how *that* piece had tarnished the city's image. Bregman protested to the *Miami Herald*: "We are not doing a film about Cubans in Miami. We're doing a picture about one gangster. The movie has more crooked Jews than crooked Cubans."

Says Bregman today, "I had a big run-in with one of the commissioners there, Perez, who thought the movie was insulting to the good Cuban-American community. I guess I blasted him a little bit in an interview [I gave in Miami], but he'd convinced some in the Cuban community that this was a Castro-financed film, being made to embarrass the Cuban-American community. Which was insane. I mean,

Lew Wasserman [then-chairman of Universal Pictures] was many things, but he was not paid by Fidel Castro to okay this film. It was a movie about capitalism, for god's sake; it was an antidrug film."

Perez was not alone. "We're very concerned about stereotyping that would cause damage to the Cuban community in the United States," said Eduardo Padron, head of the Spanish-American League Against Discrimination to the *Miami Herald* in July 1982. "The basic message of the movie seems to be drugs, killing, and criminal activities. That does not represent the majority of hard-working and law-abiding Cubans."

Yet the film production had its political supporters as well. The *Miami Herald* noted that Manny Diaz, board member of the Spanish-American League Against Discrimination, said he was "concerned

Manny shows Tony a certain technique.

A Director Is Born During *Scarface*

One notable extra in a Miami street scene was future director Brett Ratner (*X-Men: The Last Stand; Rush Hour*). The native Miamian was a young teenager when the *Scarface* crew came to town.

"I was on the set of *Scarface*—I skipped school to go to the set every day and watch them shoot—and I saw Brian De Palma telling Al Pacino what to do, and Al Pacino doing what the director told him to do.

"I shot a *Variety* cover of Al Pacino [in 2007]. I walked up to Pacino and I said, 'I was on the set when you shot *Scarface* and it's because of you that I became a director.'

"'Why's that?' he asked me, and I said, 'Because I saw you act and I could never be that good, so I wanted to be the guy who told you what to do.'"

that community 'overreaction' could drive *Scarface* away. 'I want the movie to be filmed here,' Diaz said. 'If it gets filmed in Topeka, Kansas, we won't be able to have any input in it.'"

Nonetheless, by August 1982, with shooting scheduled to start in mid-October, Commissioner Perez was apparently fancying himself a budding screenwriter, for he told the *Miami Herald* that he "wants Pacino to play not just any Mariel refugee, but a Communist agent, infiltrated into the United States by the Fidel Castro government." Bregman's response? "Preposterous."

Perez drew up a resolution that would have banned filming *Scarface* on city property—a clever move, because in other words, Bregman and Universal could rent or buy any locations they liked, but they wouldn't be able to shoot crucial street scenes or even park their equipment trucks on Miami streets. The resolution stated that Pacino's character promoted the "propagation of pernicious racism."

By early September, with a minimal amount of footage shot and increasing protests and threats from locals, Universal decided it wasn't worth the grief. Bregman announced they were packing up the production and going home to Hollywood to shoot the rest there. The *Miami Herald* reported that some politicians, having recognized all along the financial windfall that the influx of a major motion-picture production can bring, "scrambled to get the filmmakers to reconsider." Marylee Lander, Miami-Dade's film and television coordinator, estimated that *Scarface* would have meant "at least $10 million to Dade's economy," newspapers reported. Commissioner Perez, of course, proclaimed the pull-out "a victory for the people of Miami."

Says Steven Bauer now, "We didn't so much leave as we didn't get a chance to start. Before we could ever really get going, Universal got nervous about the community reaction, which is really based on one [op-ed page] editorial in the *Miami Herald* by one guy, this city commissioner." Demetrio Perez? "Yes! He was sort of this self-interested person, ranting and raving about the plot of the movie. But it was enough to scare the bosses of Universal about a potential boycott or protests, demonstrations of some sort. And the possibility of having to shut down once we started. So they made a decision to do all the interiors in Los Angeles at Universal."

Bregman told me, "Well, it's something I haven't discussed before, but there were a lot of threats, telephone calls, and in one case, a visit. I threw them out of the office. I took it seriously enough that I did not allow my wife and newborn child to come to Miami, because I thought that harm would befall them; so did the studio, and those around me did."

Bregman says it wasn't just him who was contacted. "Al once got a threat that he didn't interpret as a threat. [Someone] called him on his number, which was unlisted, and that was a pretty new thing at that point, to be able get hold of unlisted numbers. This person told him it would not be a healthy thing for him to do this film."

"They basically ran us out of town," De Palma has said.

The film's costume designer, Patricia Norris, told me, "I did think they'd have killed us if we'd stayed in Miami. There were members of the community who hated us because they thought we were doing a pro-Castro movie, which was absurd, but their anger was very serious. And then there were real drug people around, Colombians who came on the set. The day a fellow sat down in the chair next to me, and crossed his legs, and I saw a gun strapped to his ankle, I knew I wanted to get back to Los Angeles. Thank god we did, within two weeks."

Shooting *Scarface* in Los Angeles

And so, the Miami internment-camp scenes in *Scarface* were actually filmed not under Florida's I-95 ramps, but beneath the Santa Monica and Harbor freeways in Los Angeles. Tony's wedding to Elvira was shot not at some posh Coral Gables mansion, but at a thirty-five-acre mansion in Santa Barbara once owned by the novelist Thomas Mann. (Once inside, seated before a pile of cocaine, *Scarface* would give new meaning to the term "Magic Mountain.") Most of the interiors, in fact, were built and shot at Universal Studios. And when principal photography was done, De Palma and a small crew went back and shot some scenes in Miami. "We started around Thanksgiving of 1982 and finished in May of 1983," says Bauer. "So, by the time we were finishing, we could slip into Miami and pick up all the location stuff, so we did all that in Miami Beach. By then all the furor had ended. Universal wasn't as nervous." (Bregman and Loggia contradict this in the 2006 *E! True Hollywood Story* documentary, with Bregman saying he received more threats and carried a gun for self-protection, and Loggia asserting bluntly, "They wanted us out in a hurry. [Many people in Miami] were not thrilled by our presence there.")

As a result of all these moves, what was slated to be a five-month shoot ended up taking nearly seven. Loggia remembers the added shooting time well, because he says it sparked a fight with Bregman over his salary. "The pay was zilch. I'm not going to tell you what I got, but when [we went over-schedule], that went beyond my original signing agreement into a penalty period." Bregman, he says, didn't want to pony up. "He said, 'I'll give you some extra plane tickets.' I said 'Go fuck yourself.' So I had to go to the CAA lawyer [at the agency that represented him] and he took one look at the contract and said to Bregman, 'Oh, for chrissake, pay him!' It was just case closed, it was in the contract, and [Bregman] wanted to get around it for some fucking reason. Cheap or whatever, I don't know. I don't give a flying fuck. Intimidation. He picked the wrong guy to try and intimidate."

Bregman chose not to comment on this when I recited Loggia's side of the story, opting instead to praise Loggia's film performance as "gutsy." For his part, Loggia says, "At the twentieth anniversary party, when they launched the DVD [release], Marty Bregman and I shook hands; we let bygones be bygones."

Getting the Accent Right

Shooting the movie presented challenges beyond the pressures from outside influences. For one thing, there was the accent Pacino had to master. Over the years, comedians and T-shirt slogans have made a household phrase of Tony's machine-gun mini-aria, "Say hello to my little friend!" or as it is more commonly written as the actor enunciated it, "Say hello to mah leetle *fren'*!" The Cuban accent Pacino presented has been compared unfavorably to Desi Arnaz's Ricky Ricardo in *I Love Lucy*. But that ignores the fact that Arnaz was Cuban and was only slightly exaggerating the accent he had when he spoke in serious interviews. In other words, Tony's accent seems an excessive stereotype only when Tony is doing something excessively atypical to normal life, such as snorting desktops-full of coke and mowing down enemies with a gun as big as his torso.

Pacino had a number of collaborators in building the accent, chief among them dialect coach Robert Easton, and Bauer says he, as the son of Cuban parents, was also of considerable help: "I was one of [Pacino's] main teachers. There was Robert Easton, who worked with us, when Al and I spent time together for a month before we started shooting. Every day we would just go over our lines in-character, talk about Cuba, talk about society, talk about what this country, the United States, would be like to us as outsiders. It was homework of a very abstract nature, subliminal and useful because it colored what we did when we got in front of the cameras. We really became those guys."

Loggia confirms this. "We would go out to dinner, Pacino and

How Many Suits Does It Take to Make a *Scarface*?

Between nine and twelve, apparently. Patricia Norris, *Scarface* costume designer, said, "I made between nine and twelve versions of it; especially for the big gun scene at the end, we used nine [black suits] for that [scene] alone. It's a pain— they all have to match, of course, and you have to make sure the blood-spatter matches, and then they get sooty with the smoke effects and the fake gunpowder. You run through a lot of suits, especially when they're white. But that was my own fault, I wanted him in white [for the Babylon Club shoot-out]. I completely agreed with Brian [De Palma] that it was interesting to [dress] a bad guy [in white]. We think of good guys in white, bad guys in black. To put the bad guy in white, I liked that. And contrary to what you may read about that time, white was *not* a popular color to wear at night in Miami. It was *over* as a disco-suit color, even then. I like to think we brought it back [in fashion]."

Bauer and I, especially when we were first in Florida. We would continue to speak with a Cuban accent, just to have it become second nature. Accents are very tricky things. You really have to work at it because it can so easily come across as phony."

Costume designer Patricia Norris adds, "Pacino was very nice. I had been told he was going to stay in character and all that, so I was prepared for it." He spoke to her in the Cuban accent even during his wardrobe fittings. "Oh yeah—[he was] real Method, you know?"

The movie was also fortunate in many ways to have as its cinematographer John A. Alonzo, a Cuban-American who not only shot many of the film's more difficult sequences, such as the shoot-out against mirrored walls in the Babylon nightclub, but who also helped Pacino hone his impersonation. "When I first met [Pacino], we hadn't even started production, and he was using the accent," Alonzo, who died in 2001, told *American Cinematographer*. "I spoke Spanish to him and asked if it was okay. His response was, 'Please! The more Spanish I hear, the better I'll feel.' That, to me, is a prepared actor."

Bauer says that "Robert Easton would give Al notes on the grammatical rules; he would have the class-division breakdowns of the Cuban accents. And then my contribution was the realization that [Tony's accent] was my dad's accent. So I would work with Al on the conversational sound of it, and Robert Easton would give him the rules of the language. And I also taught Al that little bit of Spanish he uses in the film. Al wanted one moment when Tony bursts into Spanish with someone who speaks Spanish. Tony and Manolo, among themselves, would speak English because we were characters who didn't want to be seen as outsiders. And in terms of the movie, we didn't want to speak Spanish to each other because then you'd have to use subtitles, and we didn't want the audience to get pulled out of the drama by having to read subtitles." He laughs. "Maybe the audience for this movie wouldn't have read the subtitles!"

Bauer continues, "So Al chose to speak Spanish in the scene when he's in the car [in New York City], stuck with that guy who's talking to him in Spanish saying they have to blow up that car [containing a Colombian drug lord who's burned Tony] now, *now*! Tony's upset because he didn't plan for the wife and kid to be in the car, and that's his [moral] boundary; he hits a wall there. So Al wanted me to teach him how to say that in Spanish, so he can blow up at this guy and say no, I'm *not* killing this guy when he's with his wife and kids; it's not right.

John Alonzo shooting Roger Corman's *Bloody Mama,* 1970 (AIP)

"For me, the criticism of his accent—I just lump that into all the nitpicking that went on over the years of anything related to the movie."

Pacino suffered for his art in other ways. During one of the first times he had to handle one of Tony's machine guns, it proved not to be a little friend: The actor grabbed the recently fired weapon by its still-red-hot barrel and suffered second-degree burns on his hand, which kept him off-camera for a week.

Ego Clashes—Um, Creative Differences— On the Set

Oliver Stone was present for much of the shooting, during the brief, abortive stage in Miami, and later for a longer period in California, "because Marty [Bregman] and Al asked me to," Stone told me. "Which was a tough [decision], because I wasn't making more money by staying, but rather I was sort of protecting the script. And it turned from three months into six months."

As he saw how De Palma was interpreting his script, he became annoyed and protective of the project, and wrote a memo to Bregman and the studio listing his concerns and complaints. Bregman was furious that Stone copied Pacino on this memo, bringing the actor over to the screenwriter's side on a number of items. Stone explained to me that the memo contained "about twenty-four things. Mostly about dialogue and mood-setting scenes that were being cut because De Palma had all these elaborate camera shots he wanted to shove in there, and something had to go. To me, what was being sacrificed was narrative sense and atmosphere. That seemed crucial to me—worth fighting for.

"Bregman is a very old-fashioned producer, out of the Darryl Zanuck mold in that way: He wants control and his favorite ploy is to make someone a demon—so it became, 'Stone is impossible to work with!'; 'Pacino is a nutcase!' He'd say, 'De Palma, I'm reviving his career!' It's all ego, all 'me-me-me,' and Marty needs that ammunition in his head: He's an aggressive personality. On the other hand, I would say it's his aggression that got *Scarface* made . . .

"His method of not taking prisoners, however, was not good for me. Al and I did have a relationship going back to *Born on the Fourth of July,* for which I did numerous drafts for Al, [in collaboration] with [the book's author] Ron Kovic. We rehearsed *Scarface* extensively; it was not a normal film in that sense. And also, Bregman treated De Palma like a hired director, so in order to get my points made—if I give my letter to Bregman and De Palma, it [probably] gets torn up and forgotten—so my point of view was that Pacino is the only one who can really do something about the production, and there are some fundamental flaws here. The letter probably *did* get torn up as it went into the system. I never saw Bregman again for years. In fact, I don't really speak to him today."

Stone's irksome memo addressed what he felt were "questions of logic. The film has a realistic base onto which was put an operatic framework. Which is okay—it made the movie what it is, but for operatic purposes you don't throw out logic, and certain things were sticking in my craw. I think Brian had strayed—" Stone pauses here, looking for the right words before simply sighing and saying, "Sometimes his plot points are ridiculous. It's as if there's nobody keeping rational logic there. He's done certain things in other of his films too that are really loopy"—Stone pauses to laugh almost affectionately—"*really* loopy."

Stone elaborates upon what he felt was De Palma's excessiveness. "I'll give you an example: I think the ending was written realistically, that Tony had fucked over the cartel. And they came to get him at the mansion, and I'd written it as four or five gunmen sneaking up on him on his property, and, of course, when I got on the set"—Stone laughs and shakes his head in disbelief—"it was like thirty or forty gunmen! It could have been fifty or sixty—it didn't matter. It became a Hong Kong [action] movie at that point. And I'm surprised—but, well, people loved it! And I don't say Hong Kong idly, because after *Scarface*, Hong Kong action films started upping their numbers, shooting people much more readily and easily.

"It changes the nature of the film; it was *so* outrageous at this point, and Brian just kept going and going, and for some reason it works. Why does it work to have, I don't know, a *hundred* men go in there and shoot at Tony, all alone? I didn't know, I didn't see it, back then. [But] that's a Hong Kong action-film shoot-out before its time, right?"

Bregman and De Palma also clashed over the number of takes in any given scene. Pacino's penchant for improvisation, and for plucking out further layers of characterization through repetition, was at odds with De Palma's elaborately staged shooting. Cinematographer Alonzo struggled to shoot the nightclub sequence, during which Tony's back is to a multimirrored wall, without having any of those mirrors reflect his camera. There are only so many times one can set up and explode all that glass (and as it is, *Scarface* obsessives can, with the DVD, freeze-frame a shot wherein you'll see De Palma's reflection behind Tony's head), and therefore a limit to the number of times an actor can request one more chance to capture performance magic. "There's a lot of screaming and yelling that goes on over the course of the making of any movie," De Palma told me. "But in the end, the work gets done, tempers die down, and we all know we're working toward the same goal—to make a good picture."

The film's costume designer, Patricia Norris, says, "Let me put it this way: After *Scarface,* I almost didn't want to work in the movies again. You're making a movie that's not about nice people, being made by people many of whom aren't nice people. . . . It was tense, pretty distant. I don't like being condescended to. I worked with David Lynch for over twenty-five years [on movies such as *Lost Highway* and

The Ghost of *Scarface*: Lana Clarkson

If you look closely at Steven Bauer's dance partner in the Babylon nightclub scenes, you can recognize her as Lana Clarkson, the woman whom legendary music producer Phil Spector was accused of murdering in 2003. On her Web site, Clarkson wrote, "It was an interesting set to be on . . . though I was basically window dressing. Mr. Pacino was always in character, even when in his trailer, which was just down from mine. I often overheard him speaking to his dresser in his Tony Montana accent. Steven Bauer was dreamy, Michelle Pfeiffer nervous, and De Palma drank lots of coffee."

the TV pilot of *Twin Peaks*] because he was a nice person and an artist, and he appreciates the artistry other people bring to their work.

"I didn't get that feeling with De Palma. He was tense a lot of the time; he could be cold and rude, dismissive. I don't think he liked clothes. I shouldn't say that—the only clothes he was interested in were the women's clothes, Michelle's clothes. He and Marty Bregman both. They wanted a lot of input in how she should look—it was more than a little creepy, if you ask me. I'd overhear them arguing about how she should be dressed, how sexy, how much skin they wanted her to show."

Oliver Stone says the atmosphere on the set during the long shoot was tense and exhausting, and observes of Pacino's and De Palma's contrasting styles, "I think Al was tired from the shoot; he was on-screen all the time. But there was this need [on De Palma's part] to do a minimum of, like, seven takes every time, so it was hard to warm Al up. Which changed, by the way, as time went by: Al wouldn't warm up till take seven; that's the way he worked. [But] that's where you lose your time and your energy. And it was clear that the film was dragging [behind schedule] because Universal was coming down to the set during the last part [of shooting], urging Brian and Al to work faster, but they couldn't pull the plug—it was a shame insofar as, for me it was a great example of something that happened in those days.

"Brian is not known for his energy. He's a very methodical, scientific kind of director and he's not an inspirational type. He's not, like, 'Forward lads, into the breach!,' you know? And the assistant director took the fall [for being behind schedule], which was a shame because he was a good first assistant director, but somebody had to take the fall. New first AD came in and it didn't make much difference. Bregman was pulling out his hair, but I always feared they would ask me to make cuts, and they always did. It was an irritating six months for me. I could have been doing other things, getting on with my life, but I did feel that by being there I did force myself to make the film better, I kept working with Al and Brian, we kept digging. I learned a lot by watching Brian and by watching the crew, getting to know them, so there are two sides of the coin. It became a good picture, for all that friction."

The Ratings Controversy: An X-Rated *Scarface*

Scarface received an X rating when it was submitted to the Motion Picture Association of America (MPAA) ratings board. Its *first four times*. For "excessive and cumulative violence and for language." The MPAA board was led by Richard Heffner, whose comment to *The New York Times* in October 1983, was that "*Scarface* has no rating as yet, although thus far it has proved too violent for our R classification, which allows children under seventeen to see a movie when accompanied by an adult." Heffner concluded, "When we do see *Scarface* in its final edited form, precisely as parents will see it in movie theaters, perhaps Mr. De Palma's editing will have enabled us to classify it R. If so, we shall. If not, we won't."

"This film was always an R-rated film but it wasn't an X-rated film," Bregman told me. "*Debbie Does Dallas* was an X-rated film, which I can understand. But the guy who was the head of ratings board, a guy named Heffner, had a hair up his nose, and he decided this was an ugly film, [that] it shouldn't be shown, and nobody should see it, and it would be hurtful to young people. It was just so stupid. And they gave me an X rating."

While Bregman boasted to me that "he didn't stop us and we didn't change anything in the film," De Palma told *Playboy*, "I didn't take anything out, except for the arm that was chain-sawed off. You don't really see it, just about twelve frames. I took it out, anyway. I sent the censors four versions and kept taking things out, and finally I said, 'I'm not doing this anymore,' and all four versions got an X for 'cumulative violence,' whatever that is. So I figured, 'Hey, if we're get

---

Scarface's Most Unlikely Champion: Jack Valenti

The late Jack Valenti, creator and then-president of the MPAA and chairman of the board of appeals, was not exactly known for his championing of artists' rights—he spent his Hollywood life shilling for the industry. Yet, even he came out for an R rating for *Scarface,* telling *The Los Angeles Times* during the appeals period, "I'd want my fifteen-year-old daughter to see it, because it's a very antidrug movie." (I called his daughter Alexandra, now a director and producer herself, in 2007; through a representative, she said to the best of her knowledge, she remembers *Scarface* as an "excellent" movie.)

---

ting an X, let's go with our first version.' So I put it all back and fought the appeal on the original cut. Why fight the fourth version? I didn't even like it. And we won. I had already taken out the arm on my own. I was amazed at the brouhaha." De Palma and others have repeated the four-versions-then-going-back-to-the-original-cut litany in numerous interviews.

The rating was appealed, and in early November, reported *The New York Times*, "An appeals board composed of twenty theater owners, major studio executives, and independent distributors met in New York this afternoon and awarded Universal's $23.5 million Christmas movie a less restrictive R." Bregman was quoted as saying, " 'The board voted 17 to 3 in our favor. I guess that says it all.' "

Not quite. All of the small cuts and talk of revisions leaves out the MPAA complaint of "excessive . . . language": those notorious hundred-plus f-words. (Joan Collins was widely quoted—and, I presume, bleeped or censored in print—as saying at the movie's premiere, "They say there are over a hundred 'fucks' in this film—that's more than most people have in a lifetime.")

Industry Reaction

First came the rating kerfuffle; then came industry reaction; then came the reviews. There has been a lot of revisionist history from the *Scarface* participants about the initial reaction it received. De Palma, Bregman, and company love to talk about how it was a pariah-project in Hollywood, and how it was slaughtered by the critics.

Steven Bauer repeated to me the famous anecdote about one major director's reaction. "Marty Scorsese turned to me—he was sitting in front of me at the premiere—and he turned around and said, 'Steven, this is a magnificent film, but be prepared because Hollywood is going to hate this film, because it's about them.'" Bregman concurred about the dim view his colleagues took of the film. "Scorsese was right. Hollywood did hate it, *hated* it. We were looked at as though we were dragging filth into their living rooms."

And Bregman asserts that this was pure hypocrisy in the cocaine-fueled show-business world of the early 1980s. "I would go to house parties of some senior executives of that world, and as you walked into the lobby of their houses, there was a bowl of white powder as you entered. Cocaine was a big thing out [in Hollywood] then."

De Palma told Julie Salamon in her book *The Devil's Candy* (1991) that the Hollywood "community loathed *Scarface* because the characters were so much like them; manipulative, loathsome . . ."

Oliver Stone said, "I was in Los Angeles [when it opened] and the amount of revulsion of so many people inside the industry toward it [was immense]. It was like, 'This was a horrible thing to do to our industry.' "[9]

Bregman goes further, naming names to me. "When it came out we were brutalized by some of my peers. We had an industry screening, and the guys that ran Warner Bros. at that time walked out with incredulous looks on their faces, like, 'My god, what has this guy done? What a piece of shit.' I'm talking about Bob Daly and Terry Semel. To say that depressed me would be very mild." (Daly and Semel declined to be quoted in this book.)

"We didn't expect this terrible backlash in the first year [of its release], the first *couple* of years, actually," Steven Bauer told me. "The response from the Hollywood establishment was so, *so* negative, that Al [Pacino] was really hurting, and De Palma, too; Brian took it on the chin."

As far as the reviews went, Bauer says, "The film criticism was so negative, *so* hurtful." Bauer claims that the bad reviews hurt him and Pacino so much, "for years Al and I couldn't even talk on the phone because it was such a sad subject. So it's such a nice turn of events that history has proven us right, has elevated [the movie] to a stature that is iconic."

Bregman told me flatly, "We were shocked by the negative reaction, shocked. We did not get a good review, not one. The critics did not get the movie; the *audience* got the movie."

But a look back at the reviews proves this wasn't entirely so. *Time* magazine's Richard Corliss found the movie "exhilarating for its vigor and craftsmanship," and praised Pacino for "creat[ing] his freshest character in almost a decade. There is a poetry to his psychosis that makes Tony a figure of rank awe." In *The Times*, Vincent Canby found

Pacino's performance "not a mannered one . . . completely controlled" and the film's portrayal of the rise and fall of a drug lord "as terrifying as it is vivid and arresting." Roger Ebert in the *Chicago Sun-Times* called it "a wonderful portrait of a real louse," noting that the movie "understands this criminal personality, with its links between laziness and ruthlessness, grandiosity and low self-esteem, pipe dreams and a chronic inability to be happy. It's also an exciting crime picture."

True, the praise wasn't universal. Even Corliss's review hedged toward the end, saying that "*Scarface* lacks the generational sweep and moral ambiguity of [*The Godfather*'s] Corleone saga. At the end, Tony is as he was at the beginning: his development and degeneration are horrifyingly predictable; his death evokes not fear or pity, but numb relief." A strongly negative view came from Walter Goodman, who in a 1983 *New York Times* thumbsucker about violence in movies, wrote that "Brian De Palma evidently believed that enough gore and mayhem could save a plate of cold fried bananas fifty years after it has been served up piping hot." (The "hot" film being Howard Hawks's original.)

And Pauline Kael in *The New Yorker* swung the most solidly connecting knock-out punch, saying the movie begins promisingly, "hot and raw, like a spaghetti Western," but that "the scenes are so shapeless that we don't know at what point we're meant to laugh. The picture is peddling macho primitivism and at the same time making it absurd. It's a druggy spectacle—manic yet exhausted. . . . The whole feeling of the movie is limp. This may be the only action picture that turns into an allegory of impotence."

Still, you can't help but think that the moviemakers' poor-us, we-were-misunderstood, we-were-pummeled testimony is, at least in part, a way for the filmmakers to congratulate, to flatter, the consumers of the DVD for being savvy, independent thinkers who made up their own minds, who repudiated those mingy-minded critics, and now plunk down their cash for new versions of an old 1980s movie. In any case, *Scarface* gets the last laugh; as Tony says toward his druggy end, "You know what capitalism is? 'Get fucked.'" The movie's unending popularity stands less as a rebuke to its detractors than its afterlife renders it a more complex phenomenon than anyone could have foreseen.

4

Four Creators

The Director

"I have a high tolerance for blood," Brian De Palma once remarked. Born in Newark, New Jersey, raised in Philadelphia as the son of an Irish Catholic orthopedic-surgeon father, De Palma witnessed a few of Dad's operations as a young man and developed a strong stomach and a strong sense of both the resilience and fragility of the human form; as the movie critics like to say, this is a theme that surfaces repeatedly throughout his oeuvre. "When I was, like, sixteen, seventeen, I saw him do a lot of bone surgery, amputate legs, put in a steel femur," De

SCARFACE NATION

Marty Bregman,
Louis Stoller, and
Brian De Palma
(Universal/Kobal
Collection)

Palma told *Playboy*. "I saw some brain and eye surgery performed by his colleagues. You *do* see a lot of blood when people operate."

You see a lot of blood when De Palma makes a movie, too, much of it spurting from women. To the frequently leveled charge of misogyny (given the grisly murders of women in movies like *Blow Out, Dressed to Kill,* and *Body Double,* and the cold, harsh treatment of mistress Michelle Pfeiffer in *Scarface*), De Palma points out, a bit weakly, that he "went to a girls' school for four years" (Sarah Lawrence College), and that "I like to photograph women . . . I enjoy working with women."

The director derives some of his best effects by making his audience complicit in their unmediated identification with some of his protagonists. That's certainly true of Tony Montana—that identification, in large part, is what the entire hip-hop world's infatuation with

Scarface imagery is about. And De Palma has never entirely forsaken his avant-garde roots; as the director's most eloquent defender, film critic Armond White, has put it, "[Of] the great directors of the seventies—Altman, Coppola, Scorsese, Spielberg, and De Palma . . . it is De Palma who exhibited the fascinating complexities of both radical and commercial instincts working in counterpoint, in each [of his] pictures."[1]

Up to the point of *Scarface,* De Palma had operated as a maverick auteur, writing most of his best films, including *Blow Out, Dressed to Kill, Sisters,* and *Phantom of the Paradise.* Previous to these, De Palma's earliest films have an all-over-the-map, improvised feel, and an intentionally thrown-together look that, combined with their small budgets, resulted in a chipper cheesiness that regularly hinted at the emotional depth and technical mastery he'd eventually achieve.

Obsession, in 1976, with a script by Paul Schrader from a story idea by De Palma, was simultaneously a bald-faced homage to Alfred Hitchcock's *Vertigo*—a man falls for a woman who resembles a long-dead love—and the film in which De Palma's technique settled down into the more sumptuous, confident manner of storytelling that would serve him well in *Scarface.* This newfound confidence would pay off both commercially and artistically with *Carrie,* released the same year. A big, breakthrough hit for the director and a movie whose popularity would also boost the career of its source-novelist, Stephen King, *Carrie* starred Sissy Spacek as—in the story's brilliantly silly, yet moving premise—an ostracized high-school geek with telekinetic powers triggered by menstruation. Its bloodbath finale can be seen now as De Palma's celebration of his own freshly honed expertise in montage, delirious panning shots, and an effulgent joy in jolting the bejesus out of audiences.

The Fury, in 1978, is underrated De Palma, perceived as a letdown at the time by many critics for its (only superficial) resemblances to *Carrie*: based on another horror writer's work (John Farris), about other telekinetic teens (Andrew Stevens and Amy Irving). But there's a fierce undercurrent of emotion to *The Fury,* which features John Cassavetes as a finely calibrated bad guy and Kirk Douglas in a burst of late-middle-age action-acting as a good spy and a sadly ineffectual father trying to help son Stevens. Douglas is a CIA-like agent whose son is kidnapped by a secret government project trying to harness the powers of the extrasensory-powered youth; the chief conspirator, unbeknownst to Douglas, is a close friend, Cassavetes.

The potency of the son's powers is compared to those of "an atomic bomb." Stevens's character, Robin, makes contact with another young person with inexplicable powers, Gillian (Amy Irving), whose use of telekinesis leads to a bond between the two: "I'm like a receiver and Robin sends me pictures," she says at one point. (In this, the movie predates the theme of teen mutants among us, such as those in the *The X-Men* films.) As the shadowy agency conducts more and more stressful experiments on him, Stevens grows more frustrated and angry; De Palma expresses this visually by having the boy's powers leak out into the world: In a beautiful sequence, Stevens, out on a rare trip to an amusement park, walks past a Tilt-A-Whirl: its lightbulbs explode, the ride speeds up and people are thrown out of it, as veins in Stevens's forehead bulge. Yet he walks on past the ride, unaware of the devastation he has caused so blithely.

Similarly, when Douglas, frantic to find and rescue his son ("People around me die," he says with immense sadness), meets Irving, she comes to understand that this school she's been in has a nefarious purpose, and her own powers erupt, killing a teacher she had previously thought was a friend (Carrie Snodgress) by lifting the woman up into the air telekinetically and spinning Snodgress around and around until her body begins to fly apart (De Palma cuts to Snodgress's blood spraying across a window shade).

The climax of *The Fury* is, in its way, just as bloody and tragic and "operatic" as that of *Scarface*. Douglas finally finds his son—"I never gave up; I kept looking for you all the time," he says with groaned anguish—but the father is too late. The son, ever-angrier and ridden with guilt over the participation he's had in an evil project, throws himself out a window and dies. Kirk Douglas then does the same: Life is not worth living, having failed his son. In the movie's elegantly delirious final moments, Cassavetes tries to calm down Amy Irving and convince her to trust him, but she uses her power to make him bleed internally, blood that overflows his body and emerges through his eyes, as she consigns him with a curse: "You go to hell." She makes Cassavetes's body explode: his head pops like a balloon, and blood flies everywhere. At the moment of explosion, the movie ends abruptly: Like *Scarface, The Fury* ceases to exist—it just halts; credits roll—as soon as its antihero dies. And, it should be emphasized, De Palma, long ignorantly slammed for not being a good director of actors, elicits one of Douglas's best latter-day performances, and certainly makes wooden actors like Andrew Stevens and Amy Irving seem fully alive on-screen.

So, too, was Angie Dickinson's acting in De Palma's next, *Dressed to Kill* (1980). As a lonely, affection-starved, middle-aged Manhattan woman, Dickinson allowed De Palma's cameras to move in close, to capture both the beauty of her lined face and the still-sinuous lines of her body: This was a post–Rat Pack Dickinson who was willing to risk one of Hollywood's most inviolate rules for actresses—Thou

Must Not Age—in the service of a *Psycho*'d tale that let her be a fully formed character of tremendous pathos and yearning.

The following year, *Blow Out* proved a breakthrough synthesis of the themes De Palma returned to repeatedly, combining *Dressed to Kill*'s women-in-jeopardy scenarios with *The Fury*'s evocation of a man doomed to see the people he cares most about die ("People around me die"). But *Blow Out* was no paltry retread or cut-and-paste job. The cutting-and-pasting is what its hero does for a living: John Travolta's Jack Terry is a Philadelphia sound-effects engineer for grade-C horror movies. One night, while out recording nature sounds for his latest gorefest-for-hire, *Bordello of Blood*, he accidentally records the sounds of a car veering off a road and into a river. He manages to rescue a young woman (Nancy Allen), but the man in the car, who proves to be a governor running for president, dies.

Jack Terry is a jaded smart-aleck, whom Travolta plays with brave unlikableness—trying to do something in movies that would be a break from his early sitcom success, he may have felt he had little to lose. Or, more likely, he knew that the shape and momentum of De Palma's script, over the course of which Jack goes from callow cad to deeply invested hero, would win over audiences and prove he had range.

He was right, to an extent. *Blow Out* was a fair-sized hit, although not nearly one commensurate with the pleasures, complexities, and skill the film reveals. De Palma brought out his inner nerd, the science-fair contestant with an early interest in cutting-edge technology, and poured it into the scenes where Jack snips and Scotch-tapes pieces of his sound recordings and sequential pictures of the accident that have appeared in a magazine to create a primitive little movie that proves the car swerve was no accident, but rather the result of a gunshot to the car's tire—the blow-out of the title—that caused the river crash. (The photos Travolta uses were snapped by a fishy photog named Karp, played by Dennis Franz.)

Again like *Scarface, Blow Out* features a hero who becomes isolated—no one in authority believes Jack's conspiracy theory—and loses everything he loves in a needless morass of violence. After *Blow Out*, De Palma was in the mood to collaborate, likely for at least two reasons. One was that he had career momentum, and was willing to move so quickly from *Blow Out* to another new project because there was a ready-to-go script by Stone (still struggling to establish himself as a bankable director and, therefore, writing the *Scarface* script with both a commercial and visual flair any director could use or transmute, according to his or her whim). The other reason De Palma relied on Stone's script was that its details, borne out of research both reportorial and firsthand, seemed authentic to De Palma, who has said in a number of interviews that he, unlike Stone, had little knowledge of the cocaine world.

Immediately after *Scarface*, De Palma returned to his more personal obsessions, producing as well as directing *Body Double*, a super-Hitchcocked sex thriller. Frustrated and angered by the critical and industry drubbing he'd received for *Scarface*, De Palma went around telling anyone who'd listen that, rather than back off and make a meeker sort of movie, next time around he'd really give the MPAA something to worry about. "Yeah, there was a certain amount of 'You think *Scarface* was trouble? I'll show you trouble,' in my attitude going in to *Body Double*," he told me. "But it was also an idea I'd had in the back of my head for years, well before *Scarface*. I knew I wanted to eventually do something about sexual duplicity in the context of the sex film, the porn business. I've always been interested in the fact that there's this parallel industry to establishment Hollywood's, and that, at the time anyway, there was no overlap—if you made or performed in porn films, you were a pariah in the mainstream industry.

"I was intrigued by the subculture of porn, and also by the subculture of struggling actors in the conventional movie world. You always hear about the casting couch, and you know some actresses and actors, when they start out and they go to audition after audition for a TV series, or a commercial, or a movie and don't get it, if they're attractive, must be tempted—must be approached—to do porn. So that was in the back of my mind for a while. And I liked the idea of shooting a story with these themes in a way that forced the audience to be a voyeur."

Or, as he told *Esquire* in 1984: "As soon as I get this dignity from *Scarface* [ah, an artist can dream, can't he?], I am going to go out and make an X-rated suspense porn picture . . . I'm going to give them [i.e., his critics] everything they hate, and more of it than they've ever seen."

In a making-of featurette on the *Body Double* DVD, De Palma makes a statement that demonstrates he knows what his most influential work is, but phrases it in a way that suggests disappointment by disguising it as bafflement:

Oddly enough, the most responses I get to my movies are either *Scarface* or *Body Double*. Those are the two movies [people] seem to enjoy and want to talk to me about. It's very odd that these are also the two that opened to the most controversy, were the most jumped-on by the political-correctness critics and the media mavens of the day. These are the movies that seem to have lasted through time, that seem to have left the most lasting impression.

This remark seems wily and disingenuous. *Scarface* and *Body Double* are very deliberate, very artful attempts at popular provocation: One glorifies drug use and violence; the other revels in voyeurism and violence. These are exploitation pictures lifted to a different plane of appreciation as a result of De Palma's technical skill, the wittiness of his staging, and the deep, abiding interest he has in exploring subjects too often watered-down or made taboo in mainstream movies.

Thus, I think his comment really boils down to a way of saying, "Yes, these are good movies. I have made other good movies, too. Fuck off."

The Screenwriter

"The first time Brian came to Miami I took him to the Mutiny Club, on Biscayne Bay. It was a great drug hangout and in those days it was chic to be a druggie, and all the girls were beautiful, the clubs were rich and modern— this was new to America. It was morning in America, if you remember Reagan. If you look at the cultural patterns, I think Miami set a new tone in the '80s because restaurants be-

Oliver Stone
(Catherine Cabrol/
Corbis)

came more diverse, more multi-ethnic, the clubs changed—the '80s became fun again, whereas the late '70s were kind of stale for a lot of people. The Mutiny Club was one of these places that had forty or fifty hotel rooms, each of which had a different color. I stayed in a red- or white-colored room, but fuckin' Brian chose the *black room*! Completely black."

—Oliver Stone, interview with the author, 12/06

In the early 1980s, says screenwriter Oliver Stone, "I was down on my luck. *The Hand*"—his first directorial effort, a loopy 1981 horror film starring Michael Caine and his evil severed title appendage—"had been released and had failed. Marty [Bregman] was keen enough to hire me for my writing skills." (Stone had written the 1978 hit *Midnight Express,* won an Oscar for it, and was a hot commodity as a script doctor. He also was having a number of projects making the rounds, such as his original screenplay, *Platoon,* and his adaptations of *Born on the Fourth of July,* which was, during Stone's time, meant to star Pacino but was ultimately made with a different script and star, and *Conan the Barbarian,* eventually made by director John Milius and Arnold Schwarzenegger.)

"But I had no interest in doing an Italian gangster story, because I grew up on *The Untouchables* [the Robert Stack-as-Eliott Ness 1960s TV series] and I had had enough of that subject. So I passed on it. Then Bregman called me up and said Sidney Lumet, who I had known from [trying to develop] *Platoon,* and my *Fourth of July* days, because he was somewhat involved in those films, had the idea to do [*Scarface*] as a Cuban refugee. Now, *that* caught my interest, because it made him modern—our age.

"So I wrote the first draft with Sidney in mind [as director], and as you know, he did not like it and pulled out. It wasn't his kind of thing: It was over-the-top realism, it was based on my stories, my research. What I did was essentially go to Miami, to Fort Lauderdale, to Broward and Dade counties. I was really into all these [police] departments. I was talking to the Drug Enforcement Agents [DEA], and they led me to the prosecutors, to the U.S. federal and the state guys, who are really fascinating, because they bring the cases up and put 'em away [in jail]. There was, I'd say, ten or twelve top drug dealers in that area, and their [supply] connection was no longer Cuba [which it has been, pre-Castro]. It was Colombian back then. But the Colombians were not known to the American public . . . But the drugs were coming from Colombia and beyond that, from Bolivia and Ecuador, but the Colombians were trying to cut in on the Jamaicans and the Cubans and they were killing them. Literally. There was a chain-saw murder that I was told about that was worse than what you see in [*Scarface*], and as you can imagine drug-war crimes are brutal.

"What I did the best was, I went down and hung around with these people, down into the south, also to the Caribbean Islands, some shipments were coming here through the Bahamas by cigarette boat at night—it's only sixteen miles, I think. Once I talked to the prosecutors, I went and talked to the defending attorneys . . . but I also had to go out into the real world and find the real guys. So, I was told the places to go with a few contacts, and I wormed my way in as much as I could [partly because] I was also doing coke. Not so heavily that it was impeding my ability to take notes and research—I was never a heavy user, but I was doing it. So I had a natural entrée into places like that. You hang out, you meet the middle-management guys, they brag and you hear stories, great stories.

"Three or four grams of coke [went] for $12 in Ecuador: it was so pure you'd fall asleep it was so good, [although] they'd cut it and cut it and cut it, [watering it down] by the time it got here. It was a big business, and the DEA made it bigger by making it more [so] by getting more involved and raising their own budgets, by passing the RICO Act. [This was the federal antiracketeering act that gave the government a lot of power domestically to investigate and arrest suspects.] The RICO Act was just crap; the [government] used it politically. I mention it in the script: I have Tony say they ought to legalize drugs if they had any brains.

"The RICO Act is one of the precursors to the Patriot Act; that was the mentality—you turn drugs into a monster, et cetera. So, for me there was a political motive. That's why I brought in the cartel issue in Bolivia in the movie, because at that time there was a man in Bolivia embodied by that drug lord in the movie, Suarez. In fact, I think that was his real name. Suarez was known at that time to have a large ring inside Bolivia. He was a big deal, Suarez—he was politically connected. He had his own state: The whole goal is to get your own state, like the Al Qaeda got their state in Afghanistan? Well, Suarez had his own state. The DEA was trying to take him down, but he was protected, I think, by the CIA. That was the whole point with the [*Scarface*] scene [in Bolivia]—which was misread by De Palma when he filmed it, so people missed it—Suarez was being protected by another [U.S.] government agency of some kind. Tony is given the order to kill a guy based on Orlando Letelier [the democratically elected Chilean ambassador] who was blown up in a car near Washington Circle in D.C. So that became the subplot by which Tony comes undone, not just by his own paranoia, but because he fucks with the cartel.

"So that's why I thought it was a pretty good screenplay. Too long, too big, but that's why I would have done it, as a director, in a manner that was realistic and fast-paced, because it was more like, let's get to know this world. [But] Brian chose another approach, and I respect him for that."

"Say hello to my li'l fren."

Tony in a blaze of gunfire

"I Trust Me" *Scarface* poster

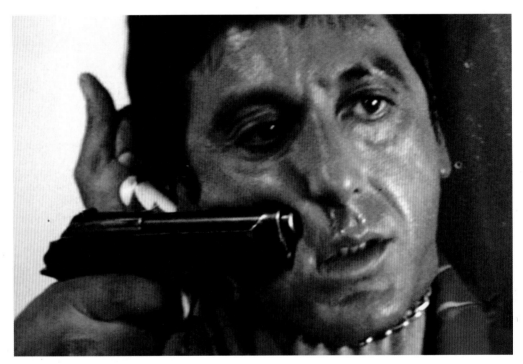

Tony is forced to watch his friend's slaughter.

Michelle Pfeiffer in club scene

Elvira (Michelle Pfeiffer) and Tony (Al Pacino) dance.

Tony and Manny (Steven Bauer) go car-shopping.

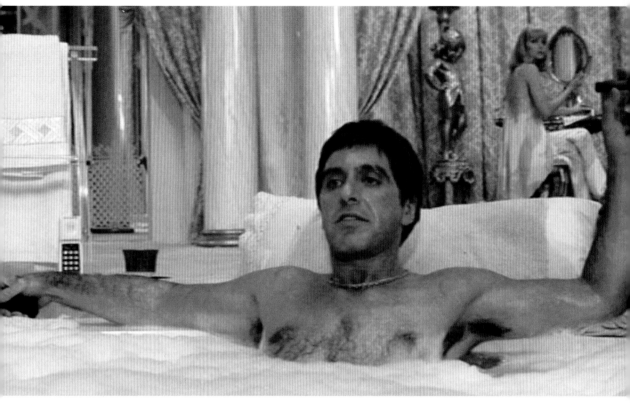

Al Pacino in the bathtub, with Michelle Pfeiffer in the background doing blow

Master of all he surveys?

Inhaling narcotics

Tony catches Gina (Mary Elizabeth Mastrantonio) with one of the punks in the nightclub.

AL PACINO SCARFACE

In the spring of 1980, the port at Mariel Harbor was opened, and thousands set sail for the United States. They came in search of the American Dream.

One of them found it on the sun-washed avenues of Miami...wealth, power and passion beyond his wildest dreams.

He was Tony Montana. The world will remember him by another name ...SCARFACE.

He loved the American Dream. With a vengeance.

A MARTIN BREGMAN
PRODUCTION

A BRIAN De PALMA
FILM

AL PACINO
"SCARFACE"

SCREENPLAY BY
OLIVER STONE

MUSIC BY
GIORGIO MORODER

DIRECTOR OF PHOTOGRAPHY
JOHN A. ALONZO
A.S.C.

EXECUTIVE PRODUCER
LOUIS A. STROLLER

PRODUCED BY
MARTIN BREGMAN

DIRECTED BY
BRIAN De PALMA

SOUNDTRACK AVAILABLE ON MCA RECORDS AND CASSETTES
A UNIVERSAL PICTURE/READ THE BERKLEY BOOK

Coming in December
to a Theatre Near You.

The iconic poster for 1983's *Scarface*

ViBe

In the summer of 1999,
the music industry floodgates
were opened and thousands
of rappers flocked from
far and wide.
They came in search
of the American Dream.

One of them found it on
the gritty avenues of
Queens…wealth, power,
and passion beyond
his wildest dreams.

He was Curtis Jackson.
The world will remember
him by another name
…50 CENT.

He loved the
American Dream.
With a vengeance.

THE
HOLLYWOOD
ISSUE

STARRING
50 CENT
AS SCARFACE

PLUS THE OTHER
49 MOVIES
THAT CHANGED
HIP HOP

MUSIC BY
JOHN LEGEND

TWEET
AS THE LEADING LADY

INTRODUCING
STAT QUO

COSTARRING
WOOD HARRIS, IDRIS ELBA,
LIL' WAYNE, MEAGAN GOOD,
THE GAME, THREE 6 MAFIA

CAMEO BY
ED BRADLEY

50 Cent on the cover of *Vibe* magazine

American poster for *Scarface*, 1932

Paul Muni as Tony Camonte in the climactic stand-off in 1932's *Scarface*

Lady Scarface poster

The Star

You have to wonder what would make Al Pacino take the risks he took—risk the ridicule that could, and sometimes did, attach itself to his performance as Tony Montana. Yet, as a business decision, *Scarface* probably seemed, on some level, like a what-the-hell proposition: What did he have to lose?

He hadn't had a decent movie role since 1975's *Dog Day Afternoon,* directed by Sidney Lumet, the director originally attached to *Scarface.* In 1979, he'd done ... *And Justice for All,* giving the first of his cheesy, over-the-top performances that would become a subtext to his career: the nature of his artistic "choices," as they say. *Scarface* as well as movies such as his Oscar-winning *Scent of a Woman, Heat, The Devil's Advocate,* and *Insomnia* would further confirm Pacino's penchant for hamminess that could be both excitingly controlled (*Heat*), excitingly uncontrolled (*Scarface*), and tediously uncontrolled (nearly all the rest).

Immediately preceding *Scarface,* Pacino had starred in William Friedkin's controversial, lousy gay-sex-'n'-murder film *Cruising* (1980), and the sub-sitcom *Author! Author!* (1982).

So, when his longtime producer-friend Martin Bregman told him about the idea to remake *Scarface* as a political refugee, an impoverished exiled Cuban who achieves the "American dream" through crime only to lose it all, in a big movie mounted as a full-scale tragedy—well, why not? Here was a significant social theme, something Pacino is always a sucker for, and a project that would reunite him with Lumet, of whom he continued to speak glowingly to *The New York Times* in 2003, in terms that you can easily imagine may have haunted him when he was busy going over-the-top with replacement-director De Palma.

Of Lumet, Pacino remarked, "What happens is, as a movie goes on, it gets more and more grueling and you really need a director who will help remind you where your character is at all times. Sidney Lumet was like that. All wonderful directors will do that. They snap you to, you know? And you need that, because sometimes you get lulled into a certain rhythm when you've been sitting around for eight hours."

Or in the case of *Scarface,* the descent must have been exhausting in just this way, as Pacino was required to lower himself into Tony Montana's ever-spiraling fall into decadence, disgrace, death. Pacino has spoken about his admiration for Hawks's *Scarface* and in particular Muni's performance, telling *The New York Times* in 2003, "I had been wanting to see it since '74, when I had done a workshop production of [Bertolt Brecht's *The Resistible Rise of*] *Arturo Ui,*" a fable about Adolf Hitler's rise to power but set in Capone-era Chicago. (Brecht was a Hawks-*Scarface* fan, too.) "The film just stopped me in my tracks," Pacino told the *Times*'s Bernard Weinraub. "All I wanted to do was imitate Paul Muni. His acting went beyond the boundaries of naturalism into another kind of expression. It was almost abstract what he did. It was almost uplifting."

Scarface, not as descent-into-hell but as uplift, was a metaphor Pacino pursued in 1991 chatting with the artist Julian Schnabel in *Interview* magazine. Pacino looked up, not down, for the source of inspiration for this character: "There's something fablelike about Tony Montana. He's just like Icarus flying close to the sun, just going a little closer and closer, knowing as soon as he gets close enough those wings are going to get burned—he's gonna soar right down. That's what attracted me to that character. When were people ever not fascinated by the gangster world, that underworld, that world that's illicit? It's always fascinating to see how and why people go to the wrong side. The idea of somebody who's flirting with the big D, you know? It just fascinates people. It fascinated me to do it."

Still, the *Scarface* shoot took its emotional toll on the actor— flirting on-camera with "the big D" will do that. He said in another interview, "When I was doing *Scarface*, I remember being in love at that time. One of the few times in my life. And I was so glad it was at that time. I would come home and she would tell me about her life that day and all her problems, and I remember saying to her, look, you really got me through this picture because I would shed everything when I came home." (Given the scrupulously private Pacino's personal-life time line, I'm guessing the love of his life at that time was probably actress Kathleen Quinlan.)[2]

In numerous interviews over the years, Pacino has honed a standard line in explaining the often garishly exaggerated acting style on display in *Scarface*. First, there is the opera comparison: "It is an operatic movie," Pacino told *The New York Times*'s Weinraub. "That was the idea of Brian De Palma. He wanted to go that way."

Next, there's the I-chose-to-make-him-a-cartoon defense, or as he casts the argument, he chose to make Tony Montana two- not three-dimensional. "I like that whole idea of being fearless in that role," he said in *Al Pacino: In Conversation with Lawrence Grobel* (2006). "I like the fact that, to me, Tony Montana was two-dimensional. I didn't want to make him a three-dimensional character. What you see is what you get . . . The fact that he didn't contemplate too much . . . That's why he dug into the cocaine." (Is it any wonder that Pacino agreed to provide his likeness for another two-dimensional version of Tony, the 2006 video game *Scarface: The World Is Yours*?)

To the charge that Tony Montana inaugurated Pacino's hammy acting style, he told interviewer Lawrence Grobel in 2005, "There's an old saying: Ham is okay as long as it's not Spam. You can tolerate more in certain characters than in others. Sometimes it's a quality you'd be surprised how many people enjoy . . . certain roles, if I was to do them over again, I know that I would take some of that stuff down. But when it's really happening, when it's energized and motivated by something real, it has size—it's not over-the-top. The way a tenor will hit a note because the note is there to hit . . . It's the call of the actor and of the director to moderate that. The whole view of *Scarface* was orchestrated that way by Brian and me . . ." Paraphrasing Shakespeare, Pacino added, "Suit the action to the word and the word to the action. I thought the combustion was there in [*Scarface*]. I don't cringe at it. But there are some other roles I've done where I cringe."[3]

Pacino also subscribes to the interpretation of Tony Montana as hero, not anti-hero or immoral thug. Asked by London's *Guardian* how he defends a guy who kills his best friend, among many other sins, the actor responded, "Well, it depends on what side of the street you are walking on," he says. "You know I'm going to say [he's a] hero. Anybody who says 'go shove it' when somebody's got a chain saw that is about to take your head off—I think pretty much that is a hero in anybody's language."

Post-*Scarface,* Pacino sought to switch it up with a dull, "classy" historical film, *Revolution,* played Marc Antony in *Julius Caesar* for Joe Papp's New York Shakespeare Festival, and found his way back into good movies with *Sea of Love,* the superior serial-killer thriller by screenwriter Richard Price and director Harold Becker, in 1989. Pacino snagged an Oscar nomination for his next film, Warren Beatty's *Dick Tracy* (1990), appearing as mobster Big Boy Caprice—a character played in heavily applied makeup to befit the Chester Gould comic-strip creation, and a character with . . . a scarred face. "I always thought it would be great to sculpt the head of that character," he told journalist Grobel. "Pow! That's three-dimensional," he said, sounding at once like an extra from the *Batman* TV series and also dipping into his "dimensional" bag of metaphors again. "I was into that; I had done *Scarface,* trying to sculpt the character, but with Big Boy I could actually put a mask on it." A mask, a comic-strip character—again, echoes: this time to the comparison I made earlier about *Scarface* (and Big Boy) as a variation on *The Spirit*, Will Eisner–style.

The Ingenue

The story goes that Brian De Palma had seen Michelle Pfeiffer in 1982's hideous *Grease 2* and resisted producer Martin Bregman's insistence that he audition her for the role of Elvira Hancock. You can hardly blame De Palma—not only was Pfeiffer a stiff in *Grease 2* (though in her defense, that was probably a conscious reaction, a way to distance herself from the idiocy of the production all around her), but her previous work had been mostly in bad TV shows. She was Sunshine Jensen in a cruddy Aaron Spelling cop show, 1980's *B.A.D. Cats*; before that, she was a nearly wordless sexpot known only as "The Bombshell" in the TV version of *Animal House*, 1979's *Delta House*. Even her one film costarring role up until *Scarface*—the lone young pretty face opposite Peter Ustinov in busy, race-stereotyping *Charlie Chan and the Curse of the Dragon Queen* (1981)—came and went without notice. Nonetheless, Bregman persisted. He told *Esquire* in 1983, "I forced that to happen against strenuous objections from al-

Michelle Pfeiffer

most everyone. But when she read the part with Al Pacino, it was magic. There was . . . an intensity."

Still, it's easy to imagine that the chilly hauteur she brought to her portrayal of Elvira—a modern-day gangster's moll kept first by mobster Frank Lopez (Robert Loggia), then freed into a new sort of captivity by Pacino's Tony—was barely suppressed panic. Or, perhaps by then, Pfeiffer, in her midtwenties, was hardened enough in the ways of Hollywood—having survived the hype and collapse of Next Big Thing-dom during the prerelease of *Grease 2*—to know that the best way to interpret this character was to play her as though she didn't expect much from any man in power, just as she'd been creatively betrayed by so many of them in show business already.

One thing about De Palma, though: The constant early-career comparisons with Alfred Hitchcock certainly clicked in one way when it came to casting instincts—he liked to employ relatively inexperienced actresses who'd do his bidding and to position them in his films as sexpots-in-jeopardy who occasionally showed flashes of spunk. He did it with Amy Irving in *The Fury*; with Nancy Allen in *Blow Out* and *Dressed to Kill*; and he'd do it again after *Scarface* with Melanie Griffith in *Body Double* and Rebecca Romijn in *Femme Fatale*. In this sense, turning Pfeiffer into a platinum-blond ice queen was De Palma's version of Hitchcock's construction of Tippi Hedren in *The Birds* and *Marnie*. Except that Pfeiffer, here and especially later on, with other, less controlling directors, would prove she could really act and had some range.

About the rehearsals for *Scarface,* Pfeiffer has said, "I was terrified, so terrified. I couldn't say two words to [Pacino]. We were both really shy. We'd sit in a room, and it was like pulling teeth to try to find any words at all. And the subject matter was so dark. There was a coldness in the [film] relationship." Pfeiffer has described De Palma as making Elvira "objectified," as she told Gerri Hirshey in *Rolling Stone* in 1992. "If there was one hair out of place . . . I remember once I had a bruise or something on my leg, and he made me go back and take off my panty hose and have makeup put on because he could see an imperfection." Pfeiffer told filmwriter Graham Fuller in 1994, "Sometimes, though, by playing an object you can actually say more about objectifying women than if you play somebody of strength. I felt that Elvira in *Scarface* was a complete object. She was a hood ornament, like another Rolls-Royce or something, for both of the men that she was with. I felt that by playing something that mirrors someone's life in that way, I could make a kind of feminist statement. It depends on the way in which it's presented. If you're glamorizing or glorifying it, then I object to that."

The objectified objecting to objectification: It's a good, solid, feminist, years-after-the-fact spin on how she dealt with the chore of being a bauble in De Palma's masterstroke of gaudiness. After spending the first part of her career looking avid and needy on both the big and small screens, *Scarface* gave Pfeiffer the opportunity to channel whatever frustration she may have felt about her career up to that point, to focus whatever sort of rage she may have felt about the men who control the industry she labored in, and transmute it into a prideful contempt as Elvira, the woman every man in the movie wants, and who makes those who win her regret it. Women in De Palma's films can be things other than sexy—funny, as Allen is in *Blow Out*; intellectual—or the movies' version of it, anyway—as Irving is in her bookish, mousy way in *The Fury*; even wily, as Penelope Ann Miller's arty dancer is in *Carlito's Way*.

But Pfeiffer's Elvira is one of the rare performances by an actress in a Brian De Palma film in which a woman is free enough to both lose control (as when Elvira succumbs first to Tony's charms and subsequently to his cocaine) and yet retain her imperious command in the battle of the sexes. It's telling that we never see Tony and Elvira having sex in *Scarface*. Beyond Pauline Kael's ever-shrewdly succinct remark about the movie in general—that it is "a metaphor for impotence"—I think there's a reason for the lack of bedroom steam in *Scarface*: For all his macho swagger, Tony is probably reduced to a babbling little boy when subjected to Elvira's potent sexuality in the most intimate of settings.

As far as I can tell, Oliver Stone has never revealed the reason he named this character Elvira—she was called Poppy in Hawks's *Scar-*

face and Vyvyan in Armitage Trail's novel—and he declined to do so when I interviewed him. But here's my theory, based in part on the fact that Stone *did* tell me he used to watch a lot of junky late-night TV when he was hammering out scripts. In 1981, Cassandra Peterson, a comic actress who used to work with Paul "Pee-wee Herman" Reubens in the L.A. improvisational group The Groundlings— brought "Elvira, Mistress of the Dark," to syndicated television. It was a late-night schlock horror movie show, done on the cheap and done many different ways earlier, with a (usually male) host who would comment sarcastically before, after, and during the "bumpers" to the commercial breaks, on the crap movie that was being screened that night.

Peterson, in Los Angeles, introduced *Movie Macabre* in 1981, gussying herself up in a black beehive wig, a black push-up bra, black stiletto heels, and a long black dress slit up the side to reveal a lot of leg: she was a female vampire who didn't suck blood but rather sucked life out of the notion of being a TV star. Elvira became something of a cult item in Hollywood. I'd wager that Oliver Stone, still in his era of cocaine-fuelled creative benders, was probably a late-night Elvira fan, and gave Pfeiffer's character this name to suggest the vampiric power of an Elvira relocated to Miami in the mid-'80s.

Whatever the source of Elvira, however, Pfeiffer made the character her own, also mining the rich source of disco as further inspiration. Knowing that she had numerous scenes in a nightclub featuring Giorgio Moroder's brassy disco music, Pfeiffer made one aspect of Elvira's character similar to that of disco queens such as Donna Summer, Gloria "I Will Survive" Gaynor, and porn actress-turned-quasi-vocalist Andrea "More, More, More" True.

After submitting herself to De Palma's "objectification," Pfeiffer emerged from it praised for a subtle performance in a movie that was rarely credited with subtlety. As a reward for her efforts, she was proceeded to be "offered every bitch that had ever been," she told an interviewer. Like a lot of actors who achieve fame in a role that seems so comfortable it threatens to stereotype the performer, Pfeiffer post-*Scarface* strove to distance herself from Elvira's chill glitz. She threw herself into a ridiculous medieval costume drama, 1985's *Ladyhawke*. She sought out female-ensemble pieces such as *The Witches of Eastwick* (1987)—it doesn't get any further from Oliver Stone than the writing of John Updike. Even when she returned to the gangster genre in 1988's *Married to the Mob*, it was with an utterly different tone, as a funny, frizzle-haired, gum-chewing widow of an organized-crime boss in Jonathan Demme's clever farce.

Pfeiffer's choices have been canny. In 1989's *The Fabulous Baker Boys*, she let herself become slinky again, but in a far more engaged way than she was as the druggily vacant Elvira. She understood that the public was still interested in seeing her with Pacino, but chose as their reunion an anti-*Scarface*, slice-of-working-class-life drama, 1991's *Frankie and Johnny*, a tepid Garry Marshall adaptation of Terrence McNally's play *Frankie and Johnny in the Clair De Lune*, playing a waitress to Pacino's lovable ex-con.

In a sense, the rest of Pfeiffer's career has been a reaction to *Scarface*, as a sustained effort to never be as manipulated behind the scenes, as "objectified," as she put it, as she was by any director since De Palma. Viewed another way, however, Pfeiffer's escape into stardom after *Scarface* has prevented her from ever revisiting the source of power in that performance: the quality of withheld hurt, of wounded anger, of playing a fundamentally powerless woman who behaves as though she has all the power she needs, because she allows herself to be defined by reaction she elicits from potent men. De Palma and Stone didn't give Pfeiffer the most politically correct role, to be sure. But it was up to that point the role of her lifetime, it gave her the mass-audience-cred to become a full-fledged movie star, and may prove better-remembered than many of her more "sophisticated," tonier projects.

5

Scarface Music

Scarface as *Saturday Night Fever*–Dream

That *Scarface* has influenced the world of hip-hop has been much
remarked upon, although usually in commentary that either deals
solely with songs or solely with the culture behind the songs. The two
need to be fused; seen and heard as inseparable. But first, I want to cel-
ebrate the trashy-glam imagination of producer Giorgio Moroder;
there's a lot of enjoyment to be gleaned from his underrated original
soundtrack. Moroder, the Italian-born synthesizer wiz who produced

SCARFACE NATION

at least one undeniable pop masterwork—Donna Summer's disco mantra "I Feel Love" in 1977—was a good choice to compose music to be played largely in the film's fictional nightclub, the Babylon. His fulsome, swirling, synthesizer-string-section-plus-dance-beats are precisely the sorts of tense-rhythmed background pulsations that enhanced so many scenes, which benefited from his serene balancing of sex and kitsch.

No element sets that rarest of *Scarface* moods—cheerfulness; its revelling in early '80s hedonism—better than "Rush, Rush," the Moroder song sung by Blondie's Debbie Harry. The one-time punk had gone disco with her own single "Heart of Glass" five years before. Here, she sings the chorus, "Rush, rush to the yeyo"—hymning, in other words, the cocaine high that Michelle Pfeiffer's Elvira needs so much. Scattered throughout Moroder's soundtrack, there's a nicely understated, self-parodic, comic tone. Melodies shade over into the romantic, in a hyped-up kind of way, but it's never old-school nightclub-romantic. This is music that Robert Loggia's Frank Lopez would probably have no affinity for—he's doubtless more of a Sinatra man, don't you think?—yet this is the club he goes to every night to feel like a younger, more vital man, to feed off its energy, a large part of which is supplied by the music.

Moroder also adds to the characterization of Pacino's Tony. "She's on Fire," played on the dance floor the first time Tony makes a clumsy move on Elvira, gives Pacino the opportunity to do an impeccable job of dancing badly. The actor has cannily thought through the way Tony would dance with Elvira in the earliest stages of their relationship, which is to say very awkwardly, with an arhythmic, herky-jerky strut and a big dumb smile plastered across his face: He can't believe he's bumping in a hot club with this hot chick.

Where Moroder flounders a bit is when he's required to make sincerely ominous music. His "Tony's Theme," reprised whenever Montana is about to do something dangerous, in its suddenly slow pace and sodden bass-synthesizer chords, owes more than a little to a disco-king's approximation of what Carmine Coppola provided more kitsch-elegantly throughout the first two *Godfather* films.

Perhaps the most recognizable *Scarface* Moroder song is "Scarface (Push It to the Limit)," sung by Paul Engemann with a full-throated, arena-rock warble in the manner of power-balladeers like Journey's Steve Perry—this is the *Scarface* equivalent of Survivor's "Eye of the

Tiger." "Push It to the Limit," with Moroder's clever, zinging urgency in dramatizing the title phrase, goes *over* the limit, in that it takes itself a bit too seriously. This tipped the song over into camp when heard back then—it was music that took you out of the movie, blaring over the montage of Tony's early rise to prominence, showing him making money and living the Miami high life. But watching *Scarface* now, "Push It to the Limit" seems perfect: Engemann's strangled tenor matches both the macho posturing and the desperation that lies beneath so much of the film.

The DVD Extra: "Origin of a Hip Hop Classic"

The stiffest acknowledgment of *Scarface*'s impact on hip-hop culture came from the man who played the title character. "Some rappers actually did a video about *Scarface*," Al Pacino told his hagiographer Lawrence Grobel in a tone that comes across on the page as simultaneously flattered and clueless. "[They did it] as a revelation; as a morality tale."

Pacino is referring to the twenty-minute minidocumentary, *Def Jam Presents: Origins of a Hip Hop Classic,* that appears on the twentieth-anniversary DVD of *Scarface.* "They" did it less as a "revelation" and more as a confirmation of certain cultural trends and inter-criminal codes: a *Chicken Soup for the Scarface Soul*; an inspirational text. And "some rappers" range from no one less than some of the hardest of hard-core gangstas, such as the Geto Boys' Brad Jordan, who took the stage name Scarface, as well as more gentrified hip-hoppers such as Sean "Diddy" Combs, who tells director Benny Boom's camera, "As time goes on, this movie gets bigger and bigger." Combs describes Tony Montana as "an upstanding gangsta, which is rare; he played by rules and morals."

Businessmen like Combs (who says in the documentary that he's watched *Scarface* exactly sixty-three times as of the interview-taping that day) and Def Jam Records founder Russell Simmons choose to interpret *Scarface* as an allegory for the way poor blacks, with no social entrée into business or high society, project themselves onto a higher plane of status and success. Combs asserts that, early on in many now-legitimate young black entrepreneurs' careers, "coming up young and black in the eighties . . . drug dealing was one of the only ways [seen] as an out"—that is, a way to make a large amount of liquid cash that could bankroll a move into lawful enterprises such as the music industry. Not just musicians but actors also chime in here in on the meaning of *Scarface*: Mekhi Phifer of *ER* fame says, "*Scarface* represented the capitalist society that we live in but it also [said] that you don't have to conform to society to, quote unquote, 'make it.' " Russell Simmons hones in on one meaning: "*Scarface* was about empowerment at all costs [and so is] hip-hop." And the rapper-songwriter Nas boils it down to a more sour essence: "We all are savages in pursuit of the American Dream."

That "savages" usage suggests a not entirely admired interpretation of *Scarface* that others articulate; some see it more as a cautionary tale. "André 3000" Benjamin of OutKast says of the coke-hoovering Tony we watch toward the end of the movie, "He got too wild, too crunk, and he kind of killed himself"—that is, he may have gone down in a hail of enemy bullets, but it was Tony's excesses, his hubris, that put him in the position of getting gunned down.

The Rules

The "rules" that Combs and others mention are the most famous lines in the movie: "Don't underestimate the other guy's greed"; "Don't get high on your own supply"; "First you get the money, then you get the power, then you get the women"; "All I have in this world is my balls and my word." The morality derives from various scenes. When Tony kills Steven Bauer's Manny for becoming involved with his sister Gina, the message, says the rapper Trick Daddy on the DVD, is fundamental: "If you're my homeboy, you're not fuckin' my sister." Seems pretty straightforward, doesn't it?

It's not, really. Many musicians claim to admire Tony's loyalty, to see nothing morally contradictory in the chain-saw scene, when Montana allows his friend Angel to be killed before his eyes rather than give up the money. This, in some of the commentators' views, just makes Tony that much more "hard" (i.e., a tough customer and a good businessman), and loyal to a higher power: not God but Frank Lopez, Tony's boss. Angel dies so that Tony can deliver the goods, ultimately, to Frank, and that makes him, as one rapper says, "a good soldier."

On the other hand, it's not long after the chain-saw scene that Tony makes a power grab and betrays and kills Frank. This, too, has the support of some of the hip-hop artists, because it can be interpreted that Tony did the dirty work that had to be done to vanquish one's chief competitor in a capitalist society. Few of the people on camera suggest what Oliver Stone was implying as one of his themes—that capitalism itself is at once part of impoverished people's solutions, and part of their everlasting problems.

In other words, *Scarface* cannot help but lead any admirer who chooses to deploy it as a life plan into confusion and contradiction, for at bottom, Tony Montana is amoral. In a 2003 interview with "Fresh Air" National Public Radio host Terry Gross, Miriam Colon, who played Tony's "mama," said her character "has standards in her house . . . The thing of honor, [her] sternness—well, she's the only one that defied Tony; [who] told him, 'Get the hell out of here'; [who] didn't wind up with her head cut off." Colon does not exaggerate by much when she suggests that not getting one's head cut off in *Scarface* is not merely a heroic achievement in an antiheroic film, it's tantamount to achieving sainthood.

The Music Inspired by *Scarface* CD

During the twentieth-anniversary year of the movie's release came *Def Jam Presents: Music Inspired by Scarface,* a CD of more than fifteen hip-hop acts who either directly or indirectly refer to the movie. The Notorious B.I.G., gunned down in a gangsta-rap feud killing in 1997, is represented by "Ten Crack Commandments," on which list number four is, "Never get high on your own supply." Mobb Deep led by Nas—who in late 2006 would try to revitalize gangsta rap through gangsta-paradox with the album title *Hip Hop Is Dead*—is heard on a cut called "It's Mine," proclaiming, "We the black mob." Mobb Deep also recorded a song called "G.O.D. Part III," that sampled Moroder's score. More intriguingly, Cam'Ron's "Yeo" uses the Moroder/Debbie Harry soundtrack refrain for its own, as Cam'Ron's backup singers coo, "Rush, rush, got the yeyo" while Cam'Ron asserts, "It's a white world"—by which he means not merely one dominated by white people but also by white powder: cocaine. "Go, go sell the yeyo," prompt the backup singers, giving new meaning to the term "go-go dancers."

Brad Jordan, the member of Houston's Geto Boys who changed his name to Scarface, chimes in here with "Mr. Scarface," sampling over and over Al Pacino saying, "All I have in this world." On top of this, Scarface boasts about dominating women (the sex scene he describes here is creepily graphic, and the detail that "the bitch has a gun" reminds one of the movie's Marta sprawled on the motel-room bed with a rifle beneath her under the covers) as well as dominating his small world of drug-selling.

Scarface Hip-Hop: Beyond the Movie and DVD

Outside of *Def Jam Presents: Music Inspired by Scarface* and the DVD minidocumentary *Def Jam Presents: Origins of a Hip Hop Classic,* other hip-hop figures have expressed the degree of esteem in which they hold *Scarface*. Snoop Dogg has said that he watches the movie "once a month," and that it's a metaphor for minority struggle: "I think any brother watching it can identify with what the main man is going through. And when you throw in Pacino—who hip-hop got mad love

for since *The Godfather*—I mean, you've got to love it. Pacino keeps it hard-core and real gangsta in all his films. I go see them all just for that Pacino flava."

Really, Snoop? Even *S1m0ne*? Even *Two for the Money*?

50 Cent, the Mike Tyson of hip-hop, posed for the April 2005 cover of the rap magazine *The Source* dressed as Tony Montana in a reproduction of the black-and-white *Scarface* movie poster. 50 Cent took one of his 2005 singles, "Gunz Come Out," and made a "Scarface Version" of it, intercutting moments from the chain-saw scene into the video's standard bragging-and-posing scenario. 50's 2006 "Till I Collapse" video includes clips from both the *Scarface* "little friend" climax as well as Michael Mann's 2006 feature film of *Miami Vice*.

Nas's 1994 song "The World Is Yours" borrows the movie's motto and its video displays the rapper in the same sort of grandiose sunken-bathtub that Pacino lolls around in. Similarly, Mariah Carey's video for her 1999 song "Heartbreaker" is a full-on *Scarface* salute to the same scene, with Jay-Z in the tub, and Carey dressed as Michelle Pfeiffer's Elvira. And more than in most homages to the film, this one also reiterates a *Scarface* theme in its lyric, as Carey/Elvira is addicted not to cocaine, as Pfeiffer's character is, but to the (implicitly abusive) love she cannot shake for her devious, duplicitous man, the heartbreaker of the title.

Mariah Carey and Jay-Z in "Heartbreaker"

MTV's Cribs

The series *Cribs* on MTV takes you into the homes of hip-hop stars, many of whom collect *Scarface* memorabilia—not just posters, but in some cases, guns from the movie set. It's become a borderline racist joke to say that no black star on *Cribs* is seen *without* some *Scarface* reference. In one 2006 so-called "Sucker-Free Edition" of *Cribs,* OutKast's Big Boi proudly showed us his collection of *Scarface* photos sharing pride of place with his group's numerous music awards. In the next segment, rapper Lil' Wayne took us through his New Orleans home. The cameras panned across a mantel adorned by photos not of family but of Pacino as both Scarface and *The Godfather*'s Michael Corleone. When we were taken into his living room, Lil' Wayne paused to expostulate. "If you haven't watched the movie *Scarface,* you need to, because in *Scarface* you will see, when Tony Montana moved up, he got the stretch-all-around-the-living-room, white sofa." Wayne proudly gestured toward a similar item of furniture in his room. "I like Tony Montana," he concluded.

In another episode of *Cribs,* rapper Trick Daddy showed us a comparatively subtle movie-based acquisition: his set of *Scarface* window blinds, the better to keep out the sun for those late-night screenings of the movie and whatever partying it might inspire.

Music and Politics

More soberly, in 1992, the rapper Paris released—or tried to release—the album *Sleeping with the Enemy* on his own label: Scarface Records. The collection became instantly notorious for containing a composition called "Bush Killa," in which the narrator fantasizes about assassinating the first President George Bush. Gunshots provide background noise over ironic shouts of a "new world order"—Bush Sr.'s foreign-policy slogan—and Paris refers to himself as "P-dog the Bush-killa." Paris creates an ugly scenario—"I pick a rooftop . . . All I wanna see is motherfuckin' brains hangin'"—over an irresistibly catchy beat that combines Public Enemy's squalling manifesto-rap with George Clinton's P-Funk-style rhythms.

"Bush Killa" cannot be separated from the then-contemporary brouhaha surrounding Ice-T's song "Cop Killer," which President Bush had taken the time to condemn in speeches as "sick," saying, "I stand against those who would use films or records or television or video games to glorify killing law enforcement officers." The album on which the song appeared, *Body Count,* was being pulled from record store shelves in the wake of widespread condemnation. Just as Ice-T had held a new conference to justify his work with a presentation that included a short film from the Black Panther Party about police assaults on black people,[1] so Paris on "Bush Killa" included a sung version of the Panthers' slogan, "No justice, no peace."

Paris's Scarface Records had a distribution deal with the major rap label Tommy Boy Records, which in turn was distributed by Time Warner (owner of Ice-T's label, Sire Records, as well). These companies

The Top 5 *Scarface*-Inspired Music and Videos

1. Raekwon, "Incarcerated Scarfaces" video,
   http://www.youtube.com/watch?v=COCmIRODuI4

The Wu Tang Clan member says "let's connect politics," asks "Guess who's the black [Donald] Trump?" and finds a lot of Scarface-wannabes in jail

2. Scarface, "On My Block" youtube video, posted September 2006,
   http://www.youtube.com/watch?v=H4pkJvD4AU

See text: the gangster as elegiac reminiscent

3. Scarface/Geto Boys, "Mind Playin' Tricks On Me"
   http://www.youtube.com/watch?v-nnRS-3AyGUs

The opposite of "On My Block": the drug dealer and drug-taker as a man whose memory has been erased, a man haunted and scared ("a paranoid sleepin' with a finger on the trigger . . .")

4. Rick Ross, "Push It," reenacting some scenes from movie using remixed "Push It to the Limit," posted September 06
   http://www.youtube.com/watch?v=a1jpQoyFEy4

Reconceiving, rechoreographing *Scarface* nightclub dancing

5. Scarface, a Minute to Pray And a Second to Die (to Marvin Gaye's "What's Going On?" riff):
   http://www.youtube.com/watch?v=ptICfgaB8

A different rapper, not Brad Jordan, samples the most *Scarface*-appropriate song title and riff ever: Marvin Gaye's "What's Going On?"

decided they didn't need the grief that Paris, a much less well-known entity than Ice-T, was sure to bring them—I mean, Paris's *Sleeping with the Enemy* album was turned in with album-cover art showing the auteur hiding in some tall grass, gun in hand, near the White House.

Tommy Boy backed out of the deal, so Paris went to producer (and future Columbia Records chairman) Rick Rubin, who was going to rush out "Bush Killa" on his label Sex Records (*also* distributed by Time Warner) before the 1992 elections. But corporate weight was brought to bear against Rubin, whose parent company, Time Warner, paid off Paris with a $100,000 settlement[2] to go away, and Paris was left to sell the record himself, his little Bay Area–based Scarface Records label soon to fade away.

The Legacy of *Scarface* Music

The use of *Scarface* imagery in music videos is wide if not deep. Gwen Stefani chose what she termed the "Michelle Pfeiffer crack-whore look"[3] as a way to brand the visual style of her 2006 album *The Sweet*

Gwen Stefani
(Gregg DeGuire/
WireImage)

Escape. On the cover, Stefani wears a platinum-blond wig and big, '80s-style sunglasses and at a fast glance, could pass for Pfeiffer-as-Elvira. *Entertainment Weekly,* in dissecting this image, referred to the disparity, the "conundrum . . . connected to the style of Michelle Pfeiffer's drugged-out gangster's moll from Brian De Palma's blood-drenched

1983 classic [and] the clean-living, gym-frequenting, new-mommying Stefani's obvious delight in being ever-so-slightly naughty. (She repeatedly uses the phrase 'coke whore' to describe her newfound fashion muse—and does so with a mischievous smirk.)"

The novelist Trey Ellis, a *Scarface* admirer who's nonetheless skeptical, if not sometimes appalled, by its influence, told me, "Like a lot of people in the black community, I think it's done some terrible things. And even in the original [Howard Hawks] *Scarface* movie, it was about how gangsterism is bad but then, people love villains and the message comes through that it's sexy and cool, and there's something ennobling about a tragic hero dying in a blaze of glory.

"And what's happening today, you'll hear in a lot of hip-hop songs about 'being a soldier,' a lot of songs saying, 'I'm looking for a soldier,' and that's what drug dealers will call it. If you watch *The Wire,* they talk about this a lot—that the kids who work for the dealers are called their soldiers, and it ennobles what they're doing as opposed to seeing that what they're doing is so obviously rooted in the slave mentality and preying upon other members of their community to sell drugs to or kill their competition. De Palma's *Scarface* ends up calling his followers 'soldiers' and transposing the honor of the military onto what they're doing, and in the process ruining lots of *real* people's lives who buy into that."

Still, it's no wonder that *Scarface* producer Martin Bregman says that for years, he has wanted to remove Giorgio Moroder's period score—that is, its disco-era glossy beats and plaintive female wails from Blondie's Debbie Harry, as well as Elizabeth Daily's polite cross between Harry and Donna Summer on two of the album's cuts—and replace it with a hip-hop soundtrack, one that would appeal to a major segment of the movie's enduring audience. "I want to do it, the studio wants to do it, the rappers I've talked to like Sean Combs have come forward to help do it, but Brian [De Palma] doesn't want to do it," Bregman told me. "I disagree with him on that. Pacino doesn't [want to change it] either. I don't want to *replace* the soundtrack; I want to give the audience *an alternative,* and with the DVD technology we can." So what's holding it up? De Palma has said he has a final-cut agreement that gives him the power to nix this. Bregman begs to differ. "De Palma has no legal [basis for holding this up]; the decision is the studio's. I think eventually it will happen."

And, of course, in a sense, it has already happened. There exists in the hip-hop genre multiple musical scores to *Scarface*; they just aren't marketed by that name. From NWA to Public Enemy to the Wu Tang Clan to 50 Cent, music that reflects the *Scarface* philosophy, its mood and anger both simmering and explosive, has informed hundreds of compositions from a wide range of artists.

In 2006, on National Public Radio's "Fresh Air with Terry Gross," OutKast's André Benjamin told the host that, as a young black man living in a poor area of Atlanta, he was grateful to his mother for enrolling him in a performing-arts school that exposed him to different kinds of culture: the theater, old musicals, dance. "Because if you're from the street and you stay on the street, you really can't blame a person—that's all he knows," said Benjamin. This is probably the most succinct answer to the question of why so many hip-hop artists took the *Scarface* philosophy—not just "Never underestimate the greed of the other guy" and "Don't get high on your own supply," but also the stoicism of Tony Montana, who won't give up the location of his drug money to the thugs that are chopping up his friend Angel with a chain saw—as gospel rather than as metaphor or as exaggerated gangster-movie hyperbole.

Out on the streets where many hip-hop stars grew up, the dangers and temptations they experienced were a lot closer to *Scarface*-reality than, say, *Die Hard*–reality or even *Saving Private Ryan*–reality. Or, at least, such is suggested by the lyrics and interviews of many working in this pop genre. The celebrity rappers attest to the movie by adding to a subculture's slang: Method Man says, "That was the first time I heard that: 'Get the yeyo' "—that is, Cuban slang for cocaine. Eventually, inevitably, just as Brad Jordan, a member of Houston's Geto Boys would change his name to Scarface, so would there be Marvin Bernard, a rapper named Tony Yayo, of Haitian descent and a member of G-Unit, the protégés of rapper 50 Cent.

In that April 2005 issue of *Vibe* with 50 Cent posed on the cover as Scarface, the film was named the number-one film among "50 Movies That Shaped Hip-Hop," noting that since its premiere it "went on to influence countless songs, samples, lyrics, fashion spreads, and video treatments. Rappers could relate to the film's core idea: The American dream could be yours; you just had to seize it."

Snoop Dogg told me that "*Scarface* laid out everything a gangsta needed to know; how to handle himself, how to live by a code of making money that may be gotten in illegal ways, but having a kind of morality. He would not kill that man's wife and kids with that bomb, you've got to remember that. He had his limits . . . You can watch it for fun, to get off on his big guns and 'Say hello to my little friend' and that funny shit. But you can also use it the way businessmen use self-help books—as a confidence-builder, as a blueprint you can apply to your life. Because the ending also tells you what *not* to do—don't get so fucked up that you can't run your organization, that you can't have a family—those are some powerful positive messages, too."

I sought out other hip-hop voices to provide some counterpoint to the Universal-approved Def Jam documentary. One of them was Cee-Lo Green, half of the Grammy-winning duo Gnarls Barkley ("Crazy"); he was also a cofounder of the Atlanta-based Goodie Mob. Green told me that "*Scarface* is a fine, exciting movie with some very

Scarface, the
rapper

bad messages." Speaking in the cadences of a minister in the Baptist church in which he was raised and whose gospel music informs his hip-hop: "I can understand why my brothers and sisters in the music would find inspiration in this kind of modern Horatio Alger story— who among us has not wanted to think that if we work hard, we will be rewarded? It's just too bad that the story [that] so many young, and not-so-young, people in hip-hop are clinging to is the story of a lawless man whose great love for his wife, sister, and mother is contradicted by his actions, his greed, which goes out of control, and his addictions, which lead him to do immoral things." Green concludes, "I have no doubt that *Scarface* has inspired a lot of good music. But that is more because our musicians are so talented, they can make good art out of bad deeds, bad thoughts, bad actions."

Scarface's "My Mind Playing Tricks on Me" and "On My Block"

Someone who has made excellent art out of invoking bad deeds is the rapper Scarface. Houston-based Brad Jordan had originally gone by the stage name Akshen (i.e., "action"), but changed it to Scarface upon seeing the movie and feeling "many similarities" to the character. One of these similarities is that sense of dread, or guilt, or doom, that weighed upon Tony Montana once his ill-gotten fortune was made. On the Geto Boys' 1991 album *We Can't Be Stopped,* Scarface contributes a haunting song called "My Mind Playing Tricks on Me." It's about a man whose every moment, his waking and sleeping hours, is disturbed by memories of past sins, of a shrouded figure of conscience and vengeance who turns out to be, of course, himself. In the song's video, rapping over a sample of the 1974 Isaac Hayes song "Hung Up on My Baby," Scarface proves a fine actor in the silent-movie manner—he acts out the nightmare scenarios with skin-crawling conviction. He seems to want to flee his own body, to cut loose from the mind that's causing such woeful hallucinations.

After leaving the Geto Boys, Jordan/Scarface titled one of his solo albums after one of the movie's key phrases, *Balls and My Word* (2003), and appeared on the cover in the image of the black-and-white Scarface poster. But he went into a deeper Scarface exploration a year earlier, with the song "On Ma Block," from the 2002 album *The Fix*. On this composition—one of gangsta rap's most elegant and simple: a voice talking over the gently repeated piano chords sampled from a Donny Hathaway–Roberta Flack song, "Be Real Black to Me"—Scarface reminisces about growing up in his neighborhood. On "my block," he says, "we probably done it all/On my block, we made the impossible look easy."

The tone is nostalgic without a trace of sentimentality; the tough, tense edge in his voice tells you that he yearns to reclaim the innocence of that time, and that he's cursed with the knowledge that that's impossible. Yet this nationwide pop star still insists, "I'll never leave my block, my niggas need me." It's left to the listener to fill in the blank—that he's already left that neighborhood years ago, and feels badly about that fact, is remembering who he left behind and how difficult lives remain on his block. For a gangsta rapper who made his fame and money with more brutal scenarios, these moments of vulnerability such as "My Mind Playing Tricks on Me" and "On Ma Block" are never, as hip-hop terminology would have it, "soft": weak or unprincipled. On the contrary, it is in songs like these that Scarface makes good on his name, coming at least as close to creating pop tragedy as Brian De Palma, Al Pacino, Oliver Stone, and their collaborators ever did on film.

Scarface Invents Gangsta Rap?

Is it going too far to suggest that the very term for the pop-music genre that came to be known as "gangsta rap" derived directly from this specific gangster movie? I spoke with Geo Santini, twenty-seven years old, who has directed scores of hip-hop music videos and who filmed, in 2007, his debut feature, a Latino gangster movie *Hotel California*. He says vehemently, "I think it influenced a whole different genre or offshoot of gangster films. Because before [*Scarface*], old gangster films were always about the mob and Italian guys, Chicago gangsters, the *Untouchables* type of stuff. And when *The Godfather* came out that brought a whole new look to those things. But what *Scarface* did was open up the genre for street thugs and a different type of gangster movie, the gangster as a loner-type, and that's why I think everybody quotes those lines, uses it in their music: it set a precedent for a new genre."

Sure, there was a lot of talk about criminals, guns, and street cred in pop and R&B well before *Scarface*'s 1983 premiere. Early proto-rap music extending as far back as Jamaican reggae music in the '60s, the Last Poets in the early '70s, and roots rap acts such as Grandmaster Flash and the Furious Five were talking about cocaine and hard times. The same year *Scarface* opened, Flash and the Five released their hit "White Lines (Don't Do It)" with an accompanying video directed by a young Spike Lee.

Lyrics in rock and country music precede this, of course: When in "Cocaine Blues," Johnny Cash sang, "Early one morning, while makin' the rounds/I took a shot of cocaine and I shot my woman down" on his 1968 album *At Folsom Prison,* he could have been describing the scene in *Scarface* where the white-nosed Tony shoots his best friend and his sister.

Still, the chronology of gangsta rap is on *Scarface*'s side for its being a prime source for the genre-name coinage. Pre-1983, it's very difficult to find any yoking of "gangster" with "rap." But in 1985, LL Cool J, on the album *Radio,* spoke of being "a hip-hop gangsta"; in the same year, the Philadelphia rapper Schoolly D released the single "P.S.K.," which stood for "Park Side Killers," and was a tremulous tale of cold-blooded murder or self-defense, depending on your point of view, since the violence in the song is incited by "police at my door." Out in California, N.W.A. was about to make the West Coast the new main headquarters of cutting-edge gangsta rap with the release in 1986 of *Straight Outta Compton,* tales of nightmarish violence that required being met by force and Scarface-like stoicism and loyalty to one's allies in all its songs, most notoriously "Fuck Tha Police."

The gangster ethos promulgated in Oliver Stone's script was based on research he'd done on Miami streets as well as on overseas trips to drug-manufacturing locations in South America. "Being on cocaine at the time, it felt natural," he told *Creative Screenwriting* magazine. "I hung out with lawyers, prosecutors, dope dealers." No matter how scrupulously he may have reported his findings, the result was a white man's fantasy of gangster life, just as all gangster movies as far back as Howard Hawks's original *Scarface* were. When the critic Robert Warshow, in his 1948 essay, "The Gangster as Tragic Hero," wrote of a scene in the 1932 *Scarface,* "We know he is successful because he has just given a party of opulent proportions," he could have been describing the visual motifs of hundreds of gangsta rap videos featuring gaudy parties in and outside De Palma–*Scarface* mansions, with champagne flowing and models in bikinis slinking around the vocalists.

Scarface principles have prevailed in both the dramas described in many gangsta rap songs and around the real-life deaths of rappers such as Tupac Shakur and The Notorious B.I.G. (The actor Vincent Laresca, perhaps best-known as the terrorist Hector Salazar in the third season of *24*, told me that Tupac, with whom Laresca appeared in the 1992 film *Juice*, used to walk around the set off camera talking in the Tony Montana Cuban accent.) In the cases of both Tupac and Biggie, loyalty, silence, and stone-faced contempt for conventional society is prized above all; betrayal of the same is punishable by injury or death. The irony is that the very movie that its makers describe as "operatic" (Bregman), "Brechtian," and "two-dimensional" (Pacino), and "over the top" (Stone) became a touchstone for musicians and fans for "keeping it real," for providing a glimpse and a game plan for how to live real lives.

Let us always keep in mind: When it comes to the cult following that developed around *Scarface*, the filmmakers had no idea what they were letting loose upon the world. You might say, well, the same could be asserted about any cult film, from *The Rocky Horror Picture Show* to *The Big Lebowski*. But no such comparison quite tracks. In this case, white filmmakers who fashioned an old property into a new melodrama set in Hispanic culture ended up inspiring devotion among diverse minority groups as well as millions of white adolescents and adults. It has been an often foolish admiration, but it has nevertheless regularly inspired a creativity that has occasionally exceeded the craft and art of *Scarface* itself.

For example: Without *Scarface,* Ghostface Killah would probably not have been inspired to write "Kilo," included on his 2006 album *Fishscale* and a remarkably cinematic song about cocaine as power, pleasure, and pain. The song climaxes with a cameo by Ghostface's Wu Tang Clan colleague Raekwon rapping, "Peace to those cooking that raw, powder white/Get your sniff on, Scarface niggas, we getting right/[. . .] Stop playing, pot slaying, baking soda and scales . . ." In the uncoiling power of its beats and its words, I would daresay "Kilo" is at least the equal of *Scarface,* its partial source. These are the kinds of small eruptions, minor miracles, of pop culture that cannot be predicted, least of all, it would seem, by *Scarface*'s own creators.

PART II

6

The Origins:
Howard Hawks's *Scarface*

"Do it first, do it yourself, and keep on doing it."
　　—Paul Muni as Scarface, reciting his own gangster rule,
　　　fifty-one years before Tony Montana

"When I made *Breathless* [1959], I thought I was making *Son of Scarface,* or *The Return of Scarface.*"
　　—Jean-Luc Godard

Accused of being too violent, plagued by censorship problems, scripted by a flamboyant writer, and starring an actor who sometimes went over the top on his accent—remind you of a movie we know? The 1932 *Scarface* both dovetails and diverges from its sequel in striking ways.

Like De Palma's version, Howard Hawks's *Scarface* begins with an interrogation of our antihero. Well, that is, after the opening credits and a title card warning us that the film we are about to see is "an indictment . . . of the callous indifference of government" to the underworld criminality that is threatening America. The on-screen text concludes with an exhortation to the moviegoing audience that "the purpose of this picture is to demand of the government, 'What are you going to do about it?' " And furthermore, redundantly: "The government is your government—what are YOU going to do about it?" This moralizing, viewed in the present day, now seems at once as radical as anything Oliver Stone has dreamed up—an American movie suggesting that government needs to be held accountable for the injustices heaped upon its citizens? Tell it to Justice Scalia, pal—and as mealymouthed as it ultimately proves to be (it's our government—i.e., we are the government—and therefore we should solve the problem ourselves: trickle-down law enforcement, as it were). The full title of this movie was, don't forget, *Scarface: The Shame of the Nation.*

The *Scarface* Nation (1932)

Director Howard Hawks, at age thirty-one, freshly powerful from the box-office success of his World War I saga *The Dawn Patrol,* worked with screenwriter (ex-newspaperman, future *His Girl Friday* author) Ben Hecht to create *Scarface.* The year before, *The Public Enemy,* starring James Cagney, had done much to

establish the gangster tale as a Hollywood genre. (*Enemy* was based on a novel by W. R. Burnett, who did a plot-structure rewrite on Hecht's *Scarface* script.) The Hays Office—the censoring board of its day, before the modern Motion Pictures Association ratings system was introduced three decades later—initially insisted that the famous *Public Enemy* moment when Cagney shoves a grapefruit half into Mae Clarke's kisser be cut. It wasn't, of course. (This losing bid to censor sensationalistic action would help Hawks in his own *Scarface* battles with Will Hays and his bluenose board.)

In 1932, the Oscar for Best Picture would go to the glossy *Grand Hotel,* but there were lots of grungier, more culturally disruptive pictures out in the marketplace along with *Scarface.* Among them: Tod Browning's *Freaks;* Josef von Sternberg's *Blonde Venus* (the one with Marlene Dietrich in an ape suit); anarchic turns by the Marx Brothers in *Horse Feathers,* and W. C. Fields in the great short *The Dentist;* and *Scarface* star Paul Muni competing against himself in *I Am a Fugitive from a Chain Gang* (a fierce performance undermined by an overlay of melodrama that Hawks, in his own movie, admirably avoided). There were also the monster movies being turned out in the wake of the previous year's success, *Frankenstein:* in 1932, there was Bela Lugosi in *White Zombie,* Carl Dreyer's gravely spooky import *Vampyr,* and *Scarface/Frankenstein*'s Boris Karloff returned in *The Mummy.*

Scarface: X Marks the Spot

The title card of Hawks's *Scarface* displays a jagged "X" slashed through the name of the movie, and this begins a visual motif Hawks usually didn't go in for: symbolism. There will be subsequent scenes including a shoot-out at a railroad crossing, with a lit neon "X" sign on the railroad track. This fades into X-shaped latticework at the top of the garage where the St. Valentine's Day Massacre occurs; the camera pans down to the wall from it, and back up to the X's when the shooting stops. The X's almost always prefigure a death, most often brutal killings—the X's become the equivalent of the notches that count off the expunging of lives.

We're shown, in the first few moments of *Scarface*, a gangland killing in front of an after-hours speakeasy; cut to a quick scene at a newspaper so that an editor can bark at an underling that they'll need a platoon of reporters to cover the gangland war that's erupting. Both scenes plus the opening credit's finger-wagging lecture-message bring us nine minutes into *Scarface,* where we first glimpse Paul Muni's Tony Camonte—or rather, we see his body: it's lying prone in a barbershop chair, his face swaddled in a hot towel in preparation for a shave. A cop car pulls up in front of the shop and in a nice silent joke, Tony instinctively reaches into his trouser pocket and hands the barber his pistol, which is tossed into a basket of dirty towels.

The cops enter and Muni unfurls his towel like the Invisible Man unwrapping his bandages—except instead of revealing empty air (a No-Face), we see the scarred face. Tony has a jagged, seared wound running down the left side of his square-jawed mug. From the first shot, Muni is in full glower, his eyes popped wide open, his brow furrowed, his mouth twisted into an angry grimace: it's a mask he'll wear for most of the movie, letting it drop only in rare moments of vulnerability and tenderness. Pacino used a blank expression as his fallback pose—while Muni signals melodrama, Pacino embodies punk-era, Blank Generation affectlessness—but the effect is the same: to convey the notion immediately that Tony/Scarface is a man who's done his best to bury his emotions, to become, above all else, a tough guy, impervious to insult or injury.

Unknown, George Raft, Vince Barnett, Paul Muni, and Osgood Perkins
(Corbis [LORES])

After another nice touch—Tony striking a match against a cop's badge to light his cigarette—the coppers haul Muni's Scarface into their precinct for an interrogation. No 360-degree De Palma camera pans around *this* Scarface, however. Hawks is already, only eleven films into a forty-seven-movie career, shooting in his signature style: at eye level, keeping the camera trained as much as possible on all the players in the room, so that our eyes are free to roam around the screen and fix on what we want, rather than have our attention drawn by the director via close-ups or quick cutting. The police tell us that Tony is a former bodyguard of the slain man, Louie, thus establishing the *Scarface* trajectory: Tony is an underling who's aiming to go over the top. Speaking of which, Muni's initial responses allow us to hear his choice for ethnic gangster-speak: a nearly vaudevillianextreme Italian accent, in its own way as ludicrous yet committed and vehement as Pacino's Cuban accent. When the police accuse Tony of killing Louie, he says (roughly approximating his dialect): "Who me? That'sa very funny. Big Louie and me, we like this!" He clamps two fingers together tightly to convey comradeship.

To those gangsta rappers who credit De Palma and Stone with laying down the code of the street, you are hereby redirected to these scenes courtesy of Ben Hecht, as well as W. R. Burnett and Seton Miller, credited with "dialogue and continuity." Tony leans forward and tells the bulls questioning him about his whereabouts and motives, "What kinda mug you think I am? I don't know nothin', I don't see nothin', and I don't hear nothin'. And when I do," he says, taking a pause here for dramatic emphasis, "I don't tell a cop," spitting the last word out as though it was poison. Then as now in big cities, snitches might as well have been walking dead men.

Dolls and Molls

At this point, Tony is sprung by a lawyer and goes to his boss, Johnny Lovo, played by Osgood Perkins (actor-father of *Psycho* star Tony). This is a scene from which Stone clearly borrowed heavily for De Palma. Muni's Tony, as when Pacino visits Robert Loggia's gaudy penthouse for the first time, comments on the swell lifestyle being lived. Lovo begins to pepper Tony with questions about the police, and a beautiful blonde in a silver dressing gown enters silently from another room. It's Lovo's moll Poppy, played by Karen Morley who, like Michelle Pfeiffer, was then a virtually unknown performer making a sexy splash here as a super-skinny, slinky-flaky siren.

Muni's Tony is immediately distracted from his boss's chatter—his eyes keep drifting over to Poppy, who seats herself in front of a makeup table, allowing her gown to fall away and reveal a shapely leg. When Tony interrupts Lovo to point at Poppy and stage-whisper, "Hey, that's pretty hot," Lovo introduces them. "Hi," says Tony, break-

ing into a rare hopeful grin. And like Pfeiffer's Elvira, Poppy gives Tony the once-over and dismisses him. Her only response to his greeting is to look down at his fingernails and murmur a dismissive, "Mmm-hmmm."

When Tony tells Lovo their pictures were in the paper (he's proud of the publicity their crimes are drawing), Poppy asks whether Tony's ran near the razor-blade ads. Slow on the uptake, Tony realizes she's referring to his face. He traces his X-shaped scar with a finger and says, "You'll get used to that," and Poppy looks up from her nails, startled that he's already assuming they'll have some future together. There's a nice give-and-take here, of the two discovering each other's personalities and of friction making sparks. Tony tells Poppy he got the scar "in the war," another detail that gibes with Trail's source-novel, but Lovo undercuts Tony's proud bravado by scoffing, saying Tony got the scar in a war, all right: "a war with a blonde in a Brooklyn speakeasy."

Scarface on the Rise

Tony, newly promoted for his no-snitch loyalty, suggests Lovo, rapidly extending his reach in Chicago's South Side, also turn his attention to the north. "Now listen, you," he tells Tony, "I say we stay outta the North Side and what I say goes!" Tony glowers, bridling at being told what to do. As always in the *Scarface* saga, Tony's pride is unbounding: the tragic flaw of hubris. But he pulls back. "Whatever you say, boss," he says mildly.

Once outside, in a car with his best buddy, George Raft's Guino

Rinaldo, Tony gives him a cut of Lovo's cash and says there's more where that came from. When Raft remarks that Lovo's got it all figured out, Tony snickers, "Who's Lovo? . . . That guy is just soft—I can see it in his face . . . This business is just waitin' for someone . . . and I got ideas . . . Some day, I'm-a gonna run the whole works." Then Tony enunciates a business philosophy that parallels Oliver Stone's proclamation for Pacino's Tony, as Muni says, "In this business, there's only one law you gotta follow to keep outta trouble."

He pats his jacket, where his gun is, then makes his hand into the shape of a shooting pistol. "Do it first, do it yourself, and keep on doing it."

The Family Scarface

Back at home, Tony wolfs down dinner prepared by his mother. Muni's uni-brow tries manfully to slant into a furrow when he hears a sound outside. He throws open the tenement-apartment door, where his sister, Cesca (a glowing-eyed, avid Ann Dvorak—a mere eighteen at the time, and who'd become Hawks's girlfriend in the course of making this movie[1]), is smooching with some well-dressed cad. Getting a load of Tony's glower, the snake slithers away. Tony bawls out Cesca, telling her he doesn't like her acting that way with men. Protesting spunkily, she says, "Who do you think you are?" "I'm your brother!" snaps Tony. "You don't act it!" says Cesca. "You act more like—I don't know, sometimes I think . . ." and her voice trails off, because there was no way the movie code at the time was going to allow her to finish that sentence—that he more often acts like a lover being two-timed.

Paul Muni and Ann Dvorak (Corbis)

Hawks's original version of De Palma's Manny is George Raft's
Guino Rinaldo, whom Cesca now sees out on a neighborhood street,
doing his trademark coin-flipping (a gesture that would be repeated
forever after by comedians impersonating Raft long after his death).
They lock eyes; we know from our modern film no good can come
of this.

Scarface Power Grabs and Business Decisions: First You Get the Money . . .

Tony smashes his way into the First Ward Social Club, proclaiming, "That's okay, boys, don't get up—just changing the name on the door!" He tells them Johnny Lovo is their new boss. Lovo tells these mugs he's taking over Chicago's beer runs, citing "half a million customers" and that "this is a business and I'm gonna run it that way." In the present day, on TV shows like *The Sopranos* and *The Wire*, it's taken for granted that illegal operations are run using corporate business models; but at the time this was a new notion explored in Hecht's script.

What follows are scenes of Tony and Rinaldo paying visits to various speakeasies, announcing that they're taking over beer delivery by fiat and extortion. "How many barrels did you say you want?" Tony asks one saloon keeper, who replies, six. "Yeah? Well, you're gettin' ten." He writes down the figure in his little book—Tony is nothing if not methodical; he also opens the saloons' beer taps and drains the supply while "negotiating." (This scene will be copped right down to the drained beer taps in Roger Corman's 1967 quickie *The St. Valentine's Day Massacre,* with an underling played by George Segal doing the threatening.)

Everyone he encounters is suitably intimidated. Tony and his guys shoot up a bar called The Shamrock (the implication: Tony is taking over the Irish mob's territory); they set off bombs in other joints.

We haven't seen Poppy in a while, so Tony looks her up one day and asks why she hasn't been around: does he scare her?, he asks with jovial pride. Poppy looks up and down at Tony in his loud checked suit—actress Karen Morley is terrific at blank-faced sarcasm—and replies drily, "Well, that outfit's enough to give *anyone* the yips."

She also observes that he's "wearing jewelry—isn't that effeminate?" Too dim to take offense, Tony proudly polishes his glittering pinkie ring against his lapel and says he got this gaudy bauble "at auction." This finally gets a laugh out of Poppy, who says, "You sure are a funny mixture, Tony." "The first time you've smiled!" Tony says triumphantly—it's the shadow-moment in De Palma's movie when Pacino's Tony puts on Michelle Pfeiffer's big floppy hat to get a laugh out of her.

After a few more murders, Tony is living high, in a new apartment, wearing silk robes. When Poppy visits him, she looks around and observes, "It's pretty gaudy, isn't it?"

"Yeah. Glad you like it!" says Tony, grinning. The movie will constantly play off of Tony's lack of education for small laughs, in much the same way the accent of Pacino's Tony made movie audiences chuckle frequently with its comic exaggeration. More significantly, we can see that fascination with gangsta-rap bling was fully in effect back in the '30s—it is important to acknowledge, at the present time when such rapacious materialism is so much identified with what some pop-social critics see as black pop culture, there was no shortage of *white* gangsters eager to show off their nouveau riche vulgarity and spendthrift ways. To consign such behavior to contemporary black youth is, as is so often the case in pop media, subtly racist.

The Great *Scarface* and *The Great Gatsby*

A provocative 2006 essay by Marilyn Roberts entitled, "Scarface, The Great Gatsby, and The American Dream," points out numerous similarities that Hecht and the other screenwriters on Hawks's *Scarface* may have drawn from F. Scott Fitzgerald's 1925 novel. Roberts points to scenes in which flower-named women—Daisy in *Gatsby*; Poppy in *Scarface*—are wooed with displays of wealth and finery, or as Roberts puts it, "won over by the lure of masculine power as signified by material possessions." Tony takes pride in his array of new suits and shirts, bragging, "What I'm gonna do is wear a shirt only once and then give it right away to the laundry; a new shirt every day." Gatsby is casually proud of his vast supply of his "pile of shirts . . . shirts of sheer linen and thick silk and fine flannel," and actually begins to cry, sobbing, "They're such beautiful shirts . . . It makes me sad because I've never seen such—such beautiful shirts before." (In turn, these women are equated with value. Gatsby describes Daisy as possessing a "voice full of money." When he first meets Poppy, Tony conveys his admiration of her to Lovo by saying simply, "Expensive, eh?")

Marshall McLuhan made a connection between shirts, Gatsby, movies, and *Scarface*-like consumerism: "Nothing is more congenial to the film form than this pathos of superabundance . . . This is the key to *The Great Gatsby* that reaches its moment of truth when Daisy breaks down in contemplating Gatsby's superb collection of shirts . . . It is, therefore, not accidental that the movie has excelled as a medium that offers poor people roles of riches and power beyond the dreams of avarice."[2]

There's another great *Gatsby* parallel that Hecht, et al, could scarcely have been unaware: the Cook's Tours neon sign with the proclamation, "The World Is Yours" that will soon loom large in Hawks's movie. This recalls the famous recurring image of the advertising sign in *The Great Gatsby*, which depicts the huge eyes and eyeglasses of the optometrist Doctor T. J. Eckleburg, staring at the main character, as though daring him to deny the power of the image. In *Gatsby*, it's Eckleburg's authority in the advertisement for a physician who may be a healer or a quack; in *Scarface*, it's the Cook's Tours ad that promises so much but which may just be a hustling come-on.

The World Is Theirs

Tony proudly shows Poppy the "steel shutters" he's had installed, hidden behind the curtains, which can be pulled shut at a moment's notice should gunfire arrive instead of pals or girls. Standing by the window, he asks her how she likes the view, and lo and behold, we see a neon sign with a globe and below it, emblazoned with the phrase "The World Is Yours" ("Cook's Tours" is below it, revealing this is an ad for a tourist agency).

"Some day I look at that sign," says Tony to Poppy with hubristic cockiness, "and I say, 'Okay—she's mine!'," referring to possessing the world and everything in it, including Poppy. He starts to put the moves on Poppy, saying, "I like Johnny, but I like you more."

A brief scene introduces Boris Karloff in a juicy role one year after his turn as the monster in 1931's *Frankenstein*—nothing less than the top-grossing film of the previous year. (He was even then so identified with the role that some *Scarface* movie posters billed him as "Boris 'Frankenstein' Karloff.") Here, he's Gaffney, a dapper illegal-machine-gun-runner—another competitor for Tony and his now-merely-nominal boss Johnny to deal with.

Then we're back to Tony courting Poppy, this time in a restaurant. "I'm not hungry for anything—except you," he murmurs. Suddenly some cars run past the café and there's a storm of gunfire: "That's O'Hara's mob!" Tony yells, pulling Poppy and himself under a table. Hawks stages this scene with vehemence: When the bullets cease, Tony and Raft's Guino, their pistols drawn, run out into the street and grab something from one of the few members of O'Hara's gang they've managed to kill. It's a machine gun, something Tony hasn't seen before. Raft hands it to him, and Tony's face beams. "Hey, looka-this—you can carry it!"

A more efficient way to kill people: Tony is elated with the new technology.

It's a turning point for Tony. Now he knows he's got both the moxie and the weaponry to make a power grab. He refers to the tommy gun as "a typewriter—and I'm gonna write my name with it in big letters all over this town!" Tony recruits some of Lovo's men to join him in doing some separate jobs. He yells, "C'mon, boys!" and his posse leaves with him. Poppy looks on, very impressed by the man with the big gun.

What follows is a terrific montage of Tony Camonte's revenge rampage. Cars shoot at each other and slam uncontrollably into walls; in a perfect, almost thrown-away noir shot, Hawks's camera is placed overhead on a street corner, and between the cross-street signpost, we see a body sprawled on the pavement, freshly shot. Then in a scant twenty-seven seconds, Hawks gives us his reenactment of the St. Valentine's Day Massacre: We see a group of men in silhouette, being ordered to stand facing a wall, arms raised. "What is this, a pinch?" asks one. "Naw, we're bringing you a valentine," says a mocking voice. Bang-bang-bang. The silhouettes drop, leaving a blank wall. That's it.

Crosses and Double-crosses

Like the X's that loom up throughout the movie, crosses also appear, although their symbolism is mercifully light-handed—crosses cast shadows in speakeasies, to advertise the illegal presence of booze, for instance. Just as Pacino's Scarface dies bloodying the life-cleansing water in his indoor fountain, with his arms thrown out in a crucifixion pose, so do these crosses in Hawks's movie bear witness to death and the immorality of the crimes being committed. In the next scene, when the cops haul in Gaffney to look at the carnage his smuggled guns have wrought in the dank garage, he beholds a grisly crime scene of bodies being removed—while a shaft of sunlight in the shape of a cross shines down upon the proceedings.

Now with the Irish mob neutralized, Gaffney moves center stage. Tony has him rattled, no doubt: he's addressing his core followers from a dingy apartment (there's another sunlight-cross thrown against the dark wall behind him). "Thinks he'll get me, huh? I'm the only one left!" he rasps—it's a fine performance; he's as feral as a wolf.

To reinforce what's gone on, cops in a police station say that both Gaffney and Lovo are now in hiding, with "Camonte behind it." "The public's interested in him. He's a colorful character," says a visiting reporter, asking the cops for quotes for a story.

" 'Colorful'?" sneers a police detective played with squat bluntness by Edwin Maxwell. "What color is a crawling louse? That's the attitude of too many morons in this country. They think these hoodlums are some sort of demigods. They sentimentalize, romance, make jokes about 'em. When I think what goes on in the minds of these lice I wanna vomit!" He mentions a daytime shooting spree that left three "kiddies playing hopscotch" with "lead in their little bellies."

This speech may strike us as a tad overwrought, but it's potent on a couple of levels. Most superficially, this is the strong anticrime message that Hecht had to be sure to insert into this movie subtitled *The Shame of a Nation,* lest it be censored by the Production Code—more commonly known as The Hays Code, adopted by the Motion Pictures Association of America in 1930 and which held, among other things, that "Murder scenes had to be filmed in a way that would discourage imitations in real life, and brutal killings could not be shown in detail. 'Revenge in modern times' was not to be justified." However, more than that, this speech holds up as the same argument that would be leveled not just at De Palma's *Scarface,* but also at the culture of gangsta-rap music that followed the release De Palma's film: the glorification of violence, even as the violent ones wear the best clothes and recite the best lines, remains central to so much of pop culture, good *and* bad.

Hammering home the point, the next scene takes place at a newspaper publisher's office, with a number of concerned citizens in attendance, where Maxwell's detective thunders, "You're glorifying the gangster by giving him all this publicity!" The publisher retorts with an echo of the film's opening-text finger-wagging: "You're the government!" he tells his assembled audience. He makes a plea for "martial law" and to "put teeth in the deportation laws—half of 'em aren't even U.S. citizens!"

Tony and company shoot and kill Gaffney.

<u>Scarface's Sister Obsession</u>

We are moved on to Tony's favorite nightspot, the Paradise Club—to paraphrase Joni Mitchell, De Palma and Oliver Stone will pave Paradise and put up a Babylon—where Tony invites himself to Johnny Lovo's table, the better to be close to Poppy. Elsewhere in the club is Tony's sister, Cesca, clad in a clingy black number; she espies Raft's Guino Rinaldo, who tries to walk past her, but she stops him. "Why are you always high-hattin' me?" she says playfully. We know why: Because Tony would slug him, or worse, if he looked any closer at this curvy kid. Flirting outrageously, Cesca tells Rinaldo, "I'm eighteen," and does an improvised, raised-arm, sexy dance to entice him—to show him her wares, as it were. Rinaldo takes it all in and scrams.

Tony, meanwhile, has snagged Poppy and brought her to the dance floor, as a morose Lovo sits back at his table, stewing. But Tony's momentary triumph is spoiled when he sees Cesca across the crowded room, also dancing with a stanger she's attracted. Tony breaks away from Poppy, grabs Cesca by the arm, pushes her out of the joint, and takes her home.

"Next time I catch you in a place like that I'm gonna kill ya!" he yells.

"I hate you!" she yells back.

By then they're back home—Cesca and her mother's home, that is—and Tony slaps Cesca for her brazen retort. Mama leads her away, moaning, "He hurt you—he hurt *everybody*!"

These scenes are the sources of two more drawn-out De Palma–*Scarface* ones: the nightclub moment in which Tony Montana roughs up a punk he catches dancing with his sister and giving her cocaine, and Montana's visit to his mother and sister.

After avoiding a post-nightclub ambush by assailants that Tony suspects were dispatched by Lovo, he arranges a trap for his old boss. Tony tells one of this flunkies to call Lovo at ten minutes after two A.M. and say, "The car got smashed and I got away"—that is, I tried to do what you told me, boss, but Tony escaped. Tony goes over to Lovo's place; the appointed time comes, ring-ring goes the phone, Lovo picks it up, listens, and says it's a wrong number. Bingo: This proves Lovo gave the orders for Tony's death. (Oliver Stone used the trick deployed in this scene in De Palma's *Scarface*; it's what leads to the murder of Robert Loggia's Frank. As in the original, Scarface has his right-hand man commit the murder—in the latter case, Steven Bauer's Manny.)

To cap off the scene, as it were, Tony Camonte brings Poppy over to the window and points out the newfound significance of the "Cook's Tours" neon sign, "The World Is Yours": with the death of Lovo, Tony is one step closer to achieving this goal.

The Fall of Scarface

The next scene occurs a month later—it's the first time the movie breaks with "real time" chronology to jump ahead, because the *Scarface* story needs to do some quick character development. Tony has been in Florida for the past thirty days or so (Florida—where the real Al "Scarface" Capone would go to get away from the Chicago pressure; where all of De Palma's *Scarface* takes place). In the meanwhile, Cesca has impressed Rinaldo with the fact that she has, as she says, "grown-up ideas"—that is, about their future together. They've become an item.

Tony returns, going first to his mother's house to check up on his family. Mama tells son that Cesca has moved out and is with "a man." Tony, coming to an instant boil, asks for the address and recognizes it when Mama tells him. He goes to Rinaldo's place where, just before he arrives, we see the couple professing love to each other. Tony rings the doorbell; Rinaldo, in a morning jacket, answers the door; Tony reaches for his gun. Hawks's camera cuts away—we hear the gunshots, but take in the murder of Rinaldo through Cesca's horrified expression as she watches what we cannot: Tony's cold-blooded murder of his best friend. "We were married!" Cesca screams. "We were going to surprise you!" About her brother, she sobs to us, or to no one: "He kills *everything*!"

The rest of the movie is shrouded in the darkness of night—the blackness of Tony's soul. Back at his "steel fortress" of an apartment, as the cops call it, Poppy calls Tony, but he hangs up on her, dazed in grief and self-recrimination. He's brought Cesca with him. The police uses Rinaldo's murder as an excuse to launch an all-out assault on him.

As the sirens blare and squads of police arrive at his address, Tony is energized by the attention he's attracted. So is Cesca, but in a hysterical, darkly romantic, my-life-is-worth-nothing-anyway manner. "I'm just like you, Tony," she says as though her grief over her brother's murder of her husband Rinaldo has carried her over to the dark side. She takes a gun from him as they both prepare to shoot it out with the coppers.

" 'Atsa way to talk!" says Tony, also verging on hysteria. "We'll take on the world!" (An echo of Jimmy Cagney's "Top o' the world, Ma!" in *Public Enemy,* released the year before.)

There's big, blasting gunplay. Cesca is shot and killed. Tony holds her in his arms as though she were *his* lover—and she is, in a sense, the only true, sustained love of his life.

Forced to emerge from his lair as the bullets come flying through his windows, Tony is ambushed by the police as he tries to escape via the back exit of his apartment stairway. His gun is shot out of his hand and he begs for mercy: "Don't shoot!"

A cop snarls, "Get you in a jam without a gun and you squeal like a yellow rat!"

Tony pushes himself down the stairs and out onto the street, where he's gunned down in a storm of bullets. The camera pans up so that the last thing we see is the neon sign: "The World Is Yours."

<u>The End, But Not Quite . . .</u>

The Hays Office overseeing the industry's Production Code found this conclusion a "glorification of the criminal," and suggested that Tony be shown finally as "a cringing coward." Hawks knew before the picture had even begun shooting that the Hays Office had problems with this gangster-hero, yet producer Howard Hughes had sent the director a note saying, "Screw the Hays Office. Start the picture and make it as realistic, as exciting, as grisly as possible."[3] Hawks had certainly held up his end of the bargain.

Now, though, to get *Scarface* released and in theaters, a compromise had to be made. An alternate version of the film—a more vindictive, adamant ending that Hughes thought would mollify the Production Code—was shot by others involved in the production, including director Richard Rosson when Hawks and Muni refused. It showed a handcuffed Scarface (a double was used in place of the absent Muni) being led to a gallows and hanged (this despite the fact that no gangster had ever suffered death by hanging in real life), with more print-on-screen exhortations for the public to do its part to enforce the law.

Even the title of the damn movie became open to debate: Hays wanted something that suggested disapproval right up-front, and the studio, United Artists, came up with *The Menace* and *An American Menace*. Hays countered with *Shame of the Nation*, while Howard Hughes was willing to go with *The Scar on the Nation*. With what one imagines were sour-pusses all around, *Scarface: The Shame of the Nation* is what went out to theaters, with the subhead in increasingly smaller type with each rerelease.

With a few final frowns of ineffectual condemnation, the then-loosely enforced Code allowed *either* version to be screened. And thus it was left up to individual states to decide which version of *Scarface* was shown in their theaters. Most of the big cities opted for Hawks's near-original. The legend, battered but only slightly bowed, continued its life, eagerly injecting itself into American culture.

The Origins:
Armitage Trail's *Scarface*

"He had learned from the movies, the only social tutor he had ever had."

Maurice Coons, writing under the pen name Armitage Trail, laid out all of the basic elements of the *Scarface* mythos in his 1930 novel of the same name.* Coons was also, by that year, dead. Raised in Chicago, he'd spent his early twenties living in Manhattan and Hollywood, churning out hundreds of short stories and a few screenplays. Coons, who weighed 315 pounds, had a fatal

*All quotes from *Scarface,* by Armitage Trail (Blackmask.com edition, 2005)

heart attack in 1930, dying at age twenty-eight in the lobby of Hollywood's Paramount movie theater—how's that for small irony?

He left behind two novels, *Scarface* and *The Thirteenth Guest.* (The
latter was made into a 1943 movie, *The Mystery of the Thirteenth
Guest,* set in a haunted house; its only notable cast members were Hel-
en Parrish, a busy actress in the 1930s and '40s who never broke
through as a star, and Frank Faylen, who later played the gloriously
grumpy grocer-father on TV's *The Many Loves of Dobie Gillis,* a
1959–1963 sitcom.) Having lived in Chicago, Coons had hung out
and ingratiated himself with the Sicilian crime syndicate, and was
well familiar with Al Capone's career trajectory, though the two
never met. The result was that Coons/Trail created Tony Guarino,
"the greatest of all America's notorious gang leaders." A pulp novel
that's equal parts cruddy melodrama and efficient thriller, it can't be
consigned to the trash heap—there's a fundamental power to Trail's
Scarface that it shares with Hawks's and De Palma's movies.

Actually, while Hawks's *Scarface* cites the book in its opening
credits as source material, the novel presages just as much of De
Palma's version as well. Trail's Tony may be referred to as both Italian
(Hawks's man) and Latino (De Palma's). In the opening pages of the
book, we're told that Guarino "loved his parents with the fierce, clan-
love of the Latin." Six pages later, we read that an Irish gang Guarino
starts hanging out with is "somewhat suspicious of an Italian in their
midst." Trail is doubtless simply lumping his character's roots in what
was once commonly called "the Latin countries."

This Tony also shares Oliver Stone's—and by extension, Tony
Montana's—whiplash contempt for an American government that is
viewed as being callous and corrupt. Guarino believes that "the only
difference between a gangster and a policeman is a badge"—the badge

against which Hawks's Scarface will strike a match two years later.

The novel is set at the start of World War I, and immediately establishes Tony Guarino's sense of himself as not merely an outsider in society, but as a self-righteous little SOB about it: in response to a movie-theater's pre-feature appeal for armed forces volunteers, Trail has Tony "wonder[ing] what sort of saps would fall for that. Not him. What did he owe the country? What had the country ever done for him?" The last line uncannily presages John F. Kennedy's "Ask not what your country can do for you" speech even as it reminds us of the early scenes in De Palma's *Scarface,* when Tony Montana nurtures his hatred of his adopted country while being detained in boiling-hot refugee holding pens in south Florida.

But Trail's Tony enlists in the army anyway—he kills a mobster, Al Spignola, and with both the police and the dead man's vengeful organization hunting for him, he figures enlistment is suddenly a smart idea, getting him out of the country until things cool down. Thus, early in his career, like Elvis Presley, Tony Guarino joins the service thinking "he'd have a nice vacation for a few months" but proves to be a good, conscientious soldier. Unlike Elvis, he comes out of the experience a more skilled killer: "Having perfected him in every branch of the fine art of murder . . . the government, in turning him loose with its blessing in the shape of an honorable discharge, seemed to expect him to forget it all immediately and thereafter be a peaceable, law-abiding citizen. Which was a lot to ask of any man, much less Tony." This theme—that the government molds its own criminals—is central to every Scarface story ever told, on-screen, in prose, in music.

In this version of the tale, however, we get a different version of the origin of the anti-hero's most telling trait. "He had come home with a new face and a lot of new ideas, ideas that were going to be profitable for him but detrimental to the community . . ." Trail writes with a typical mixture of casualness and high-handedness. Wait a minute: "a new face"? It seems an "awful night battle" in France "left him with a long livid scar down the left side of his face, a heavy scar running from the top of his ear to the point of his chin." This is the most elaborate, disfiguring scar in Scarface history; it severs "nerves and muscles" on that side of his cheek and "gave his face an amazingly sinister look." For Trail's gangster, the scar might as well be a permanent Halloween mask of horror. In real life, Capone, who'd gotten his scar face from the flick of a switchblade wielded by a guy with whose girlfriend Capone had flirted, covered his more superficial wound with powder—it was an ambivalent sign of cosmetic embarrassment as much as it was proof of a tough life. And for movie stars like Paul Muni and Al Pacino, it had to be something different—for Muni, a deep but short gouge in a cinder-block-shaped face; for Pacino, the scar was the thin flick of a knife-fight wound, a downward slash that began as a parting of Montana's left eyebrow (a touch Pacino claimed in interviews to have come up with himself), just missing his eye and then extending briefly down his cheek. As a modern movie star, the scar could not prevent the gangster from still being leading-man material.

Trail's *Scarface* novel is so pulpy it sometimes edges over into comic-book territory: specifically, Will Eisner's great, noir-influenced *The Spirit,* which would be created nine years after Trail's novel was published and share one aspect of Scarface's origin. Like Eisner's cop Denny Colt, Trail's gangster is falsely presumed dead by the people in his hometown, and uses this misinformation to transform himself into a scarier, more powerful entity. In The Spirit's case, his strategy was to put on a mask and haunt his foes; he fought crime more effec-

tively in part by the fear invoked by having a "dead" man coming after you; in *Scarface,* it's thought that Guarino died in combat, and
when he returns, his "mask" is the scar that renders him unrecogniz-
able to many, and gives him an added advantage, initially at least, of a
secret identity.

Literally a "marked man," the now-dubbed "Scarface Tony"—who
also adopts a new last name, changing Guarino to Camonte to avoid
having his family tainted with his criminal career—joins the gang run
by the weaselly crime lord Lovo, whose name we know from the
Hawks movie, and who's planning to travel to Havana, the De Palma
movie's taking-off point. In the novel, Havana is "a gay sporting place
where life is pleasant." Early on, Lovo is already like Robert Loggia's
Frank Lopez in the De Palma film: going soft, looking for relief from
the danger and pressure of the gangster life, and looking forward to
early retirement, which in this sort of saga also means death.

Like the two movies, Trail's novel also includes Tony's upstanding,
fiercely disapproving mother who lives "in squalor" but maintains "a
decent home," yet one that "spawns another gangster, as inevitably as
an oyster creates a pearl." Tony also has a virginal teenaged sister—
"Rosie, a tall, pretty girl of sixteen"—whom Tony tries and fails to
protect from the mean world out there.

And there's always a blonde, isn't there? In the case of the novel,
that blonde is not Elvira or Poppy but Vyvyan—Vyvyan Lovejoy. She
is, of course, a gangster's moll as well as a showgirl, but Tony con-
vinces her to quit and come with him. Novelist Trail reserves a rather
vehement contempt for this character among so many other, more un-
savory ones: "Being fond, like most blondes, of an easy life secured
with the smallest possible expenditure of energy, she obeyed [Tony's]
orders."

Interestingly, Trail's novel introduces a character that doesn't appear in any other form in the Hawks or De Palma movie, a character that could have been fascinating in either era of pop-culture filmmaking: Jane Conley, "the Gun Girl," a woman as ruthless as any man in her desire for power. Ostensibly a pawn who carries a gun for a male criminal, a "gun girl," the novel explains, "is usually a good-looking, well-dressed girl that nobody would suspect" whom a gangster gets "to carry his gat for him and trail him until he's ready to use it . . . He pulls off his job and runs down the street, slippin' her the gat as he goes past," because no cop is going to suspect a woman of carrying a gun, is he?

But Jane—significantly, *not* a blonde but a brunette—is an independent operator. Even Vyvyan holds Jane in grudging admiration: "Jane is the most famous of all of 'em. She's known as *The* Gun Girl." Jane allies herself with Tony during his rise, and eventually takes Vyvyan's place as Tony's true soul mate. "I've got as much guts as you—any day of the week, big shot," Jane tells Tony at one point. Tony responds by asking her to prove her loyalty by killing one of his chief rivals, Bruno, nicknamed "the Schemer."

It's clear, in retrospect, that Jane Conley, not a moll but a gunsel, would have been too potent a female presence in the movies—she might have thrown off the balance of power, shifted the focus of either movie, to see a woman making a power grab in any way other than a sexually defined role. In Hawks's film, it's unthinkable that a woman might infiltrate the "First Ward" boy's club; in De Palma's, women are disco dollies and white-silk fantasy figures, to be worshipped and traduced.

Jane the Gun Girl's weapon of choice is, naturally, the machine gun. Here again, both Hawks and De Palma (or more accurately, I guess, Hecht and Stone) were following Armitage Trail's lead in having his characters delight in newly minted firepower: "Tony lifted the machine gun to his shoulder—it was one of the new type that are operated much as a rifle—and riddled the front of the shop, both upstairs and down . . . He'd given them as good as they sent, and with their own weapon. Since machine guns had been introduced into the war, the score was even."

Another of the distinct similarities in the three *Scarface* incarnations is the portrayal of cops as either corrupt, or as dopes perennially one step behind the hoods. In De Palma's film, Harris Yulin's cop Mel Bernstein is a slimy jerk who thinks he's going to get paid off by Pacino's Tony just as Loggia's Frank had bribed him before; instead Mel ends up shot and on the floor of Frank's back office. In Hawks's *Scarface,* the police furrow their brows and have meetings to plot plans of action to neutralize the growing mob violence, to little avail (why, they don't even have machine guns!). And in Trail's novel, Tony Camonte boils it down succinctly: "If the cops were as sharp as we are, we wouldn't have a chance!" he crows.

Trail's book gives Tony a brother who's a cop, a bit of shameless, mirror-image melodrama that the filmmakers wisely ignored. What all versions share is a sister for Tony, the bright, pure girl who's just as drawn to the dark side as Tony himself, but who pays for it, because . . . well, because she's a girl, and other than Jane the Gun Girl, no woman in any Scarface saga can be the equal of a man. Is it any wonder that *Scarface* feeds the misogyny that fills so much gangsta rap, where women are most often reduced to wiggly, scantily dressed girls out to snort up the leftover cocaine and spend the money their mack-daddies make?

In Trail's *Scarface*, as in De Palma's, Tony's best friend—in this case, a tough enforcer named Mike Rinaldo—takes up with Tony's sister, Rosie, even though big brother has warned little sister to stay away from mob action of any sort. Toward the end of the book, Tony is searching for Mike and discovers the two of them in a hotel room: "He had killed for money, for vengeance, for lust, for almost every reason except a worthy one. His sister . . . Upstairs . . . With one of his own gunmen . . . Of course, Mike was the straightest and most ruthless shot in the city. Tony realized he might be facing death, probably was. Mike was touchy about his heart affairs."

"His heart affairs"—great phrase, isn't it? It's a wonder Hecht didn't pick up on it and give it a life as a freshly coined phrase that might have reverberated down into today. But Tony surprises Mike and Rosie in their room and, says narrator Trail, "in the language of their kind, Tony let him have it": from an automatic pistol Tony carried in his pocket. "Mike's jaw dropped and he gazed stupidly at his murderer through a haze of bluish smoke . . . and with a gasp abruptly fell to the floor." Tony plugs him with a half-dozen bullets, which leave "spots of red on his hitherto spotless white shirt-front. Tony watched with interest as they enlarged, then finally merged into one big red stain that grew bigger." (Again, a nice throwaway phrase that might have become a hard-boiled standby: Dashiell Hammett or Raymond Chandler or Ross Macdonald could have used "The Big Red Stain" . . .)

Tony tells Rosie to get dressed and scram before the coppers arrive. And as we know from the films, the sister will now hate the brother: " 'Oh you beast! You murdered him!' " Tony briefly reflects on "the bitter irony": "Reviled by his own sister for having saved her from the rapacity of one of his gunmen!" He wants to comfort her but "he didn't dare." Tony has crossed the final line. The former Tony Guarino "realized that the knowledge that he was the notorious Tony Camonte would kill his mother" so he just tells Rosie to leave, "and keep your mouth shut!"

In Trail's version of the tale, Tony is captured and brought to trial for murder. He beats the rap, thanks to crooked cops he's paid off, but rumors circulate that Tony may be tired of the gangster game (his men wonder whether he's become—a recurring theme—soft, looking for an easier life and an easy way out), and one underling is even bold enough to ask if it's true that Tony will "quit the racket and go into real estate. That was just talk, wasn't it, boss?"

Tony brushes off the theory, but in truth, he's come to believe that "in organizing and perfecting this powerful gang that ruled the underworld activities of a great city, he had built a Frankenstein, a monster that, acting upon the principles he had instilled into it, would feel justified in destroying him should he attempt to desert now."

In the end, though, he's betrayed by a dame—Jane the Gun Girl—who begins working in league with Tony's brother, now the police chief of detectives ("having the chief of detectives for a boyfriend would be a valuable asset for a girl like her," she reasons—and how!). Tony trips up: He becomes obsessed with the revenge killing of the assistant district attorney who tried to prosecute him, which draws his attention away from Jane and the police. Thinking he's about to ensnare the "ratty" ADA, Tony is instead drawn into a trap: " 'Jeez!,' groaned Tony. 'It's the cops!' " "Tony saw the revolver flash, then his head snapped back from the impact of the bullet. Anyway, he had always faced it." He dies; the world is no longer his, but his cop-brother's, who tells reporters "complacently": " 'Tony's old moll gave me the tip.' " (Even at the end, the woman gets no respect.) Trail's *Scarface* makes its protagonist something of a patsy in order to gin up some sympathy in the reader for his demise, but the underlying message is the old crime-doesn't-pay—or rather, it's already the modern version of that cliché: Crime pays for a while, but sooner or later, your homies betray you and you die a violent death. It's a story, written by Trail in 1930, that will reverberate from hereon, for decades to come.

When producer Howard Hughes announced his intention of bringing *Scarface* to the big screen, Coons/Trail hoped that Edward G. Robinson, who bore some resemblance to Capone, would be cast in the role which went to Paul Muni. Coons didn't live to see the final result. Capone did, and he didn't like what he saw. It was Howard Hughes and director Howard Hawks who had to wheedle and jolly-up the menacing gangster to convince him that Tony "Scarface" Guarino really wasn't Alfonse "Scarface" Capone.

As for Maurice Coons, he was a man ahead of his time. His work preceded the heyday of the hard-boiled detective novel as well as popular magazine outlets for the genre, such as Black Mask. (Coons's brother, Hannibal, was also a writer—he went on to write for TV, churning out scripts for, among other shows, *My Three Sons* and *The Addams Family*.) None of Maurice's short stories have been used as movie ideas; someone should collect and publish them in a nice fat little volume.

8

Alterna-*Scarface*s: Movies, TV Shows, Novels, and Comic Books

In his 2006 film *The Black Dahlia,* Brian De Palma, working from the novel by James Ellroy, Josh Hartnett's cop/narrator comments with a foreboding that belies his callowness: "Nothing stays buried forever—corpses, ghosts—nothing stays buried forever. Nothing."

This is the attitude of all contemporary manifestations of Scarface in America—the supposition that a man who lived his life as vitally as Tony Montana could not have died in one mere shoot-out with a bunch of imported thugs from South America; that not merely the legend but the man himself must still exist in some form, spiritual or corporeal. And so he does. In TV shows, in video games, in comic books, on the Web, and in movies that pre- and post-date the movie from which he sprang, Scarface has long haunted, and continues to haunt, America.

Movies and TV

THE UNTOUCHABLES TV SERIES

Pre-De Palma, the version of *Scarface* most familiar to mass America was the one depicted in *The Untouchables,* a TV series premiering in 1959 with a two-hour pilot directed by Phil Karlson and focusing on Eliot Ness (Robert Stack) rather than Scarface Al (embodied here by Neville Brand). "Nineteen twenty-nine: Chicago was wet," yammers the familiar staccato voice of Walter Winchell, the hugely popular syndicated columnist who made dough on the side as a radio and TV announcer. With these words—and "wet" understood as shorthand for the just-pre-Prohibition, legal-liquor era—*The Untouchables* launched its saga of what happened when a tottlin' town like Chicago went "dry." The mob moved in on speakeasies, which had sprouted up selling, as Ness's FBI boss puts it here, "beer, booze, women, and gambling." So powerful and violent had the trade become, the FBI formed a special team led by the clean-cut, no-nonsense Ness.

Before *The Untouchables,* Robert Stack had been in a slew of forgettable Westerns and did a lot of plays on TV in 1950s series such as *The Schlitz Playhouse of Stars* and *The 20th Century-Fox Hour*—the

lower-tier for teleplaywrights. But *The Untouchables* made him a star for his steady gaze and semi-hoarse bark of a voice.

The Untouchables: The Scarface Mob—broken into two hourlong halves for TV broadcast but released in some cities as a feature film—was a Desilu production; yes, that's right: the company formed by Lucille Ball and Desi Arnaz. Arnaz, as on-screen host, introduced the two hours on his *Westinghouse-Desilu Playhouse* airing in '59. Al Capone doesn't even appear until fifty minutes into *The Scarface Mob*: his introduction is meant to be the climax for the first half of the TV-movie, his menace the lure to bring the viewer back for the conclusion the following week.

As Capone, Brand—who'd also spent much of his career in TV and movie Westerns, but specializing in sneering bad guys—smoked a big cigar. His scar is almost exactly like Pacino's in that, unusually, it cuts across his left eyebrow as well as his cheek. He speaks in a stagey Italian accent: "You punks!" he bellows at his underlings after Ness's first wave of crackdowns. "You stupid-a punks! *I'll-a* take care of Ness!" he thunders.

In an attempt to intimidate Ness and make him give up on his pursuit of Capone, the mob king's men break into Ness's girlfriend's apartment and rough her up, tearing her clothes. Betty Anderson, as played by Patricia Crowley, a wonderful actress who performs with her typical combination of understated intelligence and elegant sensuality, is shaken. Her attack only inspires Ness to new relentlessness.

In *The Untouchables*, Scarface is not bigger than life—Eliot Ness is. Scarface Al is a froggy grump, one gangland leader among many whom the FBI has on its list to neutralize. The TV show is interested in Scarface primarily as a rich bully, the better to stand in contrast to Ness's government-wage citizen-with-a-badge-and-a-tommy gun. (The same is true of the Scarface portrayed by Robert De Niro in De Palma's 1987 feature film—in the movie poster, a gigantic, smug-looking De Niro/Scarface looms over a smaller but feistily heroic-looking Kevin Costner as Ness, who's pointing his gun at us, as though he'd even plug us to get to his sworn enemy.)

The Scarface Mob as it aired on TV was meant to launch a weekly *Untouchables* series, which proved to be a solid hit with viewers from

1959–1963. Among its other notable directors for individual episodes included Stuart Rosenberg (*Cool Hand Luke*), Tay Garnett (*Gunsmoke, Rawhide*), and actress Ida Lupino, still one of her era's most neglected female directors. The *Untouchables* TV show was also one of the first such series to be criticized for its violence—the show made the most of its tommy gun shoot-out sequences. Had Robert Stack not been such a calm, well-liked show business figure, the series might have made its network, ABC, more nervous. As it was, *The Untouchables* benefitted in the ratings for its guns-blazing rep, and for the fact that it could justify such action as being based on the real-life existence of Eliot Ness. FBI director J. Edgar Hoover was a big fan and viewed the show as a crackerjack recruiting tool.

The series' Ness-centric point of view was mandated by the times and the source. No TV shows of that period would have countenanced a bad guy as its pivotal character, and director Phil Karlson was working from an *Untouchables* book cowritten by the real-life Ness and Oscar Fraley, published in the late '50s. That volume was a glorified boy's-adventure book, with chapters about Ness's stalwart defeat of criminals like Capone, Ma Barker, and Baby-Face Nelson. Karlson took its thin, pulpy material and made something exciting out of it: pulp sensationalism that made it past the decorous confines of television back then. It's clear in the Patricia Crowley scene, for example, that we're really meant to believe her character was raped; Karlson has his actors signify this in the cruel brusqueness with which they handle Betty and paw at her clothes.

Karlson had made some fine, lean B-movies, some excellent westerns, but two contemporary crime pictures of particular quality—*Kansas City Confidential* (1952) and *The Phenix City Story* (1955)—that played to strengths of *The Scarface Mob*. Both *Kansas* and *Phenix,* shot in black and white as was *The Scarface Mob,* were told in a semidocumentary style with some voiceover narration and much terse hardboiled dialogue. Karlson's later career would prove more uneven and odd—he'd direct both the Dean Martin 007 spoof *The Silencers* (1966) and the lawman-revenge surprise hit *Walking Tall* in 1973—but his gift for crafting lean action films makes *The Untouchables: The Scarface Mob* the most exciting retelling of the Capone/Ness legend to pre-date *Scarface.*

Between the releases of Howard Hawks's and Brian De Palma's *Scarface*s, there were numerous attempts to capture some of this outlaw energy onscreen. Many of the following movies and TV shows favor the quasi-historical, opting to reinterpret the life of the real-life Scarface, Al Capone, the squat Chicago gang leader who ran a Depression soup kitchen to offset his bootlegger image and the murder rackets that gave him his criminal juice. A few of the others take the opposite side of the law and valorize Scarface opponents, foremost among them the TV *Untouchables*—which, in turn, was turned into a feature film by De Palma, installing Costner, an actor only slightly less wooden than Robert Stack.

What all these manifestations of Scarface lore hold in common is the notion of one man whose shining example of ambition and hard work, when used for criminal purpose, inspires many weak souls to follow him, and other, superior ones to oppose him.

Well, and then there are the ones that are actual works of art, which explore the gray areas of crime-doesn't/does-pay, such as . . .

KINGPIN

Almost a half-century after *The Untouchables,* the next best TV-Scarface appeared. *Kingpin,* which premiered on NBC in February 2003, was a brash examination of Latino machismo, a meditation on loyalty in both business and marriage. Starring Yancey Arias as Miguel Cadena, a Mexican drug lord, husband, and father, *Kingpin* revolved around a well-off clan with crime connections, occasionally capping a seriocomic scene with a moment of startling violence. (In the premiere, one thug feeds a human leg to his pet tiger; by the

Steven Bauer
and Yancey Arias

fourth hour, a kinky Englishman who wants to cane a Cadena-hired prostitute is stabbed in the chest.) But as he proved in the 2000 HBO miniseries *The Corner,* on which he collaborated, *Kingpin* writer-creator David Mills is intrigued by interracial and intercultural connections and disconnections, and explores them with exciting snap.

With his big, intelligent eyes, slim frame, and graceful movements, Arias is hypnotically convincing as a tight-lipped businessman whose inherited business happens to be running cocaine, heroin, and methamphetamines into America. Mills and his writers do a daring thing: Fully aware that television is not supposed to, y'know, "glamorize drugs," *Kingpin* nonetheless refuses to deny that for a first-generation college graduate like Miguel, it's still important to live, as one character refers to our protagonist, as "a man of honor." (The fact that said character is a corrupt sheriff only makes the distinction more knottily ambiguous.) Miguel seems to take no pleasure from his big house and fancy lifestyle; he revels only in the happiness of his eight-year-old son (Rubén Carbajal) and the love of his wife (a superbly tough/tender performance by *Twin Peaks'* Sheryl Lee). The rest of his life is all headache: keeping his hotheaded brother Chato (Bobby Cannavale, melding slickness with crudity) in line, dealing with cousins who despise his gringa spouse, Marlene. ("The women in your family . . . make me feel like the only white girl on earth," she says bitterly.) Oh, and here's a nice connection: *Scarface's* Steven Bauer was initially cast as Chato, but was replaced by Cannavale shortly before shooting began.

Kingpin had at least three strong subplots, one involving a DEA agent played by Angela Alvarado Rosa who gets shot and wounded in the debut but remains relentless in pursuing the Cadena cartel; Brian Benben as a sweaty, desperate plastic surgeon in over his head as a part-time drug dealer; and Shay Roundtree (*Drumline*) as a smart young "enforcer" who brings the viewer into fractious exchanges between black and Latino cultures.

Equal parts *Scarface* and Sam Peckinpah's *Bring Me the Head of Alfredo Garcia, Kingpin* boasted golden-hued cinematography and terrific small supporting roles, including Maria Conchita Alonso as a too chatty sex partner for Chato. Sean Young, her acting eccentricities quiveringly held in check, played Benben's harridan estranged wife. NBC made a big mistake in airing two episodes a week of this six-episode miniseries at a time when viewers' attentions were distracted by the glut of sweeps-programming stunts and reality programming. After small ratings that could have been predicted from these obstacles, the network canceled *Kingpin* hastily, as though it knew Mills was going to take the show into areas of moral ambiguity and violence that might provoke controversy NBC did not want. This show deserved a longer run, to permit Miguel's profound conflictedness (he came to seem like a more-cultured Tony Montana) to play out.

MICHAEL MANN: *CRIME STORY, DRUG WARS: THE CAMARENA STORY, HEAT,* AND THE TWO *MIAMI VICES*

The late cinematographer John A. Alonzo quoted De Palma explaining the look he wanted for *Scarface*: "If it reads dark, it reads 'film noir,'" Alonzo says De Palma told him. "'We're going to contradict it, and let the action happen within the frame. If a violent act is going to occur, the surroundings should be bright, not dark.'" Alonzo concluded from this that "if there's [an onscreen] murder, if a gun fires,

there should be bright lights with great color in the background." De Palma told interviewer Laurent Bouzereau, "I wanted to go in completely the opposite direction [from other such films]. I wanted to do kind of a high tech, neon, acrylic, vibrant pastel, instead of your usual dark 'film noir.' Because you looked at South Florida and this was what it was all about—these guys dressed in white, not black. . . . It's not all grim death and murder. It's fun. The clubs should be fun, the girls should be fun. You know there's a price to pay for all this, but you've got to show why they're there."

De Palma wasn't the only filmmaker to whom this notion had occurred. While De Palma was making *Scarface*, director Michael Mann and his producing partner Anthony Yerkovich were busy creating the TV series *Miami Vice*, which would premiere in September 1984. Where *Scarface* would be greeted with many reviews that derided its bright-color violence, *Vice* was hailed as cutting-edge TV, with its gunplay amidst bright sunlight, pink flamingos, and the pastel finery of star Don Johnson. Oliver Stone observed a tad sourly, "*Scarface* was definitely on the money, it was right-on. It was exaggerated, but it was close to the truth, but nobody got it at the time. *Miami Vice* plunged in right where we left off. Michael Mann saw it right away; he told me that. He saw the power of it. They cashed in on it more than we did. They made money on it; we didn't."[1]

Or maybe Mann knew what medium was more suited, at that moment, for such an approach (less grandiose, less exaggeratedly violent) and such colors (which looked exotic on the then-still-small TV screen). Two years later, in 1986, Mann would tackle the *Scarface* myth from another angle in his TV series *Crime Story*, which followed a Chicago gangster-on-the-rise, Ray Luca (Anthony Denison) being tracked down by a squad of police detectives headed up by real-life Chicago cop-turned-actor Dennis Farina. In this alternative scenario, Farina's Lt. Mike Torello is Eliot Ness with fewer moral qualms; his crew of good guys included the actor Billy Campbell (who'd go on to be a sensitive divorced dad in the 1999–2002 series *Once & Again* costarring Sela Ward) and Bill Smitrovich (who'd go on to be a sensitive dad in the TV series *Life Goes On*, 1989–93). In its second season, Luca, having amassed Scarface-like control over the Chicago underworld but now on the run from Farina's relentless prosecution, relocated to Las Vegas—as bright-neon and sunny a place as the settings for *Miami Vice* or the Miami of *Scarface*.

Indeed, *Crime Story* is a motherlode hide-out for *Scarface*-

influenced actors and projects. Pam Grier appeared in five episodes in the first season—the same Grier who'd starred in '70s blaxploitation gangster films like *Foxy Brown* and would star in Quentin Tarantino's most hardboiled narrative, the underrated *Jackie Brown* (1997). Ray Sharkey, who played a U.S. attorney who gives Lt. Torello grief in *Crime Story*, later appeared as one of the greatest villains in the deeply *Scarface*'d late-1980s cop show *Wiseguy,* as the jittery hood Sonny Steelgrave. And David Caruso, who appears in *Crime Story* as a red-haired, red-blooded hood, eventually took to putting on and taking off his trademark shades in the garish light of the *Scarface*-goes-forensic *CSI: Miami.*

In 1990, Mann cowrote, with Rose Schacht and Ann Powell, the TV miniseries *Drug Wars: The Camarena Story. Drug Wars* starred *Scarface*'s Steven Bauer as Ecuadorian drug lord Enrique Camarena. Schacht and Powell, not coincidentally, had coauthored several shrewd essays analyzing De Palma's movies in their short-lived, self-published 1970s film journal *Cinemabook. Drug Wars,* although low-budget and with cheaper production values, continued the *Scarface* theme of drug-running as a means of coming up in the world, combining it with a re-curring Mann theme: what it's like to live undercover, to choose to live a life in isolation (either as a cop, or as a criminal).

In 1995, Mann released his own crime epic: *Heat,* pairing Pacino with Robert De Niro for the first time onscreen, this time using Pacino as the good guy, a cop out to capture a master thief played by De Niro.

In a sense, *Heat* holds the same position in Mann's career as *Scarface* does for De Palma. Upon its release, it was frequently considered excessively long and violent, but was immediately embraced by young and inner-city audiences. Like *Scarface, Heat*'s stature has only increased as years have gone by, its cult a steadily growing mass following that has inspired everything from catchphrases to video games.

And in 2006, Mann directed the big-screen version of *Miami Vice,* dimming the bright sun even when not shooting at night. Some years earlier, speaking to a National Public Radio interviewer, Mann said that De Palma's *Scarface* was, if anything, "an understatement, a model of restraint . . . in the early to mid-1980s, Miami was unreal" in terms of outlandish crime and pervasive drugs. With Colin Farrell and Jamie Foxx as Crockett and Tubbs, Mann got to expose some of the Miami underbelly—it's not merely a TV remake; it's the unofficial *Scarface* sequel, told from the point of view of the cops.

THREE LADY SCARFACES

Lady Scarface   In 1941, RKO Pictures released *Lady Scarface,* a just-over-an-hour programmer about a female hoodlum played by the future Dame Judith Anderson. Since the movie is an undistinguished caper film the bulk of whose plot centers more on the budding romance between a cop (Dennis O'Keefe) and a nosy but cute reporter (Frances Neal) than the criminal, the title was clearly attached to cash in on the then-nine-year-old reputation of Hawks's *Scarface.*

Playing a woman named Slade whom the authorities believe throughout most of the movie must be a man, Anderson sported a scar on her left cheek that looked as though it had been grafted on from an old Universal horror movie, livid and lumpy. Slade is never referred to as "Lady Scarface," but she rules over a small band of thugs with a ruthlessness that owes more to Anderson's conviction in delivering a line like, "I've played longer shots than this before to get dough!" than to the scripted action of the thriller itself.

Most of *Lady Scarface* is actually light-hearted fare, with veteran character actors such as Preston Sturges stock-company player Eric Blore, and a running gag about dogs not being allowed in a swanky hotel. At the climax of the movie, Slade/Scarface makes her move, disguising herself as a chambermaid to bring fresh towels to a room she wants to rob. Judith Anderson—who three years later would work with Otto Preminger to costar with chilly panache in *Laura,* and play a hard-shelled "Big Mama" in Richard Brooks's 1958 adaptation of *Cat on a Hot Tin Roof*—looks sadly ridiculous here in her chambermaid get-up, her thick, make-up-caked scar a wildly distracting physical detail *no one even comments upon*. (The hapless filmmakers didn't even exploit their title effectively.) Soon after uttering a macho line of dialogue to O'Keefe's flatfoot—"You're through, copper; they shoulda put a *man* on this job!"—Anderson is mercifully put out of her misery not by a man but a dame, the plucky reporter, who seizes a nearby pistol and plugs her.

Cocaine Cowboys   Decades later, however, a Lady Scarface came to exist in real life—an actual human so colorful, so violent, it's shocking that Oliver Stone didn't come across her in his research and go running back to Bregman and De Palma and tell them he had an even *better* story to be filmed. In the 2006 documentary *Cocaine Cowboys,* the filmmakers Billy Corben and Alfred Spellman recount their version of the late-'70s/early-'80s drug extravaganza in South Florida, a lurching, rather slapdash collection of interviews with various law enforcement officials slathered with a goopy synthesizer score by Jan Hammer, who did the theme for the *Miami Vice* TV series.

Corben and Spellman's documentary is all over the South Florida map, using for its primary criminal testimony a gabby camera-hog

A scene from the documentary *Cocaine Cowboys*

named Jon Roberts, a cheap hustler who seems to have lucked into his millions before being caught, and on the side of the law, members of CENTAC, a task force that combined members of the DEA and the Miami-Dade Police Department. The filmmakers salt in interesting facts, if vaguely sourced and framed, such as the assertion that, "in the late '80s," the Miami branch of the Federal Reserve had a six-billion-dollar cash surplus, a greater surplus than all branches in the United States combined. That money, it is implied, was derived from laundered drug money.

But *Cocaine Cowboys* keeps coming back to one figure who eventually overtakes whatever narrative the filmmakers are trying to impose (and as far as I can tell, that narrative theme is: Drugs are a dead-end, folks). One person burns through all the clichés: Griselda Blanco, and what's the word for a female drug lord? Drug lady? Blanco, we are told, not only ran drugs up from South America and distributed vast amounts of cocaine—she ruled her area of South Florida with truly startling vengeance, commanding a sizable number of tough guys (including professional contract killer Jorge "Rivi" Ayala, interviewed on camera in prison telling bloodcurdling tales) to mete out her form of justice to anyone who crossed her, or whom she distrusted.

In the documentary, she's referred to as "the queen of cocaine," and her local nicknames included "La Madrina" and "the Black Widow." She had at least one common-law husband who predeceased her, had children for whom she seems not to have been a model mother, was probably bisexual, and became increasingly paranoid, violent to the point where even her most trusted lieutenants in the cocaine wars didn't want to carry out her steadily more gratuitous "hits" on real and perceived enemies. All Griselda Blanco seemed to lack to be dubbed Lady Scarface was the scar, and she probably would have cut it into herself if she'd thought it would help intimidate her foes.

At the very least, after completing *Scarface,* with Tony dead and gone, this was the semi-sequel producer Bregman could have worked on to sate the appetite of his film's growing cult following, and which has always clamored for another venture into the same red-blooded, white-powdered territory.

This, reader, is the role Michelle Pfeiffer should have played after *Scarface*—not *Ladyhawke* (1985).

Lady Scarface: The World Is Hers   Of course, there had to be a porn version. *Lady Scarface: The World Is Hers,* directed by "Daniel Dakota" in 2006, provokes only the thought, "What took them so long?" The female lead, Carmen Luvana, plays "Toni," who works her way up from menial labor (a job in a car wash that enables the occasion for a lesbian make-out scene with a coworker—I guess this is the movie's equivalent of Manny) to become a drug boss. But not before being arrested. ("Strip-search her!" says one male cop to another, leading to inevitable, non-Miranda-law-approved, action.) Although someone makes a reference to her having a scar on her right cheek, it's nowhere to be seen—not even on the right cheek of her amply exposed backside. Atrociously staged, shot on the cheap (the chain saw they use is clearly not in the "on" position, despite the whirring-noise sound effects), this three-hours-plus epic has a few amusing touches.

For one thing, as boss, this Lady Scarface straps on a dildo to show

a female subordinate who's boss. For another, when she goes into her decadent decline into cocaine addiction, she slathers the white powder all over her bare breasts before snorting. Oh, and when the movie moves to South America (which just looks like a room in another part of the house Lady Scarface was shot in), the title card tells us we're in "Columbia"—not Colombia. I guess the quality of blow is just as good at a New York college as it is in a foreign country. Added bonus: many scenes of a naked Lady Scarface puffing on a big cigar in a round white tub.

Other Movie Scarfaces

As the film's cult really took hold and grew in the 1990s, there was what amounted to a School of *Scarface* filmmaking. As a director, Oliver Stone showed us what he might have done with the action sequences when he made *Natural Born Killers* (1994)—a *Scarface*-fevered crime picture stoked by amphetamines more than cocaine. Abel Ferrara's *King of New York* (1990) proved that even so mannered an actor as Christopher Walken could be less affected than Pacino, if handed the right, down-these-mean-streets role. *New Jack City* (1991) fused the *Scarface* and hip-hop ethos into one film. And *Paid in Full* (2002) was steeped in the lore: Wood Harris's Ace says in a voiceover early on, "Things really got hot in Harlem when *Scarface* came to town." Director Charles Stone III articulated bluntly what a thousand movie and music critics had been trying to say for the previous few years when he had one character observe, "Niggers liked to see a po' ass Cuban blow up to be the man, all by himself."

Scenes of Mekhi Phifer and his crew rolling in a car are intercut

Mekhi Phifer in
Paid in Full

with moments from the final shoot-out scene in De Palma's movie—
at the moment Pacino yells, "Say hello to my little friend," Phifer's
gang shoot down a rival drug dealer. Stone wrings poignance from his
tough-love adoration: If you look closely about an hour into *Paid in
Full*, Wood Harris's innocent little brother brushes his teeth and places
his kiddie toothbrush into a bathroom cup on which is printed "The
World Is Yours." For this sweet boy, it's really not.

THE ST. VALENTINE'S DAY MASSACRE (1967)

"He is 'Scarface Al Capone,' " barks the narrator of *The St. Valentine's
Day Massacre*, director Roger Corman's 1967 film starring Jason Robards as the mighty gangster. The casting is awful: Capone was a pug-
ugly squat bully; Robards is long and lean—when he wears a

Borsalino hat and camel-hair coat, he looks like an American roue rather than a vicious mobster. (Unique among cinematic Scarfaces, his scar runs horizontally across, not vertically down, the left side of his face, as though he'd tried to grow another eye that remains closed.)

Chicago rivals of Robards's character decide to team up with "a bunch of spics" to "get" Capone—could any of these Hispanics be Cuban refugees? More believable is a young George Segal as a smiley sadist, enthusiastically beating up Prohibition-era tavern owners into paying protection money to Capone. Always in a perpetual white heat, Segal at one point smooshes a sandwich into a girl's face à la the grapefruit that Jimmy Cagney pushed into Mae Clarke's kisser.

Corman would go on to make better gangster pictures (1970's

Robards
(20th Century
Fox/Everett
Collection)

Bloody Mama, starring Shelley Winters as a lustily enthusiastic Ma Barker, and 1974's *Big Bad Mama*, starring Angie Dickinson) and worse ones—1975's *Capone*, with Ben Gazzara a more physically convincing Scarface Al than Robards, but mummified by an even more airless script.

Here, however, Corman stages the title bloodbath as though the St. Valentine's Day Massacre was just one more tedious task to fulfill if you worked for Scarface Al. His gunsels line up Capone's enemies, including a young, frightened Bruce Dern, and mow 'em down with notably little climactic drama, given that this is the title of the movie.

Instead, it's more intriguing that Robards's Capone retires to Miami—future home of Tony Montana—in a fruitless attempt to avoid the coppers.

Gazzara
(Kobel Collection)

CAPONE (1975)

"I just don't like cops, that's all," says Ben Gazzara's Al Capone in *Capone* (1975), a Roger Corman production costarring a Sylvester Stallone one year away from being Rocky, here doing tedious day-work as Capone's real-life enforcer Frank Nitti. "The Man Who Made The Twenties Roar!" went the tagline for this B-picture directed by Steve Carver, who'd made a livelier gangster picture for Corman the year before: *Big Bad Mama,* with Angie Dickinson as Ma Barker, and who probably hit his career high point with the 1983 Chuck Norris vehicle *Lone Wolf McQuade*.

As Capone, Gazzara makes the most of his square-shaped face—he may be too slender to be a convincing Al, but he's got the mug for him, and looks good in a white Borsalino hat. Susan Blakeley is his love interest, Iris Crawford, and the blond model can now be viewed as a precursor to Michelle Pfeiffer—Blakely had the slink and the sneer in place that Pfeiffer's Elvira would use so well.

Capone is otherwise notable only for the presence of another costar—John Cassavetes as mobster Frankie Yale. It was obviously just a paycheck role for the actor-director, who five years before had directed and costarred with his buddy Gazzara in the men-will-be-boys talkathon *Husbands* (Peter Falk completed the trio of macho married men there). And, of course, Cassavetes would go on to do fine work with Brian De Palma in *The Fury,* in which his evil-agent villain blows up real good in that thriller's smashing climax.

MISTER SCARFACE (1977)

Mister Scarface is a 1977 Italian-made mini-epic starring Jack Palance as "Scarface Manzari." Written and directed by Fernando Di Leo, it features atrocious American dubbing ("Now fuck outta here!") and clunky dialogue like this:

"I work for Manzari."

"Who's that?

"Scarface."

Set in Italy, *Mister Scarface* starts out as something of a *Godfather* rip-off, complete with swirling Carmine Coppola–style music, but soon takes its own peculiar course, focusing on two young Italian petty thieves who decide to rob the mob kingpin played by Palance. Palance's scenes look as though they could have been filmed in any hotel room in the world—his few but pivotal scenes are sloppily intercut with the actions of the two antiheroes. But Palance chews a cigar well, and in a rare break from the Scarface canon, his scar appears on his *right* cheek, suggesting either sloppy research and continuity, or maybe the print just got screened backward. (This Italian–West German production's German title was *Zwei Supertypen räumen auf,* or, *Two Bosses Clean Up*.)

At any rate, it's nice to know that Palance still had *City Slickers* and an Oscar awaiting him after this movie, whose high point is probably this observation made by an elderly mobster about Palance's Mister Scarface: "That Scarface—he's bad news. Just looking at him and my asshole twitches."

MOBSTERS (1991)

Don't be fooled by the rather impressive-sounding cast of 1991's
Mobsters—well, impressive for a '90s flick: Christian Slater, Anthony
Quinn, Patrick Dempsey, Michael Gambon, Lara Flynn Boyle, even
Scarface's F. Murray Abraham as a different real-life hood, mob book-
keeper Arnold Rothstein.

Abraham/Rothstein gets what amounts, in this movie, to a showy
speech: "What's the secret of America? Money! Everything is *money,*
Charlie. But you'll never make any money, because you dress like a
schmuck . . . We got balls and brains; you got those, you don't need an
army . . . One hundred years ago, Austria was run by a prince named
Metternich. Austria was weak, and its neighbors were strong; but
Metternich was a cold, calculating fox. If one country got too strong,
he organized an alliance against it. He would bring Europe to the
brink of war, and then everybody thanked him when he kept war
from happening. He barely had an army, but he had Europe by the
kishkes!"

Slater (as Lucky Luciano—with a scar on his right cheek from a
knife fight!), Dempsey (as Meyer Lansky), and *21 Jump Street*'s
Richard Grieco as Bugsy Siegel act like teenage boys who've been
given zoot suits and machine guns with which to play dress-up gangster. There's a larky atmosphere to *Mobsters* that never quite takes off
into genuine amusement for an audience. The guys go for entire decades roughhousing and working their way up the criminal ladder in
a series of aimless violent scenes.

Where's Scarface Al, you ask? He glides into view during the last
five minutes of the movie. As played by Titus Welliver (*Deadwood* and
numerous other TV series), Capone does little more than give his

benediction to the mobsters' actions—he's there simply to establish that we're about to enter a new era of gangster primacy in Chicago . . . and then the credits roll. It's a movie that's all prologue, no pay-off.

CAPONE'S BOYS (2001)

Capone's Boys (2001) was also released as *Al's Lads* (2002). It is mostly a boxing movie, a curious-in-retrospect precursor to Clint Eastwood's *Million Dollar Baby*, with Richard Roundtree (yes, Shaft) as an aging trainer who sees talent in a young Liverpool ruffian, Jimmy (Marc Warren) in Chicago circa 1927. Turns out Capone (a bland Julian Littman, who looks like a cross between Leonardo DiCaprio and John Belushi) is a fight fan—and that this Scarface's scar goes from his left *sideburn* down the length of his cheek. The subplot that eventually takes over the rest of the movie involves the kidnapping of Scarface Al's young son, named, ah, Sonny. Jimmy and his two working-stiff friends (the "lads" or "boys" of the two titles) think they'll get in good with the mobster if they locate the kid . . . but not before Jimmy is asked by one of Al's minions (Al Sapienza, who played Mikey Palmice in ten episodes of *The Sopranos*) to take a dive in his first big fight. Think the plucky young fighter goes into the tank? About as likely as Roundtree busting out some boxing moves against Al Capone—and that would have made a better movie . . . *Shaft Meets Scarface!*

Comic Books

"Your system was so amped on coke it didn't know it was *supposed* to die," says a cop to a hospital-bed-bound Tony Montana in the first issue of *Scarface: Scarred for Life,* a comic book resurrection of Tony published by IDW Comics that began in early 2007. Seems he survived the movie's final shoot-out, having taken "a total of nine bullets to the chest, and three more to the upper appendages," according to the comic's scripter, John Layman. Tony lost Elvira ("We found a Trans Am registered to her abandoned at Miami International; she's *gone,* Montana") and "two feet of lower intestines." His "poor, heartbroken mother" sends Tony a final message via the police: the cop spits in Tony's face for her.

Most important, Tony has lost all his stuff: his house, his guns, his cars, his money—"and your stash," the cop tells him. "El Gordo and

TONY MONTANA.

the Diaz brothers divvied up your operation and the overflow of *that* got commandeered by some Ukrainian ex-military gunrunner."

Tony recuperates, goes cold turkey to kick his cocaine habit, and, still wheelchair-bound at the climax of the first issue of *Scarred for Life,* begins to reclaim his previous power and glory by confronting a purple-Zoot-suited pimp who's peddling drugs on the street where Tony is recuperating in a crappy, dank apartment the hospital and the police have dumped him in. Montana reclaims a small part of his old neighborhood by telling the pimp to "Eat shit and die"—and then makes good on his command by rising up out of his wheelchair, colostomy bag in hand, only to rip it open, shove it over the pimp's head and suffocate the man to death. Taking the threat literally and depicting it visually is always a smart, vivid way to go for comic book creators. "Tony Montana is back, you fuckin' cock-a-roaches," he declares in the final panels of the first issue, "and anybody try to stop me is in for a world of pain."

By issue two, we discover that Elvira has flown the coop—to Bolivia: she's now living with Tony's arch-enemy, Sosa. And Tony confronts a rival for the Miami drug trade, El Gordo, while that immense gangster is stuffing his face in a restaurant. In a sit-down meeting, Tony orders an entire roast pig, which is placed before him on a platter, complete with apple in mouth. In a very nice touch, when Gordo pulls a gun on him, Tony puts his hand up the plattered pig's rectum to grasp a gun that's been hidden inside, and begins shooting at Gordo and his gang, the bullets emitted through the pig's snout.

At first, the script by Layman rarely strays from paraphrases of Oliver Stone's screenplay, but as the comic-book series proceeds, he builds his own amount of character development such as the twin Diaz brothers, Diego and Demario, whom no one can seem to tell apart. The art by Dave Crosland differs from De Palma's movie by necessity. Just as Pacino declined to let the 2006 video game *Scarface: The World Is Yours* use his voice, so the comic book, for legal reasons negotiated with Universal by IDW publisher Chris Ryall, was not allowed to use Pacino's likeness.

But this proves good, creatively. It forces Crosland to turn Tony Montana into someone else: a dilated-pupil, Cubist-influenced collection of 90-degree angles—his chin and jawline and eyebrows are severe slashes, his nose is broken and his mouth is set in a perpetual grimace of pain and rage. It's an exaggerated, extremely stylized look, a good, nightmarish one for a pain-fueled Tony-on-the-mend. Crosland takes full advantage of comic-book exaggeration, having one of the Diaz brothers (Diego? Demario? As Tony says, "Whoever") stuff a huge gun into Tony's mouth and ask this Scarface, "How's that gun taste, Tony, hmmm? Not quite as delicious as the bullet is going to." Tony can only respond, "Mfff Ffff!" but we get his drift . . .

The final chapter of the *Scarface: Scarred for Life* series ends with the inevitability fans of the movie have long thought a dangling thread that needed to be cut: that is, it ends with Elvira. Her hatred of Tony is by now so great, that, with comic-book Tony having reestablished himself at "the top of the heap" and having cut off both of Sosa's legs and an arm, only Elvira can confront him. She pulls a gun on him, he pulls one on her, and, off the page, we know from an earlier panel that Sosa is using his one good arm to hold his own gun trained on Tony. Elvira says through angry tears, "You're finished, Tony!" and the last panel consists of no image other than a word: a blood-red "BANG!" In theory, we don't know who dies. In my head, Elvira is lying in a heap at Tony's feet.

I like the way Crosland draws his non-Pfeifferish Elvira as a now-middle-aged woman with bony elbows who wears a dress with ruffle shoulders and midwestern housewife's sensible hairdo—she's no longer a femme fatale but she's still both hot and smart enough to keep Sosa and Tony on the hook.

One storyline of the comic-book series is entitled "City of Zeroes," which refers both to Miami's perceived population of nobodies on the make, and of the number of naughts on a check or a pay-off score that Tony wants as he rebuilds his fortune and his empire. It's doubtful the *Scarface* comic book is going to give Batman or The X-Men any sleepless nights, but as an indie comic effort, it's far more solid than the usual stiff, pointlessly solemn adaptations of movies and TV shows such as *Star Trek, Star Wars, 24,* or *Buffy the Vampire Slayer.* There's something about Scarface, no matter what medium he arrives in, that brings out the creatively disreputable in people, even those trying to make a buck off him to fans who should have outgrown his influence in a pop culture where fads live and die and stay buried within a matter of years, if not months.

The notion of the gangster who cannot be killed is a potent one in pop culture; it certainly extends to the way slain rappers such as Tupac Shakur and The Notorious B.I.G. rise from the grave again and again on "previously unreleased" tracks or as samples in other rappers' work. It informs the whole subset of horror-movie sequels (the low-budget surprise success *Saw* yields bigger budget *Saw II* and *Saw III,* whose Roman numerals are represented in ads as torturously pulled teeth and fingers).

Oddly but interestingly, the comic books this *Scarface* more closely resembles are the first-person, autobiographical comics of the writer Harvey Pekar, whose *American Splendor* comic collections have tallied the life of a low-level government drone for more than a quarter of a century. Pekar, a Cincinnati working-class file clerk, writes the scripts for artists to draw, and his perpetually frustrated, angry mug looks a lot like the way Crosland draws Tony Montana. In the end, perhaps, they're both hard-working stiffs, feeding off lessons and morals they learned in their old neighborhoods, trying to get by by—as the hip-hop-by-way-of-black-nationalism phrase has it—any means necessary.

In 2007, IDW, capitalizing on the success of its *Scarface: Scarred for Life* sequel (issues with a cover price of $3.99 were selling for $10 and more a week after their release, and selling out their print runs), announced a prequel series: *Scarface: Devil in Disguise.* The series' writer, Joshua Jabcuga, said, "My goal here is to create a ghetto opera . . . where did Tony Montana come from? He was an assassin before he even came to America. We see the scar; we see the little pitchfork tattoo on his hand. What's that all about?" Jabcuga's comic is illustrated by Alberto Dose in a dourly realistic manner that suits his subject. *Devil in Disguise* addresses questions and themes, Jabcuga says, such as "I get to show how Tony got that scar of his, but also, who gave it to him and the motive behind it. I also get to show what happens to the other guy, 'El Gancho,' who plays one of the main villains in the story. I'm also dealing with heavies like La Cosa Nostra . . . We see Tony as a young boy, we see Tony growing up on his own, since his mother and sister are forced to leave for Miami without him. We'll see Tony's involvement with the political forces of the time like Batista and Castro. The CIA has their hands in the mix as well."

It sounds to me as though Jabcuga hasn't read L. A. Banks's *Scarface: The Beginning* (see below).

But first, there's one other comic-book manifestation of Scarface we have to grapple with: Scarface the dummy, used by the Ventriloquist, a villain in some of DC Comics' Batman titles. Making his first appearance in the February 1988 issue of *Detective Comics,* the Ventriloquist is Arnold Wesker, a rather timid, addled, if criminal sad-sack born into a Mafia family. His multiple personality disorder leads him to channel his suppressed rage and lawlessness through his dummy, Scarface. Although Wesker the Ventriloquist is a contemporary character, Scarface is dressed in 1920s clothes complete with small white Borsalino hat, a gat in his hands, and a scar . . . on his right cheek, not the traditional Scarface left. Scarface orders his master around, bullying him into helping the dummy commit crimes.

One of the nice little details that the Ventriloquist's creator, British comics writer Alan Grant, built into his storyline is that Wesker is mediocre at throwing his voice—never able to master the ventriloquial trick of enunciating the difficult consonant "B," instead clumsily substituting it with a hard "G" sound. Thus in print, we read word-balloons in which the Ventriloquist refers to his "gummy." Somewhere around 2006, Wesker was killed, and in a nifty March 2007 Batman story in *Detective Comics,* it is revealed that Scarface survived, and his new ventriloquist is a shapely blond babe named Sugar, just as evil but a better "vent," as practitioners of the art refer to themselves.

But in the final pages of this story—"Double Talk," written by the nimbly witty writer-animator Paul Dini—we discover that Scarface can talk without the aid of a ventriloquist, and that he's lured Sugar into being his new "partner" in crime, preying upon her own dementia and using it for his criminal purposes. The all-pervasive Scarface nefariousness lives on and on.

Oh, and before we leave the realm of comics, one further item should be noted: Scarface in the form of Al Capone is the only real-life figure that appears in the entire, lengthy series of the internationally bestselling books about the boy adventurer Tintin. Created by the genius Belgian writer-illustrator Hergé, Tintin and his valiant little dog Snowy capture Scarface Al and a couple of his minions in 1945's *Tintin in America.*

Scarface Novelizations

In 1983, novelist and memoirist Paul Monette (1945–95), author of acclaimed books such as *Taking Care of Mrs. Carroll* (1978), *Becoming a Man: Half a Life Story* (1992), and *Borrowed Time: An AIDS Memoir* (1998), wrote a novelization of Oliver Stone's screenplay. It was obviously a paycheck job; Monette also wrote a quickie novelization of the Arnold Schwarzenegger movie *Predator* in 1987.

Monette's Scarface tale is frequently puckish—he has the corrupt cop Mel Bernstein stroke Tony Montana's cheek and say, "I like the scar. Just like Capone, eh? Real nice touch. But you ought to smile more." But otherwise it's just a piece of honorable hackwork, complete with purple (yellow?) prose: "The tall cool figure of Tony Montana, the one they would call Scarface, stood bathed in neon yellow, holding a smoking gun."

More interesting is L. A.

Banks's *Scarface: The Beginning*, a paperback original published in 2006. Banks, author of a popular series of supernatual horror, the "Vampire Huntress" books, is less of an artist than Monette and so dives more enthusiastically into the pulpiness of her subject.

Banks follows some of the clues planted by Oliver Stone's script in having Tony be a bitter young man whose loving mother had been abandoned by his father: "She had been lied to by his philandering father, a man who didn't even have the decency to make her an honest woman and give her a ring. Made a fool of, twice, yielding him and Gina to the world." Wait: Tony and Gina are bastard children??

Banks's novel plants the de rigeur, if quite awkwardly phrased, reference to Scarface's namesake, when Tony learns the ins and outs of how Havana is a port of illegal activity: "This mind-puzzle once solved helped to steady Tony's nerves. He would learn from this for the future. Figuring out the hidden angles was something he enjoyed to keep him sharp . . . bringing the cash in where Al Capone had once invested was a good omen, as well as a message: Do what another very notable crime capitalist had done to thumb his nose in the government's face, in an area where Capone had displayed his power and wealth, and do it in this current regime's phony trucks. Tony almost laughed. Perfect."

Scarface: The Beginning insists that Tony was a well-experienced criminal before he ever left Cuba; that he was the right-hand man for a Cuban crime lord named Miguel Vasquez who "Tony knew ran cigar, liquor, guns, and antiquities smuggling." Banks's attempts at Oliver Stoneish Scar-speak sometimes veer into ludicrousness—the business wisdom proffered here, for example, such as, "Friends don't let friends get fucked in the ass." And Banks, like Monette, has a penchant for sex scenes that make you glad De Palma and Stone made their Tony coked-up-impotent: Writing about one of Montana's Cuban conquests, the tempestuous Rosaliah, Banks trills, "Somewhere between this she-devil and the Madonna within her was the border of truth he'd just crossed . . . just as he lay trapped between her thighs in a new land of uncertainty." And a few sentences later: "His hands found her hair, not caring to know if it matched." Huh? *Ewww . . .*

By the end of *Scarface: The Beginning,* Tony is in a church confessional booth, telling a priest, "My problem is that I want the world, and don't feel guilty anymore for taking what's coming to me." He tells the priest on the other side of the partition, "disgustedly," "We live in two different worlds." Well, no kidding. Banks's problem in *The Beginning* is that, to make an exciting adventure story, she must ignore the fact that the Tony we see at the start of De Palma's movie, while certainly a man who has broken the law, is also a relative innocent to lawlessness on any sort of grand scale.

Stone's script clearly implies that Tony's Cuban misadventures were petty crimes, nickel-and-dime stuff, perhaps at worst a stabbing of some small-time hoodlum to earn his bones as a thug in good standing. *The Beginning* tries, by contrast, to connect Tony to a parallel universe of major crime organizations. But if Tony had learned the ropes, as he does in this book from guys named Vasquez and Ortiz, then why would he have indentured himself to Frank Lopez in the *Scarface* movie? The logic of *Scarface: The Beginning* doesn't hold up.

As an alternative view of Scarface—in comic-book terms, the "origin story" of how Tony became Tony—this novel is less useful to our purposes than the cumulative histories of all the other appearances Scarface makes in pop culture, glimpses of the cannier, more persistent, yet doomed "crime capitalist" he became, forever and ever.

9

President Scarface

In Eugene Byrne and Kim Newman's 1997 novel *Back in the USSA,* Al "Scarface" Capone becomes the leader of the United States. He is, in effect, Chairman Al—the president as dictator. "Back in '21, Chicago had been the power-base behind Mayor Al's bid for the highest office in the United Socialist States of America . . ." Not only that, our man's most salient facial mark finds an origin that cuts Tony Montana's to shreds: "Official history accepted that Capone had gotten his scar in a knife fight with William Randolph Hearst."

In Byrne and Newman's jape, politics and show business overlap. "In the Oval Office, Aimee Semple McPherson, the Chairman's mistress-helpmate, brings Scarface Al his morning mail," which includes "a couple of postcards from Secretary of State Louis B. Mayer on his European travels." Scarface Al shares the details of these missives with his Secretary of the Interior, Jimmy Hoffa." (In later years, it will come to light that Capone "muscled his way to power off the back of the big labor unions [and] the first thing he did was cut Texas loose and make a deal with [Pancho] Villa.") Although there still stands a statue erected in his honor—"a bronze [that] depicted a slimmer-than-the-newsreels Al on a rearing steed"—he is now widely reviled in Byrne and Newman's alternate-America as "a monster, a mass murderer, a thief, a lecher, a pederast."

But the point is, he made it to the top. Yes, for a while there, The World Was His.

The notion of *Scarface* as the government contributes powerfully in keeping the film's philosophy alive. In fact, it's more alive now than when it first arrived in theaters—soon after the end of the Carter administration (the Mariel Boatlift occurred under Carter's watch; a portrait of Carter hangs in the room where Tony is interrogated in the movie's opening scene), and during Ronald Reagan's years in the White House, a president who was too disengaged to publicly embody Scarface ambition or hands-dirty involvement in empire-building.

No, it's the Bush years that have revived Scarface most tellingly—this, despite the fact that it's the people behind George W. Bush (Dick Cheney, Donald Rumsfeld, Karl Rove) who exhibit more Scarface behavior than the president himself. It seems only a failure of Bush Jr.'s movie imagination that he did not give one of his closest cronies, Attorney General Alberto Gonzales, the Hispanic nickname "Manny" instead of the more Italian/*Godfather*-derived "Fredo."

What Oliver Stone's screenplay brought to Ben Hecht's original *Scarface* was a layer of politics that gives the Tony Montana myth a resonance that makes it surge from the 1980s into the present day. Tony the immigrant lives out one nasty, brutish version of the American Dream, acquiring power and wealth. But as D. H. Lawrence wrote about the heroes in James Fenimore Cooper's Leatherstocking novels, a man of strength and instinct (as Tony is) is frequently "a torn, divided monster." Lawrence writes, "When you are actually in America, America *hurts*."

And Tony is certainly in America—in it to win. Starting out a self-proclaimed "po-*lit*-i-cal prisoner," he conducts canny campaigns of ruthless social and business politics. He uses whatever sympathy he can get from being part of Jimmy Carter and Fidel Castro's Mariel mess. He courts Frank Lopez as one might a potential campaign donor, doing the crime boss favors that result in rewards of money and gangster patronage. Before Frank realizes what's happening, Tony has driven the old regime out of office—Scarface has nominated himself the new front-runner, and wins the support of the people around him (Frank's gang, once Frank himself is, in effect, assassinated under orders of the new Tony Montana administration).

The Scarface view of the world—first you get the money, then you get the power—projects itself out into the real world.

Some political observers have seized on the movie and get it wrong. The only example of Bush-as-Scarface I found in my Internet research was a lame lampoon of the black-and-white *Scarface* movie poster, with Bush's face superimposed on Pacino's white-suited body, Bush still holding Pacino's gun but he's all ruffly haired, college-era, frat-boy smiles, bearing the legend "George Bush Scarface": "He snorted all the coke in Washington, now he's after yours!"

Doesn't even make sense. In 2003, Thomas W. Hazlett, a professor of economics at the University of California at Davis, wrote an essay called "President Scarface: Bill Clinton's Press Relations," which carried the subtitle, "How Bill Clinton Runs the Press Like Capone Ran Chicago." But that's overreaching malarkey: It was the press that behaved like gangsters, teaming up initially to build up Clinton's campaign, and then, once he took office, did their damnedest to tear him down. Which is not to say that Clinton isn't somewhat Scarfacesque: You could say that Bill Clinton's downfall was following Tony's three-part advice to his pal Manny too assiduously: First he got the money (campaign financing), then he got the power (the presidency), then he got the pussy (serial adultery culminating in the Monica Lewinsky affair). Unlike Tony, however, Clinton wasn't committing actual crimes, though he was prosecuted in the press as though he had.

No, it's the Bush II era that seems to inspire especially vituperative *Scarface* comparisons. Comments pop up all over the Internet. "Outlaw Vern," on a political Web site thread, posts: "Are you telling me bin Laden doesn't have *The Godfather* and *Scarface* on his shelf? Of course he does."

During the 2004 campaign, *The Believer* magazine ran a dispatch about John Buchanan, "a marginal [Florida] candidate running in the Republican primary, but [who] gets little attention because there are no real challengers to Bush." *The Believer* reported, "Buchanan has been posting indie media articles about himself under the name Omar Suarez, the guy they lynched from the helicopter in *Scarface*. And he's been calling radio programs under the name Omar Suarez."[1]

"That's my alter ego," Buchanan is quoted as saying. Hey, cool—low-level right-wing party hack adopts the identity of low-level drug-cartel mob hack . . . *with pride*!

But let's head back up to the top—to the presidency. In 2005, Timothy Sexton wrote an essay whose title borrowed from Scarface's positive-thinking mantra: "Money, Power and Respect."[2] Sexton writes that he had spent the previous year as a high school English teacher, and had been appalled by the frequent, admiring invocations of the Al Pacino Scarface "on expensive oversized polyester shirts. As well as T-shirts and hooded jackets and jerseys and just about any other kind of clothing you can imagine . . . In addition to silkscreen printings of recreations of scenes from the movie, these shirts also often carry quotes such as the famous 'Say hello to my little friend,' 'I bury those cockroaches,' and, of course, Tony's motto: 'Money, Power, Respect.'"

Cheney
(J. Scott
Applewhite/AP Wide
World)

Sexton then poses what he calls "a hypothetical." "Let's say there's this C student. Yet he manages to get into Yale," he writes and you immediately begin to see where he's going with this. "He doesn't stand out as anything except for his ability to knock back drinks at frat parties . . . Now we certainly wouldn't expect this guy to rise to the heights of money, power and respect would we? . . . This guy is not much more deserving of being on a shirt than Tony Montana, is he? I mean all he's really got on the guy is that he doesn't have blood on his hands and he hasn't committed a series of criminal acts. Heck, that recommendation is apparently good enough to get him elected President . . . [But] now he's deserving of power and respect. Now he's got more blood on his hands than Tony Montana and has committed more criminal acts than Tony Montana."

Melodramatic? Maybe. Self-serving? Yes. But if politics is, as an advisor to President Bill Clinton memorably put it, show business for ugly people, *Scarface* has proven a potent symbol for just how ugly politics has become. Go to the Internet for a striking example.

At http://www.churchoftherobot.org/dangsquid/abd.mov, footage can be seen of Dick Cheney making a nominating speech for George Bush at the 2004 Republican National Convention. But instead of Cheney's throw-bloody-meat-to-the-base clichés, what comes out of his mouth is Al Pacino's voice telling the crowd that "you need people like me, so you can point your fucking fingers and say, 'That's the bad guy.' "

In other words, Tony's drunken, coked-up restaurant rant toward the end of De Palma's movie is used to articulate more candidly the wants and desires of the Bush administration and its supporters. This mash-up speech/video becomes all the more effective for its crudity: Cheney's real mouth is replaced by a smear of pixilation—it's either the superimposed mouth of Pacino, or just an intentional blur from which the words emerge. Who made it? It travels like virus across the Internet, its authorship unknown; in fact, it's an idea that doubtless occurred to more than one Web-savvy person, as there are scores of sites that link to it if you Google "Scarface" and "Cheney."

The version I came across most often is labeled "America's Biggest Dick," and uses footage from the Fox News Channel. It commences with Cheney saying to—no coincidence here, given Tony Montana's base of operations—a Florida audience, to wild applause, "This town like a great big pussy just waiting to get fucked." "Ain't no stoppin' me," says Scarface Cheney, "I'm makin' all the right connections. I could go right to the top." Cut to thousands of Republicans on their feet, whooping. One holds up a sign saying, "Cheney rocks!"

There's some artful editing. "In this country, first you gotta get the money," Scarface Cheney says in a snatch of dialogue we think we know well. "When you gotta make the money first, then when you get the money, you get the power," he continues. He goes further:

"Then when you get the power, you get the money." In Vice President Scarface's vision of America, sex is beside the point, if not downright repellent. All that matters is money and power, so the word "sex" is excised from his speech.

"With that kind of money, you can buy the Supreme Court," says Veep Scarface—cut to Republicans turning to each other in the crowd, winking and nodding in agreement and talking to each other, saying variations of, "He knows what he's saying."

"Me, I want what's coming to me—the world, Chico," says this old white man in a gray suit with an American flag lapel. It's probably the first time Dick Cheney has ever uttered the word "Chico" other than to thank someone for his shoeshine.

Then things go wrong. "Come on, gimme a kiss," says Cheney (the sound bite is from Tony to Elvira). Cut to people frowning, some booing—they're repulsed by the idea of kissing that mouth. "Hey, fuck you! Who put this thing together? Me!" Scarface Cheney is ranting now, thwarted, rejected, not feeling the love anymore.

He changes gears to get the crowd back: "You wanna go to war?" he asks, as Iraq burns. "I take you to war—I take you to fucking hell!" Ah, he's got 'em back—cut to throngs giving him a standing ovation. But Scarface Cheney's contempt cannot be denied. As we see a shot of a uniformed soldier in the crowd, he sneers, "You're all a bunch of fucking assholes." And: "You know what capitalism is? 'Get fucked.'"

The screen goes black; we think it's over. But then the veep's wife, Lynn Cheney, appears, and she says in the world-weary voice of Michelle Pfeiffer, "Can't you stop saying 'fuck' all the time?" She adds, "Real contribution to human history," her voice heavy with Pfeiffer's sarcasm and Lynn Cheney's stern frown. Mrs. Vice President Scarface is disgusted by her husband's venal crudity. "Can't you see what we've become?" Elvira/Lynn asks, looking out over the crowd. "We're losers, not winners."

Cut to shots of disapproving conventioneers: No one believes her . . . no one—because they know in their hearts they're winners in Scarface America.

Scarface: It's Money, It's Women, It's Power

Because it arrived swaddled in controversy and has since taken on the label of "cult film," we should look closely and with a clear eye at the business and culture into which *Scarface* was born.

Scarface premiered in New York and Los Angeles on December 1, 1983. It was reported in New York that both Kurt Vonnegut and John Irving walked out of the movie before it ended, presumably repelled, and in Los Angeles, Joan Collins said of the film's profusion of profanity, "I hear there are 183 'fucks' in the movie, which is more than most people get in a lifetime.") On December 9, 1983, *Scarface* opened in

996 theaters. It made $4,597,536 in its opening weekend, an only-respectable debut bow. By way of comparison, Clint Eastwood's thriller *Sudden Impact* opened the same weekend in 500 more theaters and pulled in $9,688,561. And James Brooks's *Terms of Endearment,* which would go on to win a slew of Oscars including best picture, had opened the previous month with an opening-weekend draw of $3,498,813—but it premiered in only a third fewer theaters and would go on to become 1983's second-highest box-office earner. *Scarface* would rank sixteenth for 1983 (pretty darn good, considering there are only four weekends in December), but wouldn't even make the Top 50 in the ranking of the following year's box-office hits.

What was the top-grossing film of 1983? It was *Return of the Jedi* (later retitled *Star Wars Episode VI: Return of the Jedi*). De Palma's old friend and generational ally George Lucas produced and wrote (with Lawrence Kasdan) this third film in the Star Wars trilogy. It was the one in the saga in which Yoda dies, Luke Skywalker finds out Princess Leia is his twin sister, and Luke engages in a fierce battle with Darth Vader armed with his little friend, his light-saber. Hmmm—if you're willing to consider Robert Loggia's Frank as Tony Montana's Yoda and the whole messed-up sister/romance angle as being analagous to Tony and Gina, you get the feeling De Palma and company would have made more money by putting everything into a spaceship and rocketing the plot to the outer-space future. A half-decade earlier, De Palma helped his then-good friend Lucas on an ambitious film project. He had a hand in auditioning and interviewing some of the mostly unknown actors. Once the movie had been nearly completed, De Palma did some uncredited writing for the opening crawl, a device De Palma cooked up at the last minutes of postproduction to help set up the history and milieu of the movie, since initial audiences has been confused by it. That film was the very first *Star Wars* (1977).[1]

Sci-fi certainly had its appeal to De Palma—he spent a number of years trying to get Alfred Bester's classic science-fiction novel *The Demolished Man* onto the big screen without success, and eventually did make a space opera, the much-derided, frequently lovely *Mission to Mars* (2000).

And what of De Palma's other friends and colleagues in 1983? Among the middle-aging 1970s ex-rebels, Francis Ford Coppola retreated to lyrical nostalgia with an adaptation of the S. E. Hinton young-adult novel *Rumble Fish,* with Matt Dillon as an adolescent street thug (Tony Montana with an American pedigree and less expressiveness?).

Steven Spielberg (who, along with De Palma and Lucas had co-financed De Palma's 1980 film-about-filmmakers-making-a-film spoof *Home Movies*) produced and directed one segment of the anthology film *Twilight Zone: The Movie* in 1983. That production remains better known nowadays by the tragic accident that occurred during the shooting of director John Landis's Vietnam-set segment: a helicopter crash killed star Vic Morrow and two child actors.

And Martin Scorsese—to whom De Palma had introduced his young *Hi, Mom!* star Robert De Niro, thus paving the way for the actor to transition from a De Palma street revolutionary in 1970 to a Scorsese street thug in 1973's *Mean Streets*—directed *King of Comedy.* This Scorsese film ranks right alongside *Scarface* as an atypical project, from an auteurist standpoint of their careers; a willful aberration—a pushing to the extremes—of the two men's standard themes of isolated characters cutting loose from society. Where Al Pacino in *Scarface* slayed 'em with bullets, Robert De Niro in *King of Comedy* tried to slay 'em with jokes as a pathetic, potentially violent, unhinged comedian who takes hostage a talk-show host (Jerry Lewis) to get a spot on the host's show. Like Tony, De Niro's Rupert Pupkin does not take "no" for an answer.

Elsewhere in 1983, it was a big year for sequels and franchise films. *Staying Alive,* John Travolta's headband-wearing, I-gotta-make-it-on-Broadway, Sylvester Stallone–directed sequel to *Saturday Night Fever,* opened to dismal reviews. Travolta's character was named Tony Manero–he could have been Tony Montana's stagestruck, glammed-up instead of mobbed-up, cousin.

Another sequel: *Superman III,* possibly the looniest installment of the Big Blue Cheese franchise, costarred Richard Pryor as a computer wiz. At the time, Pryor was so big a star, he very nearly pushed star Christopher Reeve to the margins of his own movie. As directed by Richard Lester (*A Hard Day's Night; The Three Musketeers*)—yet another 1983 director working outside his comfort zone and very nearly in the Phantom Zone—*Superman III* was met with dismay by most critics but still went on to be the fifth most-profitable movie of '83.

Superman III opened in June of that year; a month later there was *Jaws 3-D,* the third *Jaws* installment but with which, to his credit, Steven Spielberg had nothing to do. This *Jaws* was part of the odd, brief reinfatuation Hollywood had with 3-D effects—the horror films *Friday the 13th Part 3* and *Amityville 3-D* were part of the wincing minitrend, and other than the nominal presence of original *Jaws* screenwriter Carl Gottlieb as cowriter, you'd be hard-pressed to find anything similar to Spielberg's *Jaws* except for a shark, some water, and the copycat poster.

Sequels, sequels—1983 sometimes must have seemed as though it didn't have an original idea in its head. *Psycho II*? Does anyone remember this follow-up to Alfred Hitchcock's 1960 chiller classic, this one overseen by one Richard Franklin, an Australian-born director who died in 2007? *Psycho II* came replete with Anthony Perkins as Norman Bates but introducing—well, whattya know—Robert Loggia as his new guide-to-sanity doctor, and De Palma fave Dennis Franz as the Bates Motel's new, decidedly frowsy manager, Warren Toomey. As dreadful an embarrassment as it was for everyone involved, *Psycho II* still managed to make more money in 1983 than *Twilight Zone: The Movie* or Coppola's *The Outsiders*.

I'll just mention the other big '83 profit-making sequel—*Porky's II: The Next Day* (burp)—before moving on to the final two, more significant, entries in this Year of the Sequel.

Those would be the two James Bond films that opened in 1983: *Octopussy* (with Roger Moore) and *Never Say Never Again* (with Sean Connery), competing projects from different studios—MGM for the first one, Warner Bros. for the second. Except for providing fans with the opportunity to take sides on which Bond they preferred—the gracefully aging, still-brawny Connery or the slickly debonair, winkingly game Moore—both films were second-tier in the Bond pantheon . . . and both made more dough than *Scarface*.

And, oh yes—this year also saw the premiere of a movie that would yield an appalling number of sequels: *National Lampoon's Vacation*, written by John Hughes a year before he'd launch his own empire of teen flicks with his 1984 directorial debut, *Sixteen Candles*.

If we mention empire-building, we can't help but notice that 1983 was a very good year for Stephen King, who saw no fewer than three of his novels get made into movies that cracked the box-office Top 50: killer-dog flick *Cujo*, killer-car flick *Christine*, and elegant horror flick courtesy of director David Cronenberg, *The Dead Zone*. All racked up eight-figure profits, if none of them equaled the artistry of Brian De Palma's still-unsurpassed Stephen King adaptation, *Carrie* (1976).

In April of '83, the previous year's *Gandhi*—in every way imaginable the anti-*Scarface*—won the Oscar for Best Picture. What the two films have in common, however, is an air of overweening gravitas and grandiosity: middlebrow-high-minded in the case of the makers of *Gandhi*; highbrow-low-minded in the case of the makers of *Scarface*. (*Scarface*'s F. Murray Abraham would move from the latter to the former the very next year, taking the Oscar-snagging costarring role in *Amadeus*.) But this particular period found movies tilting away from those qualities. The early-'80s hits that struck mass audiences as both entertaining and different were different sorts of films—lighter both artistically and in tone, far more designed to be crowd pleasers, as well as proving to be showcases for up-and-coming stars.

Take, for example, *Flashdance*, the number-three box-office champ in 1983. If any critic or paying customer thought *Scarface* was over the top, how could he or she not have applied the same criticism at this loopy tale of a female steel-mill welder by day and exotic dancer by night? Jennifer Beals and the bucket of water she doused herself with during her night job became instant pop-culture symbols—but symbols of what? Was it a kind of garish pop-feminism, as presumably its bumptious director, Adrian Lyne, and blowhard screenwriter, Joe Eszterhas, believed, or tried to make the press believe? Or simply symbols of exuberant exploitation, and the best long commercial for the pleasures of Pittsburgh ever committed to celluloid? *Flashdance* even had something—someone—in common with *Scarface*: its rattling disco-pop soundtrack was provided by Giorgio Moroder. Was it coincidence or societal inevitability that the same year the T-shirt-soaking in *Flashdance* was revealed, the first Hooters restaurant opened in Clearwater, Florida, in October 1983?

Oh, and I almost forgot: De Palma had been offered *Flashdance* before Lyne, and turned it down. Wise artistic decision, or boneheaded miscalculation? Come on: Wouldn't you love to have seen how De Palma might have made Beals's water splash look like a bucket of blood being poured over her, *Carrie*-style?

The other pop-movie phenomenon of '83 was *Risky Business,* the movie that made Tom Cruise a top-drawer movie star three years before *Top Gun.* A teen movie whose only dangerous moments lay in whether or not Cruise's smirky suburban rebel Joel will make it into Princeton after he becomes involved with an expensive call girl (Rebecca De Mornay) and her come-to-collect pimp (Joe Pantoliano), *Risky Business,* the tenth-biggest money-maker of 1983 and the film that associated Bob Seger music with tighty-whitey underwear in a generation's collective mind, was probably the sort of commercial fare that probably could have driven Brian De Palma out of his, if he payed any attention to it at all.

But as long as we're still in suburbia, let's not forget the debatably less-profitable but certainly even more influential *The Big Chill* (opening within a month of each other, *Risky* grossed $7 million more than *Chill* by the end of 1983).[2]

Directed and cowritten by Lucas's *Star Wars* screenwriting collaborator Lawrence Kasdan, *The Big Chill* was intended to be, and for many thirtysomethings-before-*thirtysomething* was, a generation-defining document of '60s idealism gone south, to be replaced by white grown-ups recapturing their radical youths by dancing to Motown oldies and smoking dope. Its soundtrack may have been better than *Scarface*'s—it's hard to gainsay Debbie Harry's "Rush Rush" compared to the Temptations' "Ain't Too Proud to Beg"—but if *The Big Chill*'s marijuana-toking be liberty, give me *Scarface*'s cocaine death.

Another suburban-set film was a bigger hit: *Mr. Mom*, starring Michael Keaton as a stay-at-home dad at a time when the concept was still new and risible. And it was written by the soon-to-be-inescapable John Hughes.

Indeed, of all the biggest-grossing movies of 1983, the only one that even suggested the kind of outrageousness and subversion that *Scarface* achieved was the very sly comedy *Trading Places*. John Landis directed this pointed farce starring a Philadelphia commodities broker, played by Dan Aykroyd, who ends up switching his station in life with a street hustler played by Eddie Murphy. The clashing class-consciousness that underlies Landis's comedy is very similar to the theme that runs through so many of De Palma's films, whether they be his early counterculture satires or the restaurant scene in *Scarface*, in which a drug-addled Tony rages at the wealthy diners that they "need" a disreputable, low-class guy like him to feel superior to, concluding, "Say good-night to the bad guy!" No one does.

The same month that *Scarface* opened, Landis's other high-profile directorial work premiered—the music video for Michael Jackson's mega-hit song "Thriller," a half-hour mini-horror-movie. De Palma would get into the music-video game a year later, when he directed Bruce Springsteen's "Dancing in the Dark," and helped discover the then-unknown actress whom the Boss pulls out of a concert audience to boogaloo with: Courteney Cox, soon of *Friends*. It's not surprising that Springsteen was a De Palma fan (Bruce likes his auteurists), but one does wonder why De Palma, with his eye for female talent, didn't immediately sign up and then kill off Cox in a subsequent feature-length project. She would have made a great attractive-brunette substitution for the less expressive Deborah Shelton in De Palma's next movie, *Body Double*.

The Women in *Scarface*

On Valentine's Day 2008, *Attack of the Show!*, a daily round-up of technology, Internet, and multimedia news on the cable channel G4, named *Scarface* as the movie to rent if you've fallen out of love or if you hate Valentine's Day. The reference was a jokey one, to be sure—*Scarface* as the ultimate anti-chick-flick. But it had a valid point: *Scarface* is to some degree a movie about a man whose relationships with women are fraught wth anxiety—fears of disapproval and abandonment, and rage that the women in his life might change, become less dependent upon him, or respect him less.

There are, basically, only three women in the film: Miriam Colon's "Mama" Montana, Mary Elizabeth Mastrantonio's Gina Montana, and Michelle Pfeiffer's Elvira Hancock. To put it as crudely as they are frequently deployed onscreen: they are the mother, the madonna/whore, and the whore/mother/madonna, all of whom Tony adores, in his brutal fashion.

Scarface is singular among Brian DePalma's films in its portrayal of female characters. In his best movies—*Blow Out, Carrie, Body Double*, and *The Fury*—women are mostly helpless, often hapless victims, slasher killers, or supernatural forces. Sometimes they battle back (as Sissy Spacek does in *Carrie*, flinging blood at her high-school tormentors). Sometimes they moan, gasp, and die (as Nancy Allen, the squeaky-voiced girl-woman—who in real life was De Palma's girlfriend—does in *Blow Out*). De Palma may be many things, but a keen observer of female behavior isn't one of them.

In *Scarface,* with the exception of the three whose trajectories we can trace through the movie, women are either predators (Barbra Perez's malicious shotgun-shooting woman laying on the motel bed during the chain-saw scene) or simply fair game for sex for Tony and Manny. Manny is distracted from his job in the walk-up to the chain-saw massacre, for instance, while he flirts with a bikini'd babe who just naturally stroll up to his car on the street.

And let's not forget the weird, funny, ultimately pathetic scene on a Miami beach with Tony sitting with Manny, sipping drinks out of absurdly decorated pineapple husks. Tony, waxing philosophical, utters one of the key profane *Scarface* phrases so beloved by its cultists:

"This town like a great big pussy, waiting to get fucked."

They're talking about making money, but they're also talking about—well, a cute female in a bikini walks by and Tony asks her whether she'd enjoy some ice cream. The sweet-looking girl tells him to scram. Manny then demonstrates to Tony how you get American girls: He leans in close to Tony and slithers his tongue quickly in and out of his mouth.

"What the fuck is *that*?" says Tony, and Pacino's startlement probably echoed that of audiences first seeing the film in 1983. Was Manny really demonstrating what we thought he was demonstrating? Yes: how to perform cunnilingus, with a rapid flicking motion. "*Oooh, tha's disgusting!*" Tony says, who compares it to "a *bug* comin' outta your mouth!" Manny explains a cultural difference between Cuban and American women, that American girls go into ecstasy when you "fluff the pussy." Tony dares him to demonstrate his technique to another woman lounging nearby. Manny squats down beside her, murmurs some banal come-on, and does the tongue waggle. She slaps him. As Tony pulls him away, Manny spits out that she must be a "lesssbian!" The scene is all exaggerated accents and slapstick, but with a point: these guys are clueless when it comes to women. Here, it's presented as a joke; later, that misunderstanding of the opposite sex will result in alienation and death.

Say what you will about the macho muscle rippling through *Scarface* screenwriter Oliver Stone's own body of work: the man does try to make *his* female clichés lively ones. Between the two of them, De Palma and Stone created a doozy, a handful—just the sort of dame a macho mama's boy like Tony both can't resist and should run away from—in Elvira Hancock, She Who Will Not Be Controlled.

In Elvira, Tony meets a woman who, under normal circumstances, would never look at him twice. Our first glimpse of her is from Tony's point of view, as she rides down in a glass elevator to the main floor of boss Frank Lopez's mansion, and Tony is immediately riveted: She's a blond angel descending from the heavens, as far as he's concerned—no matter that this is one hard, as-yet-inexplicably bitter angel, bored and self-narcotized by liquor so that she can put up with Lopez's familiar jokes, complaints, and pats on her ass.

In a way, Pfeiffer was an odd bit of casting. So thin that her shoulder blades might pass as the wings Tony is imagining on his angel, she doesn't have the curvy sensuality you'd expect the Cuban Tony to be immediately attracted to, and her sour demeanor is nobody's idea of a turn-on. But for film buffs—De Palma among them—Pfeiffer's blond slink (she's wearing a blue-green dress slit up the side so that every stride exposes a thigh) echoes back through film-time at least as

far as Marlene Dietrich, and her page-boy cut is a platinum version of Louise Brooks's dark bob.

In any case, Elvira is certainly convincing as a Great Unobtainable, whose quality alone makes her irresistible to Tony. One of her early showcase scenes locates her in Lopez's favorite nightclub hangout, The Babylon, where Giorgio Moroder's throbbing disco music features Debbie Harry coming through the sound system chanting something about "ye-yo." Lopez takes his cronies, including a newly rewarded and spiffed-up Tony, to a prominently raised booth in the club, the mini-throne from which he talks business and dispenses advice to Tony. "Lesson number one: never underestimate the other guy's greed!" (This is punctuated by Robert Loggia's great, gravelly bray of a laugh, a sound that always reminds me of Joe Flaherty's Count Floyd on the old *SCTV* show: "Bwah-ha-ha-ha-hah!") Elvira, who's heard these bromides a thousand times, offers rule number two before Lopez can finish cackling. "Don't get high on your own supply," she says with world-weary disdain. The words mean almost nothing to her: She's so used to being provided for—by this time in her jaded young life, Elvira barely knows or cares where the money and drugs come from as long as they're there for her to consume at her bored leisure.

Throughout this, Tony is silent, drawing on a big fat cigar and maintaining a poker face but keeping his eyes panther-alert, taking in the scene, accepting Lopez's compliments and promises with polite nonchalance (in asking Tony to work for him, Frank says he's going to buy the kid "$550 suits"—I love the pointless precision there: not $500 but *$550*). This scene is where Pacino really takes hold of *Scarface* and makes it his own—until this point, he's had to act Tony's innocence about America, bottle his emotions to convey Tony's unfocused yearnings. But now, in a *Saturday Night Fever*–era leisure suit and open-necked shirt, his arms thrown across the back of the banquette as he sits next to Loggia, Pacino is all feral intensity. He's turned on by the glittering spectacle around him, by Elvira (who's separated from him only by Lopez in the booth where they sit—a visual cue for the guy he must overcome to get closer to her), and by the information Lopez is dropping in between his back "lessons" in the trade.

When Lopez declines to dance with her, Elvira asks Tony, who follows her onto the dance floor as Amy Holland sings the title phrase "She's on Fire" over and over. Really, a few words repeated over a pumping beat is all that's required for pleasure in a place like this. The disco era is perfect for De Palma's purposes: stiff dancing between two people stiffly getting to know each other over the blare of mating Muzak. The dance floor is full of people like Elvira, who has perfected one or two moves and nearly dances in place. She occasionally turns her back on Tony, keeping her arms raised to shoulder level and wiggling to the rhythm—she does a narcissistic hustle. This only makes Tony more interested, of course. He teases out of her, with her immense reluctance, that she's from Baltimore, a city of which Tony has never heard. Then Elvira deflects any further embarrassing information by tossing out snide put-downs such as dismissing Tony as being fresh off a banana boat and a contributor to a Cuban crime wave. Tony responds with his usual bullshit line, that he's a political prisoner.

Then the real courtship begins in this obscenity-besotted movie. Tony enumerates Elvira's loveliest features, complimenting her face and legs, but adding, ". . . only you got a look in your eye like you haven't been fucked in a year." The vehemence with which Pacino utters *fuck*—his confident reliance upon the word to get a rise out of the character he's playing to, and from the look on Pfeiffer's face, maybe the actress herself—acts as a jolt in the movie. Elvira, shaking off the shock, sneers that this is none of his business, that "who, how, and when I fuck is none of your business, okay?" Tony is delighted, no longer trying to play it cool to get to her. He removes the thick cigar from his mouth and purrs that he's glad he's got her dander up, that he's struck a nerve. This only makes Elvira even more belligerent. "Even if I was blind, desperate, starved, and begging for it on a desert island, you'd be the *last* thing that I'd ever fuck." Again, Tony grins: It's love at first "fuck."

Later in the film, Tony and Manny tool over to Frank Lopez's pad

in a big yellow boat of a Cadillac convertible with zebra-skin uphol-
stery (this is Tony's idea of classy), and wait for Elvira to walk out the
front door. Pfeiffer—a dream woman in a gleaming white skirt, heels,
and large white hat—says the car is too gaudy, too overdone. She's always calling attention to Tony's lack of class, and he's always absorb-
ing her contempt and turning it back at her transformed into blithe
misunderstanding and patience. *Doesn't she get it?* his attitude implies:
It's only a matter of time before she realizes she belongs with me, not Frank.
Tony is as sure of this as he is of any future dream of money and
power.

Soon enough, Tony, Elvira, and Manny are in a car dealership
showroom, picking out a sleek, silver Jaguar (a car more in keeping
with Elvira's notion of classiness), which Tony buys with cash. The
purchase made, Elvira deigns to get into Tony's Caddy, where he lays
it on thick, professing his affection. But, ignoring him, she starts
snorting coke in the passenger seat. Tony asks for some, taking his
first, and we know eventually ruinous, toot: talk about your "gateway
drug" to hell. He tries to put his arm around Elvira, like a 1950s boy
attempting to make out with his date at the drive-in. Elvira pushes
him away, still harping on his low station in life, snickering that she
doesn't make out with "the help." She removes her hat and starts
combing her hair so she won't have to look at him.

Instead of becoming angry, there occurs one of the sweetest, most
spontaneous moments in *Scarface*. Tony nonchalantly puts on her big
white hat, looking deadpan-silly. "Would you kiss me if I wear the
hat?" Elvira looks over and she can't help herself: She laughs. For the
first time, she acknowledges that Tony is a charmer, that there's something disarming about this flunky.

This is all the encouragement a truly romantic hustler like Tony needs. A few scenes later, he proposes marriage—this, despite the fact that she's still Frank Lopez's kept woman. Elvira is lounging poolside in the bright sun, and Tony sprawls awkwardly on the chaise lounge next to her. (One of Pacino's best ideas is to make Tony frequently seem dorky, placing himself in uncomfortable postures in an effort to assimilate himself into new surroundings and with new people.)

Tony asks her, as his opening gambit, if she likes kids. Now it's Elvira's turn to be thrown off-balance. Kids? Where is this guy going with this? This is a line she hasn't heard before, from Frank or the horny muscle-heads she's spent her life consorting with. "Sure, why not," she says, quickly regaining her fall-back pose: bored cynicism. "As long as there's a nurse," she adds—though the way Pfeiffer delivers the line, you know Elvira *has* thought about kids, probably a lot, especially when she's in a coked-up reverie.

Saying with gruff humility that he's risen from "the gutter," that he has no education, Tony insists he's got something better: a plan, ambition, and now—via the boss he's about to betray in so many ways—connections. "With the right woman, ain't no stoppin' me," says Tony, zeroing in on a key *Scarface* refrain: "I could go right to the top." As far as Tony is concerned, he considers Elvira to be a tiger, one to be tamed, to "belong" to him. "I want you to marry me—I want you to be the mother of my children," he concludes.

Elvira seems stunned. "Marry me?" She lowers her voice. "What about Frank?" Tony has drawn her in, ineluctably. He says he can handle Frank, and to think about what he's just said. Even behind her huge sunglasses, we know she will. It's a great little scene, one that shows, by the economy of dialogue, by the very quickness of its exchanges, how rapidly Tony can turn people around to his way of thinking. With this scene and the one before it with Frank about business matters, we know that Tony has not merely brute ambition but the subtle power that confidence builds, that emanates from people who want things—not just power, but respect and even love—in a fierce, determined manner.

And so, after a few choice murders, Tony wins her over and marries Elvira, as bridesmaid Gina and groomsman Manny look longingly at each other across the aisle. Tony the tiger gets a real tiger for his estate property (everyone in the wedding party scurries down to see the growling, chained poor thing). It's hubris time. Everything's great, unless you factor in the lousy *Scarface* theme song "Push It to the Limit," by a yowling Paul Engemann on the soundtrack during this montage.

The only sour note in this sequence, aside from Engemann's singing, is its final shot: a solitary Elvira sitting in a silk-white robe at her makeup table, snorting cocaine—she's either neurotically unhappy, or she knows no matter what happens in this life, things will not turn out well. Or both.

Cut to a key scene in *Scarface* mythology. Sitting in a bubble bath in his absurdly ornate, gold-plated, huge bathroom, Tony watches a bank commercial on his TV starring Jerry, and he scoffs. "You know what capitalism is? 'Get fucked.'" Tony says this to Manny while stationed rather comically in a chair beside the sunken tub so that he can hear every pearl of coke-inspired wisdom his boss cares to drop, but Pacino delivers the line looking straight ahead, as though to us in the audience. CAPITALISM = GET FUCKED. It's the message Oliver Stone has peddled and will peddle again, in movies ranging from *JFK* to *Natural Born Killers*. Here, it makes sense because Tony Montana is such a monster-creation of capitalism . . . and yet Tony doesn't realize the extent to which he is also a creation (a victim) of the capitalist system.

Off-camera, we hear Elvira scoff at Tony's words. Hoo boy, is *this* honeymoon ever over. He sneers in return, "How would you know, bubblehead?" (Don't you think Pacino must have looked down and noticed for the first time the bubbles he himself was sitting in and improvised the line?) The camera pulls back to reveal Pfeiffer sitting at a table breathing drug powder up her nose, painting her nails, and taking swigs from a glass of amber alcohol.

De Palma has now grounded us in Montana's world thoroughly: we have no idea whether it's 2 A.M. or 2 P.M.—there are no windows, no bright, clarifying Miami sunlight; we're trapped in opulence along with Tony and his already miserable marriage. It's Lucy and Desi as drug-addicted brawlers. "Nothing succeeds like excess," Elvira drawls sarcastically.

Tony sees a politician on a nearby TV now, a suit decrying the drug trade, and this image sends him on another slurry tear. "The politicians and the bankers—they want to keep cocaine illegal, so they can make the fuckin' money, they get the fuckin' votes . . . *they* the bad guys! They'll fuck anything or anybody to make a buck!" he bellows.

"Can't you stop saying 'fuck' all the time?" moans Elvira. Is this De Palma and Stone anticipating one of the many complaints the movie's critics will have about it, that it's tiresomely profane? Already, so early in this nouveau-riche marital arrangement, Elvira is so insulated in her druggy palace-prison that she can condemn the very stuff that enables her to be so cavalierly bored. Tony, the true working-class man, is (justifiably, when viewed on his terms) angered by this. Elvira taunts him all the more—she knows how to get under his thin skin. "Money, money, money, money, money . . . Frank never talked about money. . . . You know what you're becoming, Tony?" she asks, arising to waft over to the drink tray atop the TV. "You're an immigrant millionaire spic who can't stop talking about money." The blond Elvira is like the banker to whom Tony takes his money to be laundered: a white WASP whore, to paraphrase and put it bluntly, who believes incessant talk about money is unseemly. The true rich don't *talk* about money—they merely take it as a fact of life.

Tony protests that he works hard for the money, if I may borrow a phrase Donna Summer used in a big hit single at the time of *Scarface*'s release. Elvira responds in a crucial moment of true wisdom: "Too bad—somebody should have given it to you; you would have been a nicer person."

Tony marshals what he considers an argument, suggesting she do something useful to society (yet remain in what he would consider an essentially servile, "feminine" profession), like become a nurse. "Work with blind kids or lepers." Well, *kinda* okay so far, but then he sneers, "Anything beats lying around all day waiting for me to fuck you."

Elvira cuts him coldly, telling him he's got nothing to brag about when it comes to sack work. She exits. Tony bellows for her to come back. "I was *keeed*ing!" *Loooosi*—come back!

Manny also leaves to go conduct some business—we'll call it Snuggling with Gina—and Tony curses them both out, saying he doesn't need anyone. Here, De Palma and cinematographer John A. Alonzo pull the camera back and up, executing a slow overhead shot that shows Tony, a dark-mood man isolated in an empty white room: It might as well be the whiteness of a sanitarium.

"Say Good-bye to the Bad Guy!"
... and His Girl

This crude Miami version of *Scenes from a Marriage* hits its peak
when Tony takes Elvira and Manny to a posh restaurant. Tony and
Manny are wearing demure black tuxedos for a change; Elvira is in a
spangly gown cut like her usual white silk ones. Tony's about to go to
New York to oversee an operation he dreads: getting rid of the Bolivian informant, because by this time Tony is so cocaine-crazy paranoid
he believes only he can handle the job properly himself. But he's feeling sorry for himself for having to dirty his hands this way. He's
slumped in his chair, looking a bit drunk. Elvira keeps sniffing and
wiggling her nostrils, never touching her meal. She tells Tony grimly
that she has no appetite—she's more deeply than ever into the cocaine
diet. Tony looks disgusted about his entire situation.

Is this all there is? he wonders. "Eating? Drinking? Fucking? Suck-
ing? Snorting? . . . This is what I work for?" He's puffing on a big sto-
gie, eyes looking glazed. "I got a fucking junkie for a wife . . . sleeps all
day and won't fuck me 'cause she's in a coma." And now he really
goes in for the kill—we're in *Who's Afraid of Virginia Woolf?* territory:
"I can't even have a kid with her . . . her womb is so *polluted*."

Elvira throws a drink at Tony, snapping that he's no better than she
is. Her voice rising, patrons are looking at them now. She doesn't care;
she's too far gone. Yelling that her husband sells drugs and kills people, she says sarcastically, "*Real* contribution to human society!"
Elvira's conclusion is that they've become "losers [. . .] not winners,
Tony." She leaves alone.

What Happens to Elvira?

Elvira makes her exit two hours and ten minutes into *Scarface*, forty minutes before the film ends. It's as though she's irrelevant to the film once she's served her purpose as Tony's verbal sparring partner and punching bag. She also vanishes from the final version of Stone's screenplay. When I asked Stone about this, he paused for a moment, and laughed. "You're right—as a character who brings the action to a certain peak there in the restaurant, she's fulfilled her role. I like to think that if I was writing it now, I'd figure out some cool way to bring Elvira back, but if I'd tried it at the time—and I probably did, I just can't remember—I probably would have just had one of Sosa's men take her out [i.e., kill her]." Stone grinned. "I was in a *Scarface* frame of mind myself while writing this, you know? So as Elvira left Tony's consciousness, she left mine, too."

Which makes the questions only more intriguing. Where does Elvira go? What does she do next? What happens to her? When it comes to the women in the film, De Palma shifts his gaze to Gina.

In the 2007 comic-book miniseries *Scarface: Scarred for Life*, writer John Layman has Elvira escaping Tony to live with Sosa—she goes from being the kept woman of one thug to the trophy-whore of another. This seems to me to sell Elvira short.

Here's what I like to think happened.

Elvira, coming out of her drug stupor, goes back to the mansion, packs up, and scrams before Sosa's gun toters arrive. She flies to Los Angeles and checks into rehab. While living with Tony, she had set up a bank account in her own name and funneled enough money into it to keep her going for a while, and so she pursues her dream: to become an actress.

It's the mid-'80's, and she'd really like to get into a franchise like the *Indiana Jones* or the *Romancing the Stone* movies. (She fancies herself both a smart-cookie businesswoman, and a slimmer, smarter Kathleen Turner, whom she admired from her tough-broad performance in *Body Heat*.) But Hollywood is a tougher nut to crack than even the jaded Elvira expected. She auditions for the lead in *King Solomon's Mines*, but loses the role to Sharon Stone. The best she can do is play one of the many female victims in 1985's *Friday the 13th: A New Beginning*, narrowly aced out of the meatier role of "Pam," the head of the sanitarium where the movie's killer re-dons his hockey mask.

That movie proves not much of a new beginning for Elvira, though. After losing another costarring role, this time to Rosanna Arquette in *8 Million Ways to Die*—"Hey, I've already died a thousand small deaths," she jokes to director Hal Ashby at the audition. "What's a few thousand more?"—she turns to TV, playing a blond bimbo in one episode of the then-new 1987 ABC sitcom *Perfect Strangers* and lands a recurring role on the same network's cop parody-show, *Sledge Hammer!*, only to see the series canceled after its second season. At a party, Elvira meets one of the producers of David Lynch's *Blue Velvet* (not Elvira's kind of picture—too "out there"), and finds the guy charming. They date, she tells him about her past, he gets her a chunk of money to develop a project to which they give the working title "Lady Scarface," about a woman who rises up in the drug trade. A British independent film company trying to crack the American market options it, but the Brits go bankrupt before they can get the movie made.

Elvira marries the producer. Turns out she's not barren. They have two kids: a boy and a girl—Ethan and Hayley.

Elvira never sets foot in Miami again.

That's how I imagine it going down.

Going Home, Leaving Home: Mama Montana and Sister Gina

About fifty minutes into *Scarface*, after the chain-saw scene, after Tony has been taken under Frank Lopez's wing and is wearing "$550" suits, he pulls up in front of a dilapidated bungalow. It's his mother's house. Her blunt greeting is to say she's surprised she hadn't received any postcards from him from jail recently. Miriam Colon's quiet, emotional performance as Tony's mother isn't at all as tough or as mean as that line—she's verbally slapping him for his absence of five years, but her huge hurt eyes tell us how much she misses her son, his physical presence, and how she hates the distance he's placed between them in the life he's chosen. Still framed in the half-open doorway, Mama Montana is joined by a younger woman. Tony sees her and, nearly an hour into the film, Pacino allows his character to become vulnerable for the first time in *Scarface*.

Tony greets his beloved sister, the movie's symbol of innocence (however fleeting), played by Mary Elizabeth Mastrantonio. He hasn't seen her since she was a little girl and now, he tells her, she's a beautiful woman. He talks to her like a father as much as a brother; there is no father in this broken, lower-middle-class home, and De Palma makes clear in just these few seconds that Tony has had to fill both

225

roles, even in his absence. Although separated from his sister for many years, in Tony's mind he has always been her protector. She hugs him, tearing up, while the mother leaves the room grimly, silently.

Soon the three of them are in the kitchen, where Gina is chattering happily about her present life. Mama, she says, still works in a factory—doubtless some sort of sweatshop, and a lifetime of onerous toil is thus tossed off in one comment. Gina is proud to tell him that she's going to school to become a beautician and has a job lined up at a beauty parlor and . . .

Tony cuts her off. Leaning back in his white disco suit and removing a Cuban cigar from the corner of his mouth, he says that kind of striving is over for both of them. His money will take care of them. Tony, of course, cannot see that his largesse isn't the solution to his family's problems, but rather, a curse that he's extending onto his loved ones. He's about to inject their lives with the misery and damnation of the crimes he has and will commit.

Tony explains his absence by saying he didn't want to return until he was successful. He reaches deep into his suit pocket, uttering an inadvertent rhyme: "I want you to see, what a good boy I be." And he pulls out a thick wad of cash and plops it onto the small kitchen table, offering his mother a gift of a thousand dollars.

Mama wonders aloud who Tony has killed for this money, and she fingers the money as though it was oil to be washed from her hands. She asks him if he's sticking up banks or bodegas. That's how she imagines Tony's life to be.

Can you imagine how a son must feel in the presence of such a mother, a mother who expresses such a complete lack of—never mind love—a *lack of humanity* in her own offspring? This is what makes

Miriam Colon

Most of the auditions for *Scarface* were held at the Puerto Rican Traveling Theater, the Manhattan Off-Broadway company cofounded by Miriam Colon. A recurring character on the soap opera *The Guiding Light* from 1999–2002, the Puerto Rican–born Colon has appeared in scores of TV shows and movies, usually as a Mexican, including *The Dick Van Dyke Show, Gunsmoke, Bonanza,* and she costarred in Marlon Brando's *One-Eyed Jacks* (1961).

Tony Montana the monster he will so fully become by the end of this tale.

Still clinging to the high-minded justification he has used from the start, Tony says no, he's with an anti-Castro political group, that he's an organizer, that he gets a lot of—and he has to pause here, to make an imaginative leap he almost can't surmount, but does—"a lotta political contributions." No matter that a legitimate organizer wouldn't be doling out contributions to his family; Tony is, beneath a barely maintained cool, trying to make his mother and sister proud of him. Mama doesn't believe him, of course, and goes in for the emotional kill, saying she reads all the time in newspapers about "animals" like him. She, too, knows how to play the game, using the old you're-a-disgrace-to-your-ethnic-heritage line. The clichés cascade with increasing ferocity from her: "It's Cubans like you who give the rest of us bad names . . ." When Gina protests, "He's your son!" Mama spits that he's a bum, and we simultaneously know that Mama is speaking the truth but we also identify with Tony, who's looking like a sulky boy, not wanting to listen to clichés that sting because they are truths.

Mama not only rejects Tony's affection and money, she insists that he not "destroy" Gina with his glam and his easy money. She tells him to leave the house and throws his money at him. Tony walks out and we notice that he's leaving through a small white-picket fence (De Palma can be so shamelessly, effectively pointed sometimes) as Gina chases after him. She hugs Tony passionately—and De Palma cuts to Manny, who's been waiting in the car, watching, seeing how lovely Gina is. We know that he's suddenly wishing *he* was the one being hugged. After pressing the money on Gina, Tony gets back into the car, and Manny says, "She's beautiful," and Tony immediately explodes: "You stay away from her! She not for you!" That is, no one is good enough for his pure, virginal sister. "Okay," agrees Manny, his glance back at the house conveying precisely the opposite.

A few scenes later, some months have passed, and our next glimpse is of a much-changed Gina. Tony enters the bright, blaring Babylon Club: Tony is moving fast, literally glad-handing people who now know his name and greet him jovially, slapping him five and clapping him on the back. The guy has the wafting smell of success coming off him—he's on the verge of taking the bright world and spinning it the way the disco ball spins in the center of the dance floor.

The first thing Tony notices after he is seated in a booth, however, is his Gina, now with a frizzed-out Latin Afro in the shape of a globe (subliminal message: *this* world is hers), shaking her groove thing with a slick-looking dude. "Who *issss* that guy?" Tony hisses to his sidekick Manny. Before taking in the answer (some petty hood who works for Lopez—harmless, Manny assures him), Tony fixes his eyes on Gina, as the swell of a single synthesizer chord rises ominously in the background. In case we miss the point that Tony is concerned that his Virgin Mary of a sister is in the wrong place, De Palma now, instead of moving away, tracks the camera in, in, in closer to Tony's face, until it seems as though the lenses are pressing against his eyeballs like an optometrist's examining machine. He's lost in a trance of slowly enveloping anger until . . .

The camera advances on Tony's eyeballs again as De Palma cuts to another close-up: the punk cradling Gina's backside with his hand as he guides her out of the club. That's all Tony needs to see. He's up and out of the booth like a flash, following them, with Manny scrambling to keep up. Gina, giggly and probably more than a bit drunk or high, is pulled by the punk into the men's lavatory, and from there into a stall where they do some contortionist combo of making out and snorting coke.

Tony slams the stall door open. He throws the punk aside. He grabs Gina by the throat and tells her that she can't do this anymore, as she tells him it's none of his business. Tony threatens to punish her if he catches her again—as though she's still a little girl. Gina, perhaps emboldened by the blow she's consumed, says, "You think you can

come in here *now* and tell me what to do?"—coming down hard on the word "now" to instantly lodge in Tony's head that he's neglected her and her mother for years. It's a signal Tony immediately picks up on and which only further enrages him—with guilt, with excessive protectiveness. Gina says she's not a kid anymore and that "if I want to fuck him"—presumably that dreadful little punk with his sad little pencil-thin moustache—"then I'll fuck him." What can a proud macho man with family pride—someone like Tony—do except what he does, which is slap Gina across the face so hard she falls to the floor? (I must say, as violent as Tony is, as much as he's dealing with the fact that his kid sister, whom he hadn't seen for years, has turned into a hot babe he cannot resist noticing, he *did* give her the money she's wasting on wanton nights on the town; I'd be annoyed, too, wouldn't you?) It's left to Manny to pick up Gina off the floor and lead her out.

He drives her home, rattling on about how Tony, being her brother, is naturally protective of her. Pounding home the scene's message, Manny says, "You're the only thing in his life that's any good, that's pure . . . so he has this father thing for you." (Virginity is what

Manny's getting at, but as always with De Palma and Stone, there are obvious subtexts: beyond the Freudian "father thing," she's "pure" in the same way the drugs Tony sells are.) Gina protests that she's twenty years old, that the slug she was dancing and tooting with (he has a name: Fernando) was fun, a guy who "knows how to treat a woman." Then Bauer's Manny delivers his most winning, common-sense line in the entire movie, saying with a chuckle, "By taking you to a toilet to make out?"

By the time they reach Gina and her mother's house, Gina is telling Manny that she sees the way he looks at her. (Really, if this girl wasn't set up in her first scene with her mama to be viewed by us as a good girl, we'd be thinking she was quite a little tramp by now.) Manny is obliged to trace lineage: "Look, Tony and I are like brothers and you're his kid sister, and that's where it ends." Gina taunts him by narrowing her eyes to a sexy cat's gazing stare and asks Manny if he's afraid of Tony. Button pushed, Manny is flustered and says only, "*I'm not the point here!*"

Although the rest of *Scarface* will be uncharacteristically discreet about Gina and Manny's attraction to each other, we sense it's not a subplot that will fade away—even if first-time viewers probably never supect just *how far* it will go. This entire subplot is lifted directly from the Howard Hawks movie pretty much intact with entirely new dialogue; Oliver Stone knew that this was a potent theme to explore about an essentially impotent power-seeker like Tony.

Other than a brief scene in which we note that Tony has bought Gina her own beauty salon (there's a brief, no-dialogue glimpse of the pink-ribbon-cutting ceremony), we don't see or hear much about Gina until Tony has entered his coke-crazed, control-freak stage later in the movie. That's when he revisits Mama Montana's house, where she tells Tony that Gina is missing, that it's his fault, that with all the money he gives her, she got her own place and she won't tell Mama where it is. We've figured out what they haven't: that Manny is the one who's keeping Gina from her family now. Tony goes to leave and we're outside—we can see the little white-picket fence around the perfect little house in Nowheresville—with Mama screaming after Tony, "Why do you have to destroy everything you touch?"

Tony goes to the last address Mama knew where Gina was, on Citrus Avenue. He knocks on the door, and Manny answers the door in a white bathrobe. Looking over Manny's shoulder, Tony sees Gina on a second-floor balcony, also in a robe. Moroder's ominous, pulsing *Scarface* theme is starting to play under the action, slowly rising in volume. Now De Palma removes the sound of dialogue. Tony shoots Manny in the gut and all we hear is the gunshot and the music; Manny and Gina's "No's!" are just mouth movements. We're inside Tony's fevered brain. He can't hear anything except the blood pounding in his own head. Tony shoots Manny again, Gina rushes down to hug Manny in death. Now we hear her sobs.

"We got married just yesterday—we were going to surprise you," she murmurs to Tony, cradling Manny in her arms. Two of Tony's henchmen come. "We gotta get outta here, Tony!" they say upon seeing the bloody scene. They drive Tony and the moaning Gina back to Tony's home.

Meanwhile, outside, stealthy gunmen invade Tony's palace, taking out his guards. Inside, Tony takes another huge snort, as Gina enters the room. "Is this what you want, Tony?" she asks, running her hand along her breast beneath the robe. She's talking softly, seductively. "You can't stand for *another* man to be touching me." She's making overt the incestuous-sibling undercurrent that has run through the movie. "You want me, Tony, huh?" She undoes her robe . . . and pulls out a gun, taking a shot at Tony that misses.

"Here I am, Tony," she says, still calm—narcotized with grief—advancing on him. "I'm all yours now," she says, laughing bitterly, taking aim again. "Come and get me, Tony—we do it now before it's too late." She shoots again and wings Tony, who's backing up, unnerved. He falls to the floor holding his leg. "Come on, Tony: Fuck me," says Gina, using the f-word in a more powerfully obscene way than Tony ever has. As he hides behind his desk, Gina alternates shooting her gun with shouting, "Fuck me, Tony!" She's out of her mind with misery.

Then, one of the trespassing gunmen enters through the window behind Tony's desk and machine-guns Gina dead. Tony whirls around, dives at him, and pushes him back through the upper-floor window, throwing the gunman down to the ground below. Tony has this guy's machine gun now. He riddles the corpse with bullets. Outside, more gunmen arrive and kill off Tony's men. Inside, Tony hugs Gina's corpse. He moans for her to talk to him, he says desperately that he loves her, that he even loves Manny—all for naught, now. Tony's enemies swarm the property, shooting everyone in Tony's crew they see. They enter through the front door; Tony can see them on his bank of security cameras. Tony kisses Gina's body and says he'll be back. He won't.

He's lost all the women in his life—either pushed them away, or drawn them too close to his corrupting world. The man who lied to the immigration officials at the start of the film that his mother was dead is now a man whose mother has rejected him, whose wife has vanished from his universe, whose sister lies dead in his arms. What is it again about this movie that renders its hero a role model? There are probably a lot of women who've sat through *Scarface* and pondered just that question.

The Violence in *Scarface*

Violence is the element for which *Scarface* is most famous, most cultishly prized. It's the engine that drives the narrative, but not the film's motives (those would be ambition, pride, lust, and extreme family loyalty carried to the brink of incest).

The film's violent scenes occur at regular intervals, with an ever-increasing ratcheting-up of blood and anger, and what we can see in retrospect as weapons carefully chosen to up the ante in destruction power as the movie proceeds.

The first example of this occurs about eleven minutes into *Scarface*. We witness a makeshift village, an open-air detention center—a concrete-buttressed holding pen, basically, in northern Miami (and actually shot under an exit ramp of the Santa Monica Freeway in Los Angeles)—where Tony (Al Pacino) and his friend Manolo, nicknamed Manny (Steven Bauer), are being held. This pal pulls Tony out of a basketball game. (When people talk about any implausibilities in *Scarface*, I sometimes first think not of Pacino's accent or his character's cocaine binges, but of the likelihood that Tony—at Pacino's five-foot, five-inch height—would be a decent basketball player.) Manny tells Tony he knows a way out of this trap contemptuously called Freedomtown. Manny says they'll get illicitly obtained green cards— their magic tickets out of this Latino hell, an anti–Disney World—if they kill Rebenga (Roberto Contreras), once a top Castro confidant now expelled into the same American mass holding pen, because Castro felt threatened by Rebenga's increasing power in Cuba.

Tony Montana, Po-*lit*-i-cal Prisoner, speaks decisively. "I kill a Communist for fun. But for a green card, I gonna carve him up *real* nice." Shortly thereafter, during a mass riot at the detention center, Manny singles out their target (a trembling middle-aged gent with large eyeglasses that emphasize his vulnerability) and comes at him slowly with a knife. All around them, detainees are ripping up the makeshift camp, setting mattresses on fire, and smashing everything with wooden planks, but Manny and the Castro loyalist move slowly as hunter and hunted. You think Manny is going to kill him with his knife, but suddenly Tony enters the frame and thrusts his arm into the man's stomach—you know immediately that there is a knife in Tony's hand as well, and that he hasn't carved him up nice; instead, he's just stuck Rebenga once, and lets the guy flop to the floor so that De Palma can have cinematographer John A. Alonzo pull his camera up overhead. From this vantage point, we note that part of Tony's American dream has now been realized: his first victim on these shores is bleeding red against a white shirt, wearing blue pants. This is Tony Montana's true assimilation into his new homeland—via an all-American, patriotic thrill-kill.

The Motel Scene

A half hour into *Scarface* is precisely when we get the movie's most disputed chunk of violence, timed almost to the minute to when they teach you in screenwriting school you have to come up with some scene of action that increases the audience's involvement. In a blindingly bright blue-and-pink Miami Beach, we see Tony in a car with Manny, and their pals Angel (Pepe Serna) and Chi Chi (Angel Salazar). Tony and Angel climb out to get the coke; Manny and Chi Chi stay in the getaway car. We are now about to enter the first major set-piece in *Scarface,* the scene that will forever set the tone not only for the rest of the movie but for much of the media coverage and the artistic evaluation of the film. De Palma begins the scene as though he was trying out for a future episode of *Miami Vice,* the Michael Mann cop show that would premiere the following year. De Palma's site of battle is the Sun Ray, a shabby motel painted in peeling pastel blues and faded cream-white.

De Palma has said in interviews that you have to put a violent scene before the first half hour of a thriller like this to prove that "you mean business." Tony and Angel enter a dingy room occupied by Hector the Toad (Al Israel), who grins too widely, and Marta (Barbra Perez), a gaunt, grim woman who's curled around a pillow on the room's bed; when Tony says hello to her, she glances up briefly from the cop show she's watching on TV (sirens blare from a chase scene on the box). She gives Tony a silent, sour look, and reaffixes her gaze to the television. Hector asks him if he has the money; Tony asks Hector if he's got the "stuff." Hector says, sure, just not here—it's "close by." Tony instantly changes his tune and tone, saying "I don't have the money, either," that he has the desired product but that it, too, isn't on him . . . it's close by. He is cool and collected, acting as though nothing is throwing him off, but you can tell from his quick glances at the now off-camera Marta that he's trying to figure out just what the hell is up in this motel room, wondering what's going to happen next. It's one of the most subtle bits of acting Pacino does in the entire movie.

In an attempt to increase the tension, De Palma inserts a sly little scene to contrast with the normal life going on outside that motel room. It's a quick cut to the car outside, from the motel balcony point of view: Manny nonchalantly gesturing to a girl in a teeny blue bikini to stop walking and come over to talk to him. Cut back: the tension back in the motel room increases. Hector is trying to cool down an increasingly steamed-looking Tony by asking him where he's from. You don't ask Tony Montana about his roots without getting some fury with it. Tony dimisses this query, asking Hector what difference does that make. Business and place of origin: two subjects Tony takes very seriously.

Standing just outside the room, Angel is watching the two men; we see an arm holding a gun suddenly move into the right lower corner of the frame, advancing behind Angel. No sooner does Tony tell Hector to stop delaying things when the gunman grabs Angel by the hair and jabs the gun in his back, pushing him into the room. Then Marta pulls a shotgun out from under that pillow and kneels up on the bed, pointing it at Tony, Hector pulls a gun on Tony as well, and a third armed man enters the room as backup. They drag Tony and Angel into the bathroom.

The two men put Angel into the bathtub, standing him up and taping his arms to the shower spigot. Hector tells Tony he'll kill Tony's "brother," as he mistakenly refers to Angel, and that he'll then kill Tony, too. Tony's face is blank; his body has gone semi-limp as he leans against a wall, Hector's gun at his throat. He looks at Hector with dead eyes. "Why don't you try sticking your head up your ass? See if it fits," he says in one of Pacino's more nonchalantly stylized line readings. (It comes out more like, "Why don' you try stickin' jo head up joo ass? See if it feets.") The accent somehow only adds to our suspense: not only is there going to be some bad violence going down, but we know that after *Scarface* opens nationwide in '83, the Movie Police are going to bust Pacino for bad verbal impersonation as well.

Hector turns away and goes over to a brown suitcase nearby, opens it, puts down his gun, and lifts out a bright yellow chain saw. The camera focuses on the chain saw as Giorgio Moroder's approximation of monster-movie music rises up on the soundtrack. Hector pushes Tony into the bathroom with Angel. Marta raises the volume on the TV, as De Palma and cinematographer Alonzo execute one of De Palma's favorite sort of shots: a sweeping, single-take move in which the camera

ELIZABETH DAILY turns out to be E. G. Daily, a minor but vocally recognizable fix-
ture on the L.A. music and movie scene for at least two decades. She tried to
launch a pop-rock career with a brief contract on A&M Records (the dance-pop
tune "Say It, Say It" was her only dance-floor hit), but Daily turned to other employ-
ment.

She became a prolific voice-over actor, for fifteen years providing the cartoon
voices for Tommy Pickles on *Rugrats,* as well as voicing Buttercup on *The Power-
puff Girls* and many other animated characters. As an actress, she had the dubious
pleasure of playing Paris Hilton's mother in *National Lampoon's Pledge This!,* a
straight-to-DVD effort in 2006.

glides from the cop show on the TV, goes out the motel window, rises
momentarily to take in the crayon-blue Miami sky, then gracefully dips
down to the sidewalk below, where once again we see Manny in the
convertible, oblivious to what's going on just a few hundred feet away,
still flirting with the aqua-blue-bikinied blonde, fondling her ass as she
waggles it into and out of his grasp. The primary sound out here in the
street is on the soundtrack: "Shake It Up," not the putrid hit song by
the Cars, but a putrid Moroder disco tune sung by a skilled vocalist
billed as Elizabeth Daily, blaring tinnily from the car radio.

The music fades down as the roar of the chain saw fades up; it's
momentarily hard to know which sounds worse.

Then, suddenly, we *know* what's worse: Tony and Angel are facing
each other, standing in the tub, and Hector's asking again for the
money, holding the chain saw menacingly near Angel. Tony maintains
his poker face—only his eyes, glancing at Angel, betray any anxiety,
but he's fighting to remain utterly emotionless, and succeeding.

This is one of the key moments in *Scarface* history, in the sense that it will enter gangsta rap culture in particular as a code of behavior: this is how you should act when threatened, or when your comrade is threatened—you never give in to your enemy, you stand your ground, and keep focused on the future, on revenge.

What follows are a series of contrasting facial close-ups, as the chain saw revs up its volume and an unseen Hector goes to work on Angel, who tries to scream through a mouth that's been covered with duct tape. We know instinctively that the chain saw is ripping into Angel's body, but we don't see it. What we see is Tony's sickened reaction as he tries to turn away, but a gunman uses his weapon to push Tony's face straight ahead, so that he's forced to witness the dismemberment of his friend. We see blood fly and spatter across Angel's face—his own blood flying back against him. De Palma, pushing his luck with such repetition, makes another quick cut outside to Manny, who's just been given the brush-off by the blonde; he settles back in his seat, glancing up at the motel room, wondering what's taking so long. He looks bored. His boredom is meant to crank up the movie's suspense, but viewed now, it just looks like a rather lazy way of extending the scene with heavy-handed stalling tactics.

Back inside, it's all blood-blood-blood. Copious red stuff dripping from the walls, and a blood-soaked Hector is holding the blood-soaked yellow chain saw. Blood has flown across the tub and landed on the shower curtain, and on Tony. Outside (De Palma is cutting faster now, building up steam for a showdown), Manny (*finally!*) decides it's taking too long and tells his passenger-mate Chi Chi they should go see what's happening; they get out of the car and cross the street, holding guns discreetly low as people pass by. Inside, Tony's hands are being

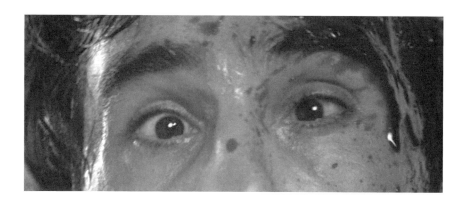

chained to the shower-curtain rod; he's drenched in Angel's blood, and Hector is now turning his attention to Tony. Hector holds a red-dripping blade to Tony's nose and says he wouldn't mind killing Tony, too.

"Fock you!" Tony snarls, and spits in Hector's face. (You can almost hear the cheers erupting from the younger members of the film's audience during its theatrical release; and in the fist-pumping "*Yesssss!*"es of couch potatoes nationwide as they watch this scene for the 485th time on DVD at home.) Hector yanks on the chain saw's throttle to get it going at the highest, loudest speed. Meanwhile, Manny and Chi Chi, now aware that something bad is going down, are flattened against the outside walls, guns out, ready to make their move. It's at this point that *Scarface* becomes almost like a Western—the cavalry arrives to help the threatened soldier.

Manny machine-guns his way through the glass door, shooting Marta and the two other men as he enters. Hector is about to apply the chain saw to Tony when Manny appears in the bathroom doorway and blasts at Hector. Manny stops firing—his gun is jammed, or out of ammunition. He looks down at his weapon and one of the gunmen

THIS IS ONE OF THE crucial scenes that required De Palma to submit four different versions to the MPAA ratings board in order to obtain an R, not an X, rating. De Palma has pointed out repeatedly that you never see the chain saw ripping into anyone's skin—his defense is that this is the old Hitchcockian, it's-all-in-your-imagination editing technique. Nonetheless, De Palma has also maintained that because of this, the editing was easily manipulated in his dealings with a ratings board he clearly holds in contempt, and while in some interviews says that he made thirty to forty tiny cuts to appease the MPAA appeal board, he put those frames back in, and what we see in the released version is actually his first, original, and desired cut.

The director told *Playboy* in 1984, "I didn't take anything out, except for the arm that was chain-sawed off. You don't really see it, just about twelve frames. I took it out, anyway. I sent the censors four versions and kept taking things out and finally said, 'I'm not doing this anymore,' and all four versions got an X for 'cumulative violence,' whatever that is. So I figured, Hey, if we're getting an X, let's go with our first version. So I put it all back and fought the appeal on the original cut. Why fight the fourth version? I didn't even like it. And we won. I had already taken out the arm on my own. I was amazed at the brouhaha.' "

De Palma decided he could pull a fast one over on the ratings board. Because the graphic violence was more in the board members' minds than onscreen and thus having been *told* they were seeing a different version, they were gulled into thinking they'd agreed to a more-trimmed-down cut.

shoots him in the side. As a gunman keeps Tony pushed against the bathroom wall, Hector decides it's time to flee: He runs to the opposite side of the room and uses the chain saw to *slash a hole in the wall into the adjoining apartment.* (De Palma is channeling his inner cartoon-animator, his R-rated Chuck Jones: He's got his hero snipping holes into walls for escape like the Road Runner painting holes on walls to dive through and escape Wile E. Coyote.)

Hector jumps into that room, where a woman screams in surprised fright, then he uses the chain saw to smash a window in *her* apartment. (Kirk Douglas will make a similar escape a few years later in De Palma's *The Fury,* to equally fine comic-suspense effect.) He jumps through it and falls one flight, onto the outside pavement. Chi Chi enters the apartment (*finally!*), and shoots one gunman while, inside the bathroom, Tony wrestles a gun away from the other man and shoots this guy in the chest. Tony goes over to Manny, who says the bullet that got him just pierced his side, and that he's okay.

Tony is getting some perspective on this bright nightmare now: he hears the screams that are erupting throughout the motel and knows it's going to be all chaos 'n' cops soon. He says, "Chi Chi, get the ye-yo"—remember that small phrase; tons of rappers did, and sampled or quoted it in lyrics. What Tony means is grab the drugs now just lying on the motel-room floor in plastic bags. Tony runs outside in pursuit of Hector as we see scores of white-haired Florida senior citizens cowering and screeching. (De Palma never misses a visual cliché—in this case, scandalized retirees—if it will provide a concise shortcut to the frantic mayhem he wants to create.) Hector staggers out—shot, sans chain saw—into the middle of the street. Tony, bloodied but unhurt, doesn't care about the public site now. In fact, all the better to make his point: He runs around Hector and positions himself in front of the toadlike thug, so that this enemy can see him clearly, and shoots Hector through the forehead.

More screaming and wailing all around. Tony hops into the convertible as police sirens—real ones, that echo the TV ones we heard on Marta's TV earlier—erupt in the background: the cops are about to arrive on the scene. Tony pulls a U-turn on the street, pulling up in front of the motel just as Manny and Chi Chi emerge. They get in and Tony speeds off.

Like clockwork, the next set-piece of *Scarface* violence occurs an hour into the film. Tony has, at Frank's request and to Omar's chagrin, accompanied Omar to Bolivia, where they are to meet with the merchant supplier Alejandro Sosa (Paul Shenar). F. Murray Abraham's Omar is just a well-heeled messenger boy, dispatched only to make Sosa an offer and receive Sosa's counter.

After some business talk, Omar says he will take Sosa's offer back to his boss, Frank, in Miami; they all get up to leave. Sosa asks that Tony stay behind—Omar hestitates, but he can't offend Sosa by disagreeing with him, so he leaves. Sosa tells Tony when he has him alone that he likes him, that he feels Tony doesn't lie, a vibe he doesn't feel from the rest of Frank Lopez's crew. Puzzled, Tony asks what he means. They're now outside; we start to hear helicopter blades rattling on the soundtrack. Sosa explains what he means: that he's convinced Omar is a rat, a police informer. Sosa whips out a pair of binoculars and hands them to Tony, who looks up at the now-hovering copter just in time to see a beaten, tied-up Omar pushed out of the helicopter, hung by his neck. The helicopter then flies off into the distance, the body flailing a warning to, one can only suspect, some very unnerved Bolivians.

(I went through the Los Angeles phone book and found the stunt man who doubled for Abraham in that shot, Dick Ziker. A semiretired Hollywood old-school pro and a legend among stuntmen [he did the "triple lindy" swimming pool dive doubling for Rodney Dangerfield in *Back to School*], Ziker says amiably, "Stunt men were stupid back then—we'd do anything. That was the most dangerous stunt of my life. We did it on Stage 12 at Universal, 4,000 feet in the air. De Palma was okay to work for—he didn't smile or make small talk, but I don't need either of those things. What I liked was that he was very methodical about how to set up the shot; he knew what he wanted. No one had ever done a shot like this before, dangling someone out of a helicopter by the neck. I had a big rig on, a whole neck-and-spine brace to keep me from separating my head from my shoulders when they pushed me out of the chopper. It still hurt like hell . . . They shot the hanging scene twice—a week apart! Which was kind of annoying, since both De Palma and I thought we got it right the first time, but the producer insisted, so that we'd have 'coverage' from a different angle in the editing room. It's a nice stunt. I'm proud of it, and other stunt men still ask me how it was done, even today.")

So, if you're keeping score—we have death by knife, by chain saw, by hanging.

Another half hour later: another violent tableau. De Palma takes us back into the nightclub, the Babylon, where after a long night, after Loggia's Lopez has left, Tony's eyes have closed; he's slumped in the booth. He rouses himself, probably wondering about Octavio, a masked-fool nightclub entertainer who's picking women out of the audience to dance with—to Tony, it seems like some kind of bad dream. The cuts get faster, the syntheizer goes up a register to start approximating a Bernard Herrmann violin riff out of *Psycho,* and suddenly two thugs stand up and starting blasting machine-gun fire at Tony, who dives under his table as the multimirrored wall behind him shatters. Tony stays under the table and shoots the two guys' legs out from under them, and scrambles to escape amidst the chaos this causes in the disco.

Tony's assumption here, when the dust and glass shards settle, is that this was a Frank Lopez set-up—that Frank thinks Tony has gotten too big for his leisure suit. Thus, Tony plots his revenge with Manny. Wearing a sling on his left arm, Tony goes to Lopez's office, where his cronies and the corrupt cop Bernstein are sitting around guffawing over life. Upon seeing Tony—sling; bloody shirt; toting gun in his good hand—Lopez expresses shock and dismay, half-feigned, half-real, since if Tony's correct, Frank assumed Tony was dead by now. Lopez acts angry on Tony's behalf, blaming the attack on a number of possible enemies, and vowing revenge on Tony's behalf. (This is one of the rare scenes in which Loggia actually tries to approximate a Latino accent—it was as though, hearing Pacino's rich overripeness, the veteran character actor had opted out of trying to come up with an accent that was either more subtle or more outlandish than the star's—in any case, it's an odd lapse that only calls attention to itself here.)

Frank asks Tony why he's holding the gun. Looking at the pistol in his hand, Pacino gives his accent a workout: This thing? I dunno, says Tony, "I'm—how you say?—paranoin.'" The phone rings. In order to trick his old boss into revealing he was behind the abortive Babylon Club hit, Tony had told an ally to call and say that Tony got away. Lopez doesn't want to answer it, but knows he must; he pretends it's his wife calling and hangs up. Tony calls him a "fucking cock-a-roach." There's some angry give-and-take about loyalty, and then Frank admits he was the one behind the attack. Tony cocks the gun and points it at Frank. Frank is totally freaked; he asks/pleads/lies/vamps for Tony's forgiveness, for a second chance.

Frank gets down on his knees and tries to grasp Tony's leg, ostensibly to kiss his foot. Tony pulls away, says he's not going to kill him, but it's just semantics: he has *Manny* plug Lopez dead. Too bad— Robert Loggia added a lot of lusty energy to this baroque exercise thus far. But it makes sense dramatically: offing Frank is Tony's next step in grasping more power. He now turns to Det. Mel Bernstein, who's still sitting at Lopez's home boardroom meeting table, arms crossed, cool as a piña colada. Bernstein says Lopez messed up—that he, Bernstein, told Frank it made no sense to try and kill Tony.

Tony's in the mood to murder, though. He says, no, *you* messed up, Mel, and Tony shoots him in his soft, white Lacoste-shirted belly.

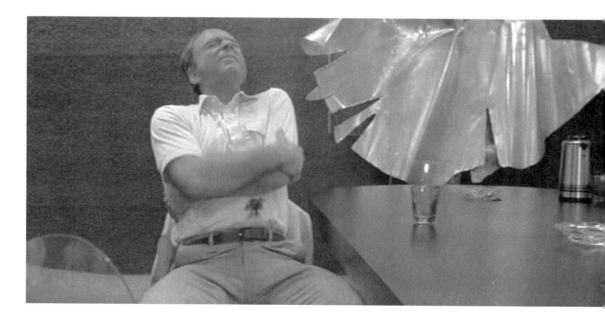

Mel, an old-school reprobate, goes down calling Tony a cheap punk. (You can almost hear Jimmy Cagney's echo in the line—it's a variation on the impersonation comedians used to do of Cagney: "You dirty rat!") Again, too bad: In his way, Bernstein was living by the gangster code even though he was a cop—he goes out defiantly, cursing, and the picture loses some more good middle-aged-character-actor talent in Harris Yulin. Tony then goes to collect his trophy: to Elvira's bedroom, where the ice-blonde is sleeping in ice-white silk sheets, and where he murmurs that Frank's gone, and she is to come with him.

As I said, action occurs in almost precise half-hour increments in *Scarface*. And so, at the two-hour mark, it's time for De Palma to rev it up again. We move to Manhattan, where the Bolivian politician who's prepared to testify before a U.S. commission about Sosa's drug empire is getting out of a car at night to enter his home. Tony is in a nearby car, watching Alberto—an emaciated Sosa emissary we first met back in Bolivia—now crawl under the guy's car to plant a bomb under the car. The next morning, Alberto and Tony are in their car, waiting for the guy to emerge. Alberto says they're to follow the car and blow it up in front of the place where the politician is about to give an anti-drug-ring speech: the United Nations building (the bomb is to be detonated by a remote-control device Alberto is fingering with sadistic love).

But then the man comes out and his wife and kids also get into the car. Tony, who's been snorting coke, is rattled: family means a lot to him still—as depraved as he's become, it's the one thing that still tethers him to humanity. Now, he may be behind the wheel, but he's not in control of this scenario; Tony insists that Alberto not harm those innocents. Alberto insists right back that Sosa gave the order—they have to do it now. Tony seethes, squeezing the wheel: it's one of Pacino's better moments—and rare for this movie—of Tony trying to control his emotions, of *suppressing* his rage. He also communicates just through a succession of facial expressions that he's become full of self-loathing for what he's doing with his life.

De Palma has a very Hitchcockian—which is to say, nonchalantly phony-looking—process shot here of the car that's moving ahead of Tony: the guy's two kids are in the backseat, facing Tony, but oblivious, happily playing patty-cake. (This is what Hollywood filmmakers thought kids still did in 1983?) Tony mutters over and over that this is the wrong thing to do, thinking about the grave sin he's about to commit with Alberto sitting in the passenger seat, a box with a cherry-red detonator button in his lap. Tony asks whether Alberto feels good killing a mother and her kids, trying to appeal to Alberto's human side, forgetting that Alberto doesn't have one. Alberto couldn't care less one way or another. He will very soon.

Tony says he doesn't want these deaths on his conscience. "*You* die, motherfucker!" He pulls out a gun and shoots Alberto sitting next to him, pressing the gun against his foe's head. Tony talks to the corpse, yelling over and over, that he shouldn't have messed with Tony Montana.

A vetitable machine of a movie, *Scarface,* now two hours and thirty minutes in, enters the final phase of Tony's life. He's hurt everyone he's ever loved. He's in his big manor house, alone except for his employees, and they ask him what are they to do now. Montana, slumped in his big office chair in his black pinstripe suit, says they're going to go to war against Sosa's minions, whom only Tony, despite all the camera secuity set up all over his house, correctly believes are closing in on him. Still, good intuition aside, he's also clearly out of his head; coked up and in the only reaction-mode he knows: rage. A few minutes before, he has murdered his best friend Manny for getting too close to his sister, Gina—he doesn't realize they've done things the "right" way and married. All this has contributed to Tony's angry guilt and despair.

Outside, stealthy gunmen invade Tony's palace, taking out his guards. Inside, Tony takes another huge snort, as Gina enters the room to make a scene. Half out of her mind, she accuses Tony of loving her so much, he's crossed the line. (See "The Women in Scarface" in this chapter.) Gina unties her robe, pulls out a gun, and takes a shot at Tony, which misses.

After one of the trespassing gunmen enters and machine-guns Gina to death, Tony pushes him out the window and riddles the corpse with bullets with the man's machine gun. Tony then hugs Gina's corpse and sobs. When he sees his enemies approaching, Tony kisses Gina's body and says he'll be back.

He takes a big machine gun from a nearby cabinet and, looking at the security cameras, vows to get this encroaching army of assassins. He loads his gun, frantically, clumsily. He stuffs pistols in his pockets as well. Knowing some gunmen are right outside his office door, he hefts the huge machine gun and utters the line that will put *Scarface* in pop-culture history:

"Say hello to my little friend!"

He starts blasting through the door, splintering it with pure firepower. On the other side, the gun detonates a virtual explosion—Tony's foes don't merely die, they get blown off their feet and die in a tremendous blast. Tony strides through the door, letting out bursts of gunfire on already dead bodies as more live ones advance. This is Tony's last stand; he knows it.

He's on the second-floor balcony of his home now, standing at the railing. He's taking a few bullets himself, but so far, he's giving more than he's getting. But more and more men are piling in, and Tony's alone. He reloads and blasts the giant machine gun again, momentarily silencing everyone. We see a lone gunman in sunglasses slowly sneaking up on him through the smoke and confusion. Meanwhile, some other minor punk takes an easy potshot at him and Tony zaps him dead.

"You fuck with Tony Montana, you fuckin' with the best!" he proclaims.

Then a gaggle of gunmen all begin shooting. Tony's big gun is blasted out of his hands, and we see his body start to take multiple shots, but he's still on his feet. He seems unstoppable, invincible; here, De Palma presaged the video-game era by making Tony look almost inhuman, waxy but implacable—like an avatar of violent power.

But the guy with the sunglasses is now tiptoeing right up behind him, and levels a double-barreled shotgun at Tony's back. He shoots once, the camera goes into slow motion, and Tony falls face-first down into the shallow pool that decorated his home's lobby. Red blood starts filling the blue water as De Palma's camera rises up to take in the gold statue at the head of the pool: the one with the globe ribboned with the phrase THE WORLD IS YOURS.

The camera pulls up and back, and we see the mess of devastation that has just occurred. The final words appear on the screen: "This film is dedicated to Howard Hawks and Ben Hecht." Fade to black, with the credits scrolling up in blood-red. The violence can go no further, and when De Palma has run out of people to kill, he stops filming. It's over. The *Scarface* world is now ours, forever and ever.

A Meaning of *Scarface*

How did what is on its surface an antidrug movie become, in its pop-cultural afterlife, a pro-thug movie?

In *Scarface,* the cocaine upon which Montana builds his fortune causes nothing but unhappiness and trouble. No one, especially Tony and Elvira, ever snorts cocaine for mere pleasure—rather, it is to escape momentarily, to draw a hazy veil over private pain.

No, the true source of exhilaration for the characters in the movie is business—success in business, ruthlessness in business, the glory and power that derives from succeeding in the material world. Two old-fashioned, time-passes-via-montage sequences occur in the movie:

the first is when we witness Tony's quick rise to job security and new wealth within Frank's drug empire (shots of Tony being greeted like a king in nightspots; buying new cars with cash; overseeing the building of his garish mansion); the second occurs when we are shown the ways the profits from drug-selling are converted into cold cash (the mechanical and human money counters; the trips to banks carrying duffel bags of cash to be laundered).

Both of these aspects are rooted in a fundamental selfishness: an array of characters (not just Tony himself) tells us, through words and actions: my misery is so acute, it takes precedence over family and friendship, so get outta here and let me bury my snout in a mound of coke. Or: I came from nothing; I'm a self-created person; I made you what you are today; I gave you everything you ever wanted and this is how you repay me . . . everything is an endless string of first-person-singular assertions, the I-I-I-I's of the Me Generation. It's no wonder 1980s kids dug the movie more rapturously than the Greatest Generation, and baby-boomer moviegoers and film critics.

On the most superficial level, *Scarface* went from being a warning against the evils of drugs to a primer for thug life because being preached to is less exciting than being shown how to have a good time. On a subtler level, *Scarface* came along—quite coincidentally, since the moviemakers had no connection with or feeling for hip-hop culture—at a time when hip-hop was going "gangsta." Previously, rap and R&B, as well as blaxploitation movies, had included themes of street life that played out both humorously and brutally; these consisted largely, however, of material about hustling and pimping. Guns were certainly wielded by the gangsters in, say, a 1973 film like *Black Caesar* (soundtrack courtesy of James Brown), but drug consumption was very much a fringe-theme or subplot. Jamaican reggae, especially in the 1972 film *The Harder They Come* and in songs such as Junior Murvin's 1976 "Police and Thieves" (covered by The Clash), spun out the Scarfacian scenarios of poor boy-turns-outlaw. But these examples remained rooted in the idea that the central figure was an essentially sympathetic person, a suffering young man forced into a bad life, not an impoverished fellow who's chosen the criminal life and drug-taking as the means to a monomaniacal power grab resulting in a tragic fall.

No, *Scarface* uncannily predicted—and then, in its afterlife as VHS/DVD fetish cult-item dovetailed very precisely with—the mid-to-late '80s, during which time there was a small explosion of music acts articulating minority culture's vehement belief that law enforcement was either nonexistent (Public Enemy's "911 Is a Joke") or oppressive (NWA's "Fuck Tha Police").

People like rules, dictums, aphorisms, credos; such things are used as inspiration, as codes of discipline and honor. In the absence of either a legal system that served or protected the vulnerable—whether we're talking about a fictional Cuban immigrant like Tony Montana or a real young black or Hispanic youth scraping by in Los Angeles, New York, Philadelphia, Miami, or any big city—the rules as set down in *Scarface* had an irresistible allure.

Certainly, most of the audience interpreted them on the same dual level as Oliver Stone wrote them: half macho joke, half dead-serious wisdom. By the early 1980s, when cocaine was one major recreational drug of choice among both Hollywood players *and* street-level sellers, *Scarface* teased out two interpretations: it operated as an in-joke scolding of its own industry (an industry that specifically, tacitly condoned Oliver Stone's own cocaine habit until he took responsibility for himself and fled the country to kick the habit and write the movie), and as

one of those movies whose surface message was "Don't do this!" even
as its action and subtext sniggered, "Isn't this cool?" (It was exactly
the same sort of mixed message Howard Hawks's 1930s *Scarface* sent
out about bootlegged liquor and the then-burgeoning use of the
tommy gun as a weapon of mini-mass destruction.) And so even if
producer Martin Bregman was completely sincere in his capitalistic
notion that one could make a profitable drugs-have-gotten-out-of-
control gangster update, you can bet that De Palma, former counterculture subversive, and Stone, armed-services vet and more than a
dabbler in coke, knew that *Scarface* would play as excitement: an
incitement at least as much as an indictment.

Ultimately, the movie itself is its own Scarface; the movie behaves
like Tony Montana—it's a celluloid/digital/televised organism that
stubbornly, furiously, refuses to become a mannerly part of film history,
to leave the popular consciousness. When in June 2007, another great
gangster tale, HBO's The Sopranos, came to an end by cutting off its final scene abruptly, leaving only a blank, black screen and doubt about
the fate of its central mobster, Tony Soprano, creator David Chase
pulled an arty move that neither Brian De Palma nor Tony Montana
would ever have put up with. Where The Sopranos increasingly became
a story about inner turmoil and quietly resigned fate, Scarface remains
a loud, livid, pulsating thing.

There was no *Soprano*-ish doubt about what happened to this anti-
hero: you saw Tony Montana go out in a drenching rain of bullets and
blood. Yet, even as he fell into a pool, his arms outstretched in a typi-
cally cheesy, self-pitying Montana swan dive, this Tony was Christ-

like, immediately resurrected. He instantly entered the kingdom of pop, where all things exist in an eternal present. Hey, I liked *The Sopranos* immensely. But I also would put money on the fact that De Palma's Tony will outlive HBO's Tony as a face, a body, a collection of lines quoted and scenes cited, in more various permutations than *The Sopranos'* Tony ever will.

All that the taciturn actor James Gandolfini wanted to say when *The Sopranos* ended was that he was glad to be able to move on; that it was time. When in 2007, the American Film Institute honored Al Pacino for his entire body of work, the televised event included about twenty-five references to *Scarface* and a sheepishly cheerful admission by Pacino that Tony Montana was the one role everyone always wants to talk to him about.

It's no surprise that *Scarface* lives on. Look at it today. Look at it again even if you've watched it two hundred times, either all the way through, or in bits and pieces when it pops up on TV. The goddamn thing is indestructible—it remains as exhilaratingly funny, vulgar, gaudy, violent, surprising, and angrily unruly as it was the first time it unspooled in 1983. *Scarface* is like, as Tony would say, a cock-a-roach: stamp out one version of it in your head, and five more will come at you—if not as the movie itself, then as a video game, or as a joke on a sitcom, or as shorthand for violent thug life, in every medium that exists now and in whatever medium yet to be invented. *Scarface* finds a dank little corner in any piece of pop culture, no matter how shiny-clean and bright it might be, and takes up residence; it moves like a virus without a cure.

Scarface encroaches upon various territories of popular culture in a way that is unparalleled in film history. Director De Palma's remake (rethinking, or reinvention, is more like it) of Howard Hawks's 1932 movie has taken on a life that has ranged far beyond the careers of De Palma, Oliver Stone, Al Pacino. Other gangster movies have surpassed it in artistry—Francis Ford Coppola's first two *Godfather* movies being the obvious examples; Raoul Walsh's 1949 James Cagney film *White Heat* the now-lesser-known but still magnificently potent one—but none has had the influence *Scarface* has. *The Godfather* and its 1974 sequel were quickly enshrined as class Hollywood acts—Oscar-worthy productions—in a way that *Scarface* never was. There is something unshakably low-down and seedy, disreputable and sneaky, about *Scarface* as a piece of art, an antistatus that only adds to its pervasiveness and longevity. Everybody who connects to *Scarface,* from inquisitive academic to hip-hop philosophizers to bloggers both enlightening and blithering, claims *Scarface* for his or her own. It's as though, unlike the way Francis Ford Coppola wrested *The Godfather* from its Mario Puzo source-novel and created a piece of Coppola art, *Scarface* belongs to no single author, and therefore we are all free to be the auteurs of Tony Montana's saga, and his life everlasting.

As a viewing experience, it's no wonder people want to watch the film over and over: As soon as you see it, you want to experience it again, to figure out just how you got drawn into this hyperbolic pageant of brightly colored, funny, sexy, wrenching, wretched excess.

Chances are, you never will.

Appendix

Scarface as a Business Plan (or The 8 Habits of Highly Successful but Tragic Gangsters)

1. Know Your Goals Tony lays out the real rules of America to Manny; he makes it clear, early on in the film, when he's still hungry and disciplined, that he has his priorities straight. "In this country, you gotta make the money first; then when you get the money, you get the power; then when you get the power, you get the woman. That's why you gotta make your own moves."

No other moment in *Scarface* distinguishes so sharply the difference between not just Tony and Manny, but Tony Montana and the rest of the hustlers and poor people he came up from: his instinctive understanding of how the game is played, how individuals shape their own destinies, and how power must be grabbed, not merely lusted after or yearned for.

2. Old School Versus New School   Tony commences his business education under the tutelage of Frank Lopez. Frank's hard-won wisdom consists of a couple of "lessons" plus the business model Tony observes and improves upon.

Says Frank, "Lesson number one: never underestimate the *other* guy's greed!" (punctuated by actor Robert Loggia's gravelly laugh). In other words, be proactively suspicious and match greed with greater greed. This sentiment was very much in the 1980s air: What is Frank's phrase if not a warm-up for *Scarface* screenwriter Oliver Stone to polish these words into the Gordon Gekko *Wall Street* mantra, "Greed is good"?

Frank's cocaine empire consists of striking the best deal he can with his suppliers in Bolivia and Colombia, getting the product into this country via his own men, and then distributing the product through his long-cultivated network of sellers.

Tony gets his first opportunity to realize he has the instincts of a good businessman when he travels to Bolivia, accompanying F. Murray Abraham's Omar, who is Frank's mouthpiece/emissary in cocaine negotiations with the sleek drug kingpin, Paul Shenar's Alejandro Sosa. Sosa wants Lopez to guarantee he'll take 150 kilos a month to sell—he needs a regular buyer to keep his operation afloat. Omar sees this as a huge commitment, and one he doesn't have the authority to decide upon. But Tony, along for the ride as muscle and lackey, seizes the opportunity. "You got good stuff here—class-A shit," says Tony boldly, speaking out of turn. Sosa and Omar take notice—Sosa with amused approval, Omar with dagger-eyed annoyance.

Sosa offers the price of $750 a kilo for its pickup and distribution by Frank Lopez's organization. Omar is worried about "cutting out the Colombians"—i.e., Lopez's other source of cocaine. There's some back and forth, and Tony interrupts, cutting through the bull, saying they should *share* the risk of alienating the Colombian cartel, proposing that Sosa deliver the drugs "as far as Panama, and we'll take it from there."

Omar is royally pissed that Tony would make such a proposal without Frank's authorization—but it almost doesn't matter, because as we soon see, Sosa believes Omar is ratting on him and Lopez to the police, and, after asking Tony to stay behind, has Omar take a little helicopter ride that will reach its height with Omar dead, dangling from a noose tied to the aircraft. (Question: *Was* Omar an informer? It's never really proven—one of a number of plot threads in *Scarface* that are left as dangling as Omar's body.)

Back in Miami, Tony assures a Frank who is livid that his minion has conducted business in his name without consulting him first. "Look, Frank, the time has come—we gotta expand the whole operation," says Tony. He's in a gray sharkskin suit now—just like Frank's, in fact. Tony is more tanned, he's taken on a gravitas that he didn't have even in just the last scene. He's facing down Lopez, the aging boss who's getting "soft." Tony tells a man set in his local Miami ways that he has to think bigger; Tony even ventures that they need to work in big northern cities like New York and Chicago. Lopez grows belligerent, calling the smooth, articulate Sosa "a greaseball," and telling Tony he bought Sosa's "line," implying that Tony isn't seasoned enough to know when he's being played.

Tony's heard enough; he gets up to leave. But Frank has one

more bit old-school advice: "The guys who last in this business are the guys who fly straight, low-key, quiet. And the guys who want it all . . . they don't last." This is heavy—oh, I'll just say it: clumsily obvious—foreshadowing of what is to come for Tony, who "wants it all."

Soon enough, Frank's rules—including the other cardinal one, "Don't get high on your own supply"—will be irrelevant to Tony (but certainly not to viewers of *Scarface*, who will be making mental notes of everything Frank lays out). Tony will make his own move, in a more expensive suit: he'll kill the man who mentored him and deal directly with Sosa.

3. "Begin with the End in Mind"   This is a tenet held by Stephen Covey in his business bible, *The Seven Habits of Highly Effective People*. Manny reminds Tony early on that "just a year ago this time you were in a fucking cage," and Tony's response—"*You* remember; I like to forget that"—shows him to have already become as pure an American character as anyone Mark Twain or F. Scott Fitzgerald or Philip Roth has created. Like Huck Finn, Gatsby, and Zuckerman, Tony Montana is a self-*re*-created man, one who throws off the shame and limitations of his low upbringing to enlighten and empower himself, to give himself some control over his world. "Me, I want what's coming to me . . . *the world* . . . and everything in it."

4. Think and Act Positively . . . and with Balls   Tony's rules, as opposed to Frank's:

* "This town like a great big pussy, waiting to get fucked."
* "I never fucked over anybody in my life didn't deserve it . . . All I have in this life is my balls and my word, and I don't break 'em for nobody."
* "The only thing in this world that gives orders is balls."

We're now at a tipping point in the movie, as Tony's giddy rise and fall commence; to emphasize this, we're reintroduced to the film's mantra: a zeppelin, moving across the night sky, whose illuminated message is THE WORLD IS YOURS. There's renewed burst of visual energy, a flashy montage of drug money being counted by sorting machines that riffle the bills into bundles; Tony on the phone sharing a laugh with the Bolivian supplier Sosa; Tony's minions hoisting duffel bags full of cash and toting them into a bank. Montana is a big player, on the upswing, reveling in the control he's grabbed. Even the banker is glad to see him.

5. Always Be Moving Forward   When is Tony most in danger? Whenever he's still: At the start of the movie, when he's sitting in the government interrogators' chair, submitting to their grilling. When he's tied up in the bathroom in the chain-saw scene. When, at the end, he sits motionless at his desk, stunned by cocaine and impending doom. Clearly, Montana and all would-be Montanas must maintain the metabolism of a shark—keep that forward momentum going. Aside from his grandiose "the world and everything in it" goal, Tony chops up his ambition into a series of individual, manageable goals and pursues them like nobody's business. "Kill a communist": check. That gets him into Frank Lopez's organization. Kill Frank and steal his wife: check. Negotiate his own terms for drug importation: check. Marry Elvira, amass a fortune, and stock the backyard with tigers: check. It's only when he slows down (too many broody bubble baths!) that Tony gets into trouble. To borrow from another movie: Always be closing. Or you die.

6. Lawyers, Guns, and Money   Tony is initially a hands-on guy. He gets down in the money-counting chamber of his operation midway through *Scarface*. It's a concrete-block-wall purgatory, surrounded by flunkies with machines that riffle through the bills and record the profits. Tony totes up figures while sitting across from a low-level bank representative; Tony comes up with a $1,500 discrepancy in his favor; he argues for it. (He's a thorough if petty guy.) He tells the guy to make out his check to the "Montana Realty Company" as the camera pans up to a clock on the wall.

There's a fade-cut on the clock—we see that hours have passed and they're still counting money. We also see that the number "12" is missing on the clock: it's a hole through which Tony and his gang have been observed by law enforcement, who now burst in with guns drawn. Tony and company are arrested for "violation of the RICO statute"—the racketeering law. Tony's lawyer tells him he'll get him off on the conspiracy charge if he gives him, the lawyer, $500,000, but that the government will come after Tony for tax evasion and Montana may get five years in prison, out in three for good behavior.

"Three fuckin' years for what? For washin' money? The fuckin' country was *built* on washin' money!" Tony fulminates in a spontaneous lecture on our Founding Fathers.

7. Know When to Delegate   This is a hard lesson Tony fails to learn. The next time Tony goes to Bolivia to see Sosa, he's the big shot. He meets various bigwigs, including the head of the ministry of the interior, a local sugar-industry executive, and a "friend from Washington." Sosa explains that if Tony has a problem (i.e., his pending RICO charge and the disruption in service caused by the drug raid), "we" have a problem. Sosa says he has contacts in Washington that assure him Tony's tax and jail problems can be taken care of. They watch a video of what Sosa thinks is their biggest threat: a Bolivian journalist and a politician who've done a TV report revealing the names of the men Tony is now in the room with, part of a report de-

Saddam Hussein and *Scarface*

After the fall of Saddam, it was discovered that the Iraqi dictator had named one of his holding companies "Montana Realty Company," in homage to one of his favorite movies.

signed to expose them and shut them down. "He's going on *60 Minutes* next," says Sosa portentously. (Whoa—those were the days, when the implication of Mike Wallace and a film crew at your door meant impending doom.)

Sosa's solution is to assassinate the Bolivian politician when he goes to New York City to give an anti-drug-ring speech to the United Nations. In a very poor-judgment move, Tony, now back in Manhattan, accompanies Sosa's hitman, Alberto (the same guy who put the noose around Omar's neck) to plant a remote-control bomb under the guy's car. Why Tony feels he needs to be the wheelman for this enterprise—which only causes him major agita when he discovers that the man's wife and children are also in the car, and this being macho Tony, he cannot be responsible for killing so he kills Alberto instead—why Tony is in the the middle of this mess, well, as I said: *delegate*!

8. Happiness Is a Warm Gun, but Money Can't Buy You Love   Tony Montana is one of the most miserable human beings in all of cinema; Charles Foster Kane has nothing on him. *Scarface* is an

Appendix

almost unremittingly bleak depiction of nouveau wealth. Really: other than being able to afford a house upon whose property one can keep a few tigers, where did it get him? Once rich, the sex with Elvira was bad-to-nonexistent; his largesse to his family resulted in tragedy.

Recall the restaurant scene, well into Tony's cokehead period, when he squabbles with Elvira and makes a scene in the posh eatery that leaves people gawking at him. Tony looks around at the shocked patrons and curses them out for their haughty stares. "You don't have the guts to be what you want to be. You *need* people like me"—he's up on his wobbly feet now, Manny helping him out of the restaurant—"so you can point your fingers and say, '*That's* the fucking bad guy.'" Manny's pushing him out now, and Tony delivers another *Scarface* special, now available as a ringtone (oh, if only Tony had lived long enough to get a piece of *that* revenue stream): "So say good-bye to the bad guy!" he says slurrily, throwing open his arms. It's Tony's version of Sinatra doing "My Way," in spoken verse.

This atmosphere of gaudy dread permeates the *Scarface* mythos, on one of its many levels, turning it into a business manual for Getting Things Done . . . in a hell on earth.

Notes

3. Making a *Scarface*

1. Norman Kagan, *The Cinema of Oliver Stone*.

2. James Riordan, *Stone: The Controversies, Excesses and Exploits of a Radical Filmmaker.*

3. Andrew Yule, *Al Pacino: A Life on the Wire* (1991), p. 211.

4. *Inside the Actors Studio,* 10/2/06.

5. Ibid., 8/6/07.

6. *Creative Screenwriter,* 2006, p. 414.

7. *E! True Hollywood Story: Scarface,* 10/2/06.

8. Ibid.

9. *Creative Screenwriter,* 2006, p. 414.

Notes

4. Four Creators

1. Armond White, *The Resistence* (Overlook Press), p. 176.
2. Andrew Yule, *Al Pacino: A Life on the Wire* (1991), p. 219.
3. Al Pacino in conversation with Lawrence Grobel (2006).

5. *Scarface* Music

1. Jeff Chang, *Can't Stop, Won't Stop,* p. 396.
2. Ibid., p. 399.
3. *Entertainment Weekly,* 11/22/06.

6. The Origins: Howard Hawks's *Scarface*

1. Todd McCarthy, *Howard Hawks: The Grey Fox of Hollywood* (1997), p. 135.
2. *Understanding Media,* 1964.
3. McCarthy, ibid.

8. Alterna-*Scarface*s: Movies, TV Shows, Novels, and Comic Books

1. *Creative Screenwriting,* 2005, p. 415.

9. President Scarface

1. Joshua Bearman, *The Believer* (Dispatch Four—Tuesday, January 27, 2004).
2. AssociatedContent.com,
   www.associatedcontent.com/article/7953/money_power_and_respect.html?page=3.

10. *Scarface*: Its Money, Its Women, Its Power

1. Netglimse.com,
www.netglimse.com/celebs/pages/brian_de_palma/index.shtml.

2. Boxofficemojo.com,
www.boxofficemojo.com/yearly/chart/?yr=1983&p=.htm.

Acknowledgments

Deep thanks once again to my wily, riotous agent, John Campbell. Also to my intimidatingly intelligent and witty editor, Elizabeth Beier, and her exceedingly helpful, thoughtful assistant, Michelle Richter. And effusive thanks to my photo editor and art-friend, Michele Romero.

Throughout the writing of this book, I consulted Bill Fentum's invaluable Web site, briandepalma.net, as well as Geoff Songs's superb "De Palma a la Mod" Web site (angelfire.com/de/palma).

My quotes from De Palma come from a brief conversation I had with him about my project while we both attended the 2005 Toronto

Acknowledgments

Film Festival. At that time, he said he would sit down for a more extensive interview. He subsequently declined all my follow-up requests. I will refrain from using a Scarfacian imprecation regarding this behavior, and simply say good night to the bad guy.

Index

Alonzo, John A., 60, 61, *62*, 167

American Film Institute, 256

"America's Biggest Dick," 199–201

Amis, Martin, 27

Archibold, Randal C., 13–14

Arias, Yancey, 29, 30, 165

Armitage Trail. *See* Coons, Maurice

Back in the USSA (Byrne and Newman), 193–94

Banks, L. A., 188, 190–92

Bauer, Steven, 48, *49*

Benjamin, André 3000, 103, 114

Bernstein, Mel, 155, 248

Big Boi, 109

Bilson, Rachel, 27

Blanco, Griselda, 173–74

Bloody Mama, 62

Blow Out, 43, 47, 80–81

Body Count, 110

Body Double, 47, 81–83

Bregman, Martin, 41–42, 48

Buchanan, John, 196

Byrne, Eugene, 193–94

Index

Cadena, Miguel, 165

Camonte, Tony, 128
  business decisions by, 135–36
  death of, 145
  interrogation of, 129–30
  power grabs by, 135–36
  pride of, 132
  revenge rampage of, 139

Cam'Ron, 106

Capachi, Casey, 14–15

Capone, 180

Capone, Al, 158

Capone's Boys, 183

Carey, Mariah, 108

Carrie, 77

cartoons, 22–23

Carver, Steve, 180

Cash, Johnny, 23–24, 120

Cassavetes, John, 78

catchphrases, 2–3, 104

Cee-Lo Green, 116–17

Cheney, Dick, *198*, 199–201

Clarkson, Lana, 66

Close, Glenn, 50–51

clothing, 24–25

cocaine, 253
  Hollywood and, 70
  price of, 85
  shipments of, 85
  Stone and, 44, 45, 85

Cocaine Cowboys, 172

Collins, Joan, 203

Colon, Miriam, 37, 49, 105, 225, 227

Combs, Sean, 103

comic books, 184–90

Conley, Jane ("the Gun Girl"), 154–55, 157

conscience, 47

Coons, Maurice, 149, 150, 151

Coppola, Francis Ford, 258

Corman, Roger, 177, 180

Cox, Courtney, 210–11

Crime Story, 169–70

Crosland, Dave, 186

Cuban Linx, 29

Daily, Elizabeth, 239

Dakota, Daniel, 174

David, Larry, 20

De Niro, Robert, 170

De Palma, Brian
  on blood, 75–76
  energy of, 67
  excessiveness of, 64–65
  on film noir, 168
  on ideal viewership, 27–28
  on violence, 236
  women in films by, 94

Def Jam Presents: Music Inspired by Scarface,
    106, 107

*Def Jam Presents: Origins of a Hip Hop
    Classic*, 102–3

Detective Comics, 189

Diaz, Richard, 19

Dickinson, Angie, 79

Didion, Joan, 52

Dog Day Afternoon, 87

Dressed to Kill, 79–80

Dvorak, Ann, *134*

Easton, Robert, 59

Ebert, Roger, 72

Eisner, Will, 152–53

Ellis, Trey, 113

Entourage, 20–21, *21*

The Fabulous Baker Boys, 96
The Family Guy, 23
50 Cent, 108, 115
Fitzgerald, F. Scott, 137
Flashdance, 208–9
The 48 Laws of Power, 28
"Fresh Air with Terry Gross," 105, 114
Fuller, Graham, 93
The Fury, 78–79

gangsta rap, 119–22
"The Gangster as Tragic Hero" (Warshow),
     120–21
Gazzara, Ben, 179, 180
Geto Boys, 106, 111, 117–19
Ghandi, 208
Ghostface Killah, 122
The Godfather, 258
Gold, Ari, 21
Grand Hotel, 127
Grand Theft Auto: Vice City, 19
Grandmaster Flash and the Furious Five,
     119
Grease 2, 91
The Great Gatsby (Fitzgerald), 137
Grobel, Lawrence, 102
Guarino, Tony, 150–51
   death of, 157

Halloween costumes, 25
Hancock, Elvira, 213–23
   exit of, 223
   withdrawal of, 38
The Hand, 84
Harry Potter fan-fiction, 23
Hawks, Howard, 126
   dedication to, 252

Hays Office, 127, 141, 146
Hazlett, Thomas W., 196
Heat, 170–71
Hecht, Ben, 130
   dedication to, 252
Hollywood, 70
Hotel California, 29, 119
Hughes, Howard, 146, 158
Hussein, Saddam, 265
Huston, John, 46–47

Ice-T, 110
Irving, Amy, 78

Jabcuga, Joshua, 188
Jay-Z, 108
"Johnny Cash Meets Scarface," 23–24
Jordan, Brad. *See* Scarface

Kael, Pauline, 1, 72, 94
Kasdan, Lawrence, 209
King of Comedy, 205–6
Kingpin, 165–67
Kington, Tom, 16–17

Lady Scarface, 171–72
Lady Scarface: The World Is Hers,
     174–76
Lander, Marylee, 56
Landis, John, 210
Laresca, Vincent, 31
Law & Order: Criminal Intent, 26
Layman, John, 184
Lil' Wayne, 109
Lipton, James, 42
LL Cool J, 120
Loggia, Robert, 51, 58

Index

Lopez, Frank, 51
  death of, 247
  rules of, 36, 214–15
  takeover of, 37–38
Lumet, Sidney, 42
  Pacino on, 88

Mann, Michael, 167–71
Manny, 48
  death of, 38, 232, 250
  demonstrating cunnilingus, 212–13
Mariel Boatlift, 6, 52
Marielitos, 44
Maxwell, Edwin, 140–41
McKenna, Dave, 17
merchandise, 24–26
Method Man, 115
Meyers, Seth, 26–27
Miami
  rising crime rate of, 52–53
  Scarface pull-out from, 56–57
  Scarface shooting in, 52–57
Miami (Didion), 52
Miami Vice, 169, 171
micrography, 26
Mister Scarface, 181
Mobb Deep, 106
Mobsters, 182–83
Montana, Gina
  changes in, 228–29
  death of, 233, 250
  as symbol of innocence, 225
Montana, Tony
  on capitalism, 219–20
  death of, 39, 251
  as hero, 90
  lack of class of, 217
  loyalty of, 105

promoted "propagation of pernicious
    racism," 56
  stoicism of, 114
  as two-dimensional, 89
Morley, Karen, 130, 136
Moroder, Giorgio, 99–102, *100*, 113, 208
Motion Picture Association of America
    (MPAA), 68
MPAA. *See* Motion Picture Association of
    America
Muni, Paul, 128, *134*
Murphy, Eddie, 210
MTV's *Cribs*, 109

Nas, 103, 108
Nelson, Brian, 14
Newman, Kim, 193–94
N.W.A., 120
Norris, Patricia, 57, 60, 65–66
Noth, Chris, 26
Notorious B.I.G., 106, 121, 187
novelizations, 190–92

Obsession, 77
The O.C., 27
O'Neill, Shaquille, 17

Pacino, Al, 30–31, 42–43, 87–91, 170
  accent of, 51, 59–62, 238
  artistic "choices" of, 87
  on exaggerated acting style, 87, 89
  honors for, 257
  improvisation of, 65
  on Lumet, 88
  risks by, 87
  on *Scarface: The Shame of a Nation*, 88
Padron, Eduardo, 54
Paris, 110, 111–12

Pearson, Felicia, 22
Pekar, Harvey, 187–88
Peterson, Cassandra, 95
Pfeiffer, Michelle, 91–97, *92*
    audition of, 50
    career choices of, 96
    casting of, 49–50, 213
    previous work of, 91
Phifer, Mekhi, 103
politics, 45
    music and, 110–12
pop culture influence, 27–32
pop parody, 8
porn, 82, 174–76
posters, 26
"President Scarface: Bill Clinton's Press
    Relations" (Hazlett), 196
Puerto Rican Traveling Theater, 49

Rabe, David, 43
Raekwon, 111, 122
Ratner, Bret, 55
Reagan administration, 45
RICO Act, 85–86, 264
ringtones, 19–20
Robards, Jason, 177, *178*
Roberts, Marilyn, 137
Ross, Rick, 111
Rosson, Richard, 146

Santini, Geo, 29, 119
Saturday Night Live, 26–27
Scarface, 102–3, 106, 111, *116*, 117–19
Scarface (1983)
    atmosphere on set of, 67
    auditions for, 49, 50
    as business plan, 259–66
    casting for, 48–52

chain-saw scene in, 35, 105, 108, 236–44
core idea of, 115
ego clashes over, 63–67
gangsta rap and, 119–22
on hip-hop culture, impact on, 102–3
as Hong Kong action movie, 64–65
industry reaction to, 70–73
as insult to Cuban-American community,
    53
key moments of, 35–39
as metaphor for impotence, 94
as metaphor for minority struggle, 107–8
Miami pull-out, 56–57
Miami shooting of, 52–57
morality in, 104
origin of, 41–43
premiere of, 203
principle photography on, 52
principles of, 121
ratings controversy, 68–70, 242
rehearsals for, 51–52, 93
restaurant scene in, 222
reviews of, 71–72
rules of, 104–5
as *Saturday Night Fever* dream, 99–102
selfishness in, 254
shooting in Los Angeles, 57–58
soundtrack of, hip hop, 114
soundtrack of, replacing, 113–14
suits in, 60
summary of, 33–35
theme of, 46–47
Scarface (Coons), 150
    setting of, 151
"Scarface Casino," 19
Scarface: Devil in Disguise, 188
"Scarface: MPR (Money, Power, Respect)",
    20

Index

Scarface: Scarred for Life, 184–87, 223
Scarface: The Beginning (Banks), 188,
    190–92
"Scarface, The Great Gatsby, and The
    American Dream" (Roberts), 137
Scarface: The Shame of a Nation
    anticrime message of, 141
    beginning of, 126
    "glorification of the criminal" in, 146
    Pacino on, 88
    title card of, 128
    title debate, 146–47
Scarface: The World Is Yours, 17–19
scarfacemobile.com, 19–20
Schiavone, Walter, 16–17
Schoolly D, 120
Schrader, Paul, 77
Scorsese, Martin, 70, 205–6
Sexton, Martin, 197
Shakur, Tupac, 121, 187
Simmons, Russell, 103
The Simpsons, 22
Snoop Dogg, 107, 115
The Sopranos, 20, 256–57
South Park, 22–23
Spanish-American League Against
    Discrimination, 54
The Spirit (Eisner), 152
The St. Valentines Day Massacre, 177–79
Starwave Mobile, 19
stereotyping, 54
Stone, Oliver, 43, 83–86
    cocaine and, 44, 45, 85
    complaints from, 63–64

on Elvira's exit, 223
    research by, 44
Superman III, 206
The Sweet Escape, 112
symbolism, 128, 140

tax evasion, 38, 264
Trading Places, 210
Trail, Armitage. *See* Coons, Maurice
Travolta, John, 80
The Treasure of the Sierra Madre, 46–47
Trick Daddy, 104, 109
Trouvile, Mark, 52

The Untouchables, 160–64

video games, 17–19
violence, 234–35
De Palma on, 236
    half-hour increments of, 248

Warshow, Robert, 120–21
Wasserman, Lew, 54
Weinraub, Bernard, 88
White, Armond, 77
The Wire, 21–22, 113
women
    in De Palma's films, 94
    in jeopardy, 80
    objectifying, 93–94, 95–96
    as predators, 212
    as sex objects, 212

Yule, Andrew, 46